Gender in History

Gender in History

Merry E. Wiesner-Hanks

BLACKWELL
Publishers

Copyright © Merry E. Wiesner-Hanks 2001

The right of Merry E. Wiesner-Hanks to be identified as author of this work has been asserted in accordance with the Copyright, Designs and Patents Act 1988.

First published 2001

2 4 6 8 10 9 7 5 3 1

Blackwell Publishers Inc.
350 Main Street
Malden, Massachusetts 02148
USA

Blackwell Publishers Ltd
108 Cowley Road
Oxford OX4 1JF
UK

Library of Congress Cataloging-in-Publication Data

Wiesner, Merry E., 1952–
   Gender in history / Merry E. Wiesner-Hanks.
      p. cm. — (New perspectives on the past)
   Includes bibliographical references and index.
      ISBN 0–631–21035–0 (hardcover: acid-free paper) — ISBN 0–631–21036–9
      (paperback: acid-free paper)
   1. Sex role—History. 2. Social history. I. Title. II. New
      perspectives on the past (Basil Blackwell Publisher)
   HQ1075 .W526 2001
   305.3′09—dc21

                                                              00-013063

British Library Cataloguing in Publication Data

A CIP catalogue record for this book is available from the British Library.

Typeset in 11/13pt MBembo
by Kolam Information Services Pvt. Ltd, Pondicherry, India
Printed in Great Britain by TJ International, Padstow, Cornwall

This book is printed on acid-free paper

For my premodern/postmodern women's reading group

Contents

Acknowledgments

Each book that I have written has encouraged me to range wider chronologically and geographically from my original home base in early modern Germany, which has meant I have entered territories in which I know less and less. Fortunately, I have found my scholarly colleagues to be uniformly gracious in sharing their expertise, providing assistance and advice, and often in the process turning from colleagues to friends. For this book I would first like to thank the series editor, Constantin Fasolt, who asked me to write it, and Tessa Harvey, the development editor at Blackwell Publishers, who encouraged its progress. Anne Hansen, Susan Kingsley Kent, Jeffrey Merrick, and Susanne Mrozik read drafts of chapters and provided invaluable suggestions. My thoughts on the issues discussed here have been influenced over the years by a great many people; my list could go on for pages, but I would particularly like to thank: Barbara Andaya, Judith Bennett, Jodi Bilink-off, Renate Bridenthal, Elizabeth Cohen, Natalie Zemon Davis, Mary Delgado, Lisa Di Caprio, Scott Hendrix, Evelyn Brooks Higginbotham, Grethe Jacobsen, Margaret Jolly, Susan Karant-Nunn, JoAnn McNa-mara, Mary Elizabeth Perry, Allyson Poska, Diana Robin, Lyndal Roper, Anne Schutte, Hilda Smith, Ulrike Strasser, Susan Stuard, Larissa Taylor, Gerhild Scholz Williams, and Heide Wunder. My husband Neil and my sons Kai and Tyr have become accustomed to my need to write, and "Mom is writing" is a normal explanation in our house for its failure to live up to Martha Stewart standards; Kai also loaned me his computer when the one I had worked on since the year he was born died, for which I am very grateful. Finally, I would like to thank the present and former members of my women's reading group, which began as one exploring medieval and Renaissance women and now knows no bounds: Margaret Borene, Martha Carlin, Janet Jesmok, Deirdre Keenan, Gwynne Kennedy, Gretchen Kling, Jennifer Sansone, Sandy Stark. None of us anticipated when we started getting together seven years ago what an important part of our lives those monthly meetings would become. Further on in the book I consider the issue of women's informal communities; the meaning of such groups in the past may be lost to us as they have left no records, but those in the present provide great sustenance, both intellectual and gustatory. This book is thus dedicated to our group.

1 Introduction

The title of this book would have made little sense to me when I chose to be a history major nearly three decades ago. I might perhaps have thought it an analysis of linguistic developments, as gender was something I considered (and bemoaned) largely when learning German nouns. The women's movement changed that, as it changed so much else. Advocates of women's rights in the present, myself included, looked at what we had been taught about the past – as well as what we had been taught about literature, psychology, religion, biology, and most other disciplines – and realized we were only hearing half the story. Most of the studies we read or heard described the male experience – "man the artist," "man the hunter," "man and his environment" – though they often portrayed it as universal. We began to investigate the lives of women in the past, first fitting them into the categories with which we were already comfortable – nations, historical periods, social classes, religious allegiance – and then realizing that this approach, sarcastically labeled "add women and stir," was unsatisfying. Focusing on women often disrupted the familiar categories, forcing us to rethink the way that history was organized and structured. The European Renaissance and Enlightenment lost some of their luster once women were included, as did the democracy of ancient Athens or Jacksonian America. Even newer historical approaches, such as the emphasis on class analysis using social science techniques termed the New Social History which had developed during the 1960s, were found to be wanting in their consideration of differences between women's and men's experiences.

This disruption of well-known categories and paradigms ultimately included the topic that had long been considered the proper focus of all history – man. Viewing the male experience as universal had not only hidden women's history, but it had also prevented analyzing men's experiences as those of men. The very words we used to describe individuals – "artist" and "woman artist," for example, or "scientist" and "woman scientist" – kept us from thinking about how the experiences of Michelangelo or Picasso or Isaac Newton were shaped by the fact that they were male, while it forced us to think about how being female affected Georgia O'Keeffe or Marie Curie. Historians familiar with studying women increasingly began to discuss the ways in which systems of sexual differentiation affected both women and men, and by the early 1980s to use the word "gender" to describe these systems. At that point, they differentiated primarily between "sex," by which they meant physical, morphological, and anatomical differences (what are often called "biological differences") and "gender," by which they meant a culturally constructed, historically changing, and often unstable system of differences.

Most of the studies with "gender" in the title still focused on women – and women's history continued as its own field – but a few looked equally at both sexes or concentrated on the male experience, calling their work "men's history" or the "new men's studies." Several university presses started book series with "gender" in their titles – "gender and culture," "gender and American law" – and scholars in many fields increasingly switched from "sex" to "gender" as the acceptable terminology: "sex roles" became "gender roles," "sex distinctions" became "gender distinctions" and so on. Historians interested in this new perspective asserted that gender was an appropriate category of analysis when looking at *all* historical developments, not simply those involving women or the family. *Every* political, intellectual, religious, economic, social, and even military change had an impact on the actions and roles of men and women, and, conversely, a culture's gender structures influenced every other structure or development.

Sex and Gender

Just at the point that historians and their students were gradually beginning to see the distinction between sex and gender (and an increasing number accepting the importance of gender as a category of analysis) that distinction became contested. Not only were there great debates about where the line should be drawn – were women "biologically" more peaceful and men "biologically" more skillful at math, or were such tendencies the result solely of their upbringing? – but some scholars wondered whether social gender and biological sex are so interrelated that any distinction between the two is meaningless. Their doubts came from four principle directions.

One of these was from biological scientists attempting to draw an absolute line between male and female. Though most people are born with external genitalia through which they are categorized "male" or "female" at birth, some are not. Their external genitalia may be ambiguous, a condition medically labeled "hermaphroditism." In earlier times most hermaphrodites were simply assigned to the sex they most closely resembled, with their condition only becoming a matter of historical record if they came to the attention of religious, medical, or legal authorities; in the nineteenth and twentieth centuries this gender assignment was sometimes reinforced by surgical procedures modifying or removing the inappropriate body parts.

Because the external body could be ambiguous, scientists began to stress the importance of internal indicators of sex difference. By the 1970s chromosomes were the favored marker, and quickly became part of popular as well as scientific understandings. In 1972, for example, the International Olympic Committee determined that simply "looking like" a woman was not enough, but that athletes would have to prove their "femaleness" through a chromosome test; an individual with certain types of chromosomal abnormalities would be judged "male" even if that person had been regarded as "female" since birth, and had breasts and a vagina but no penis. The problem with chromosomes is that they are also not perfectly dichotomous, but may involve ambiguous intermediate categories, so that more recently the anatomical roots of sex differences have been sought in prenatal hormones.

The intensity of the search for an infallible marker of sex difference, and the uncertainties in most "biological" markers, have indicated to many scholars that cultural notions are certainly influencing science in this area, and that "gender" may actually determine "sex" rather than the other way around. It is certainly cultural norms rather than biology which allow us to make gender assignments during the course of a day; not only are chromosomes and hormones not visible, but in most of the world's cultures clothing hides external genitalia. (Of course the clothing of men and women may be very different, but that is a culturally imposed gender distinction.) Children are taught these gender norms from a very young age – long before they learn anything about hormones and chromosomes – and even blind children share their culture's ideas about gender differences, so that these lessons are not based on external physical appearance alone, any more than they are based on internal body chemistry.

A second source of doubts about the distinction between sex and gender is anthropology. Though most of the world's cultures have a dichotomous view of gender, occasionally cultures develop a third or even a fourth gender. In some cultures, gender is determined by one's relationship to reproduction, so that adults are gendered male and female, but children and old people are regarded as different genders; in such cultures there are thus four genders, with linguistic, clothing, and behavioral distinctions for each one. In a number of areas throughout the world, including Alaska, the Amazon region, North America, Australia, Siberia, Central and South Asia, Oceania, and the Sudan, individuals who were originally viewed as male or female assume (or assumed, for in many areas such practices have ended) the gender identity of the other sex or combine the tasks, behavior, and clothing of men and women. Some of these individuals are hermaphrodites and occasionally they are eunuchs (castrated males), but more commonly they are morphologically male or female. The best known of these are found among several Native American peoples, and the Europeans who first encountered them regarded them as homosexuals and called them "berdaches," from an Arabic word for male prostitute. Now most scholars choose to use the term "two-spirit people," and note that they are distinguished from other men more by their work or religious roles than by their sexual activities; they are usually thought of as a third gender rather than effeminate or homosexual males. (Third genders will be discussed in more detail in chapter 8.) Comparative ethnography thus indicates that in many of the world's cultures, gender attribution is not based on genitals, and may, in fact, change throughout a person's life.

The arbitrary nature of gender is also noted in a third source of doubts, psychology. Individuals whose external genitalia and even chromosomal and hormonal patterns mark them as male or female may mentally regard themselves as the other, and choose to live and dress as the other, a condition the medical profession calls "gender dysphoria." In the 1950s sex-change operations became available for gender-dysphoric people who could afford them, and they could become transsexuals, thus making their physical sexual identity fit more closely with their mental gender identity; by the 1980s more than forty clinics in the United States were offering such operations. (Even this enterprise is shaped by gender in complex ways, as the vast majority of those who undergo sex-change operations go from male to female.) In the 1980s some people also began to describe themselves as "transgendered," that is, as neither male nor female or both male and female. The relationship between sex and gender is further complicated by sexuality, for persons of either sex (or transgendered persons) may be sexually attracted to persons of the other sex(es), persons of their own, or everyone. The transgendered movement – loosely organized in the United States within an umbrella organization of local groups called the Congress of Representatives – is politically often associated with gay, lesbian, and bisexual groups, though some adherents dispute this link, noting that the issue for them is gender, not sexual orientation. (The boundaries between the physical body and cultural forces in the issue of sexual orientation are just as contested as those in the issue of gender, of course, as some scientists attempt to find a "gay gene" and others view all such research as efforts to legitimize an immoral "life style choice" or a futile search for something that is completely socially constructed.)

The fourth source of doubts came from within history itself. As historians of women put greater emphasis on differences among women and became increasingly self-critical, they began to wonder whether "woman" was a valid analytical category. Some asserted that because gender structures varied so tremendously, and women's experiences differed so much depending on their race, class, and other factors, there really is nothing that could be labeled "woman" whose meaning is self-evident and unchanging over time. What we commonly call "biology," from this perspective, is also a socially and historically variable construct – the word "biology" itself did not appear until 1802 – and those who argue for a biological or physiological basis for gender difference (or sexual orientation) are "essentialists." These historians noted that not only in the present is gender "performative," that is, a role that can be taken on or changed at will, but it was so at many points in the past, as individuals "did gender" and conformed to or challenged gender roles. Thus it is misguided to think that we are studying women (or men, for that matter) as a sex, for the only thing that is in the historical record is gender.

Theoretical Trends

All of these doubts came together at a time when many historians were changing their basic understanding of the methods and function of history. Under the influence of literary and linguistic theory – often loosely termed "deconstruction" or "poststructuralism" – some historians focused their attention on the words of the past rather than on events, individuals, or groups. This trend is usually labeled the "linguistic turn" or the New Cultural History and its focus described as "discourse" because it incorporates visual materials such as paintings and film along with written texts. The most radical proponents of this point of view argue that the only thing we can know in history is discourse: that is, because historical sources always present a biased and partial picture, we can never fully reconstruct what actually happened. Historical documents and other types of evidence are "constructed," produced by particular individuals with particular interests and biases that consciously and unconsciously shape their content. They are thus no different from literary texts in their discursive nature, and historians should simply analyze them as texts, elucidating their possible meanings. Historians should not be preoccupied with searching for "reality," in this viewpoint, because to do so demonstrates a naive "positivism," a school of thought whose proponents regarded the chief aim of knowledge as the description of phenomena. (Both advocates and critics of positivism often quote the words of the nineteenth-century German historian Leopold von Ranke, who regarded the best history as that which retold events "as they actually happened.") Some poststructuralist historians assert that language determines, rather than simply describes, our understanding of the world; the body, for example, is not an objective reality, but changes according to the way people perceive their bodies.

The linguistic turn – which happened in other fields along with history – elicited harsh responses from many historians, including many who focused on women and gender. They asserted that it denied women the ability to shape their world – what is usually termed "agency" – in both past and present by positing unchangeable linguistic structures. Wasn't it ironic, they noted, that just as women were learning they *had* a history and asserting they were *part* of history, "history" became just a text and "women" just a historical construct? For a period it looked as if this disagreement would lead proponents of discourse analysis to lay claim to "gender" and those who opposed it to avoid "gender" and stick with "women." Because women's history was clearly rooted in the women's rights movement of the 1970s, it also appeared more political than gender analysis, and programs and research projects sometimes opted to use "gender" to downplay this connection with feminism.

As we enter the first decade of the twenty-first century, however, it appears that the division is less sharp; gender analysis is increasingly recognized as an outgrowth of women's history rather than its replacement, and viewed as a related but separate approach. Historians using gender as a category of analysis no longer feel compelled to adopt an extreme poststructuralist approach, but many instead treat their sources as referring to something beyond the sources themselves – an author, an event, a physical body – while recognizing that they do not present a perfect reflection. They do tend to use a wider range of literary and artistic sources than did earlier women's and gender history, so that their work is more "cultural" in that sense. Conversely, scholars of literature and art now pay greater attention to a text's or painting's relationship to an historical location or setting than they did in earlier decades – a movement labeled "New Historicism" in English literature – and they are beginning to pay more attention to variables that have been central to historical analysis for decades, such as class. Thus New Cultural History is evolving into the interdisciplinary field of Cultural Studies as the boundaries between history, literature, and art history are becoming less distinct or disappearing altogether.

New theoretical perspectives are adding additional complexity and bringing in new questions. One of these is queer theory, a field which began in the 1990s as in some ways a combination of gay and lesbian studies and poststructuralism. The gay liberation movement encouraged both public discussion of sexual matters in general and the study of homosexuality in the past and present. Like women's history, it challenged the assumption that sexual attitudes and practices or gender roles were "natural" and unchanging. Queer theory built on these challenges and on the doubts about the essential nature of sex, sexuality, and gender created by biology, psychology, anthropology, and history to highlight the artificial and constructed nature of all oppositional categories: men/women, homosexual/heterosexual, black/white. Some theorists celebrate all efforts at blurring or bending categories, viewing "identity" – or what in literary and cultural studies is often termed "subjectivity" – as both false and oppressive. Others have doubts about this (somewhat akin to doubts among many feminists about the merits of deconstruction), wondering whether one can work to end discrimination against homosexuals, women, African-Americans or any other group, if one denies that the group has an essential identity, something that makes its members clearly homosexual or women or African-American.

Related questions about identity, subjectivity, and the cultural construction of difference have also emerged from postcolonial theory outside of the United States and Critical Race Theory within it. Postcolonial history and theory has been particularly associated with South Asian scholars and the book series Subaltern Studies, and initially focused on people who have been subordinated by virtue of their race, class, culture, or language. Critical Race Theory developed in the 1980s as an outgrowth (and critique) of the civil rights movement combined with ideas derived from Critical Legal Studies, a radical group of legal scholars who argued that supposedly neutral legal concepts such as the individual or meritocracy actually masked power relationships. Both of these theoretical schools point out that racial, ethnic, and other hierarchies are deeply rooted social and cultural principles, not simply aberrations that can be remedied by legal or political change. They note that along with disenfranchising certain groups, such hierarchies privilege certain groups, a phenomenon that is beginning to be analyzed under the rubric of critical white studies. (This is a pattern similar to the growth of men's studies, and there is also a parallel within queer theory that is beginning to analyze heterosexuality rather than simply take it as an unquestioned given.)

Queer theory, postcolonial studies, and Critical Race Theory have all been criticized from both inside and outside for falling into the pattern set by traditional history, that is, regarding the male experience as normative and paying insufficient attention to gender differences. Scholars who have pointed this out have also noted that much feminist scholarship suffered from the opposite problem, taking the experiences of heterosexual white women as normative and paying too little attention to differences of race, class, nationality, ethnicity, or sexual orientation. They argue that the experiences of women of color must be recognized as distinctive, and that no one axis of difference (men/women, black/white, rich/poor, gay/straight) should be viewed as sufficient. These criticisms led, in the 1990s, to theoretical perspectives that attempted to recognize multiple lines of difference, such as Critical Race Feminism and postcolonial feminism. Such scholarship has begun to influence many areas of gender studies, even those which do not deal explicitly with race or ethnicity. It appears this cross-fertilization will continue, as issues of difference and identity are clearly key topics for historians in the ever-more-connected twenty-first century world.

This discussion of scholarly trends may make it appear as if focusing on women or using gender as a category of analysis has swept the discipline of history, with scholars simply choosing the approach or topic they prefer. This is far from the actual situation. Though investigating gender may seem self-evident to students in some graduate programs, there are also many historians who continue to view this as a passing fad, despite the fact that such judgments become more difficult to maintain as the decades pass. Others invoke "gender" without really thinking through its implications for their interpretations of the past. Though titles like "man the artist" have disappeared, as most authors – or their editors – have recognized their false universality, books still divide their subjects into "artists" and "women artists" or "rulers" and "women rulers." I have yet to see the phrase "the man artist Michelangelo" or "men philosophers such as Confucius" or "men governors." (One might argue that this is because women in such positions are generally the exceptions. In cases where the opposite is true, however, "male" rather than "man" is used; we speak of "male nurses," for example, not "men nurses." I am not sure why the habit of using a noun – woman – as an adjective started, nor what the implications are, as this is not done in other European languages. I experimented with such labeling by gender in the classroom, but it became too annoying, and I eventually resolved simply to try to avoid it, using "male" and "female" where these were appropriate.)

Studies of women and gender are also very unevenly distributed geographically and chronologically. Books on women's experience or that use gender as a category of analysis in the twentieth-century United States or in early modern England, for example, number in the hundreds, while those that focus on Portugal or Pakistan in any period may be counted on the fingers of one hand. This unevenness is related, not surprisingly, to uneven growth in women's studies programs, which is in turn related to the structure of higher education around the world and the ability or willingness of institutions of higher education to include new perspectives and programs. By the late 1970s hundreds of colleges and universities in the United States and Canada offered courses in women's history, and many had separate programs in women's history or women's studies. Universities in Britain, Israel, and Australia were somewhat slower to include lectures and seminars on women, and universities in western and eastern Europe slower still, with scholars in the 1990s still reporting that investigating the history of women could get them pegged as less than serious and be detrimental to their future careers. In Japan much of the research on women has been done by people outside the universities involved with local history societies, who have not used gender as a category of analysis for other historical topics. Universities and researchers, whether professional or non-professional, in developing countries have far fewer resources, and this situation has hampered all historical research and limited opportunities for any new direction. Thus an inordinate amount of the work in women's history and gender studies, including that which focuses on the continent of Europe and many other parts of the world, has been done by English-speaking historians, and the amount of research on English-speaking areas far outweighs that on the rest of the world. There is also imbalance within English-speaking areas, for studies of the United States vastly outnumber those of anywhere else; as one measure of this imbalance, more than two-thirds of the proposals to present papers at the Berkshire Conferences on Women's History during the 1980s and 1990s (the largest women's history conferences in the world) were on US topics.

There are signs that this imbalance is changing somewhat, as organizations to promote women's history and academic women's studies programs are gradually being established in more countries. Yet the head-start of English-language scholarship, combined with the ability of many students and scholars throughout the world to read English – and the inability of many English-speaking students and scholars to read anything but English – has meant that the exchange of theoretical insights and research results has to this point been largely a one-way street.

Structure of the Book

The dominance of English-language scholarship is both a blessing and a curse for the purposes of this book. Because of the sheer amount of materials available and the book's intended audience of students as well as scholars, I decided to include only English-language materials in the lists of further reading that end each chapter. You can trust that they contain much of the newest and best research available, but that they also represent only a small fraction of what is there. To explore any topic fully, you will need to go far beyond them, and in many cases, as with any historical topic, to read source materials, analyses, and theoretical discussions in other languages as well.

Organizing a brief book on a subject this huge was a challenge, made even greater by the fact that a key theme in women's and gender history has been the arbitrary and artificial nature of all boundaries – chronological, national, methodological, sexual. One of the central concepts in feminist history is that of intersection – most commonly used in the phrase "the intersection of race, class, and gender" – which highlights connections rather than boundaries. I thus decided to organize the book topically rather than geographically or chronologically, in order to highlight the specific connections between gender and other structures and institutions. Each topical chapter investigates the ways in which what it meant to be male and female was shaped by such aspects of society as economic or religious structures, and also explores the reverse – how gender in turn shaped work, for example, or religious institutions. This organization risks presenting gender as monolithic and ahistorical, however, and to lessen that tone most chapters are arranged chronologically to stress the ways in which gender structures have varied over time. Each chapter includes material from many of the world's cultures, notes both distinctions among them and links between them, and suggests possible reasons for variations among cultures and among different social, ethnic, and racial groups within one culture. I certainly could not cover every topic in every culture, so I have chosen to highlight specific developments and issues within certain cultures that have proven to be especially significant.

The order of the chapters is in some ways arbitrary, though it seemed appropriate to begin with the family, the smallest, oldest, and arguably most powerful shaper of gender. Thus chapter 2 explores the ways in which experiences within the family group differed for boys and girls, men and women. Taking insights from anthropology and demography, it notes changes in family structure and function over time, and discusses marriage patterns, family size, links between the family and other institutions, and norms and traditions of family life. Chapter 3 focuses on the economy, tracing the ways in which changes in economic structures – such as the means of production, patterns of work and consumption, and ownership practices – and in the meaning of those structures, shaped and were shaped by gender. Chapter 4 looks at ideals, norms, and laws, observing the ways in which groups defined what it meant to be a man or woman, linked these meanings with other cultural categories, and developed formal and informal means both of heightening and lessening distinctions based on gender. Chapter 5 investigates one type of particularly powerful institution, religion, and looks at the ways in which traditional religions and the major world religions have simultaneously strengthened and questioned existing gender patterns through their basic doctrines and the structures established to enforce those doctrines.

Chapter 6 considers another type of institution, politics, and explores how different forms of government have both shaped and been shaped by gender, from the earliest evidence of state formation to the contemporary political scene. It takes a broad view of political life, discussing civic and voluntary organizations along with local, national, and international political bodies, and it traces the movement for women's rights. Chapter 7 focuses on how gender figures in what is normally described as "culture," such as literature, art, architecture, and music, investigating the differing opportunities for men and women to be involved in education, training, and cultural production. Chapter 8 switches from a focus on institutions to a more individualized topic, sexuality, and traces the ways in which sexual attraction and sexual activity have been viewed and shaped, noting also how these interact with gender to create a historicized body.

The main themes and questions within each chapter often link with many of the other chapters, as one would expect for an issue as complex and pervasive as gender. This is particularly true as one goes further back in history, for most of the records we have refer to institutions that had multiple functions: Buddhist or Christian monasteries that owned land, supported cultural endeavors, and ruled territories, for example, or noble families who supported particular religious groups, organized work on their land, and used their children's marriages to increase family power. This interconnection is especially strong when looking at what many people regard as the key question in all of gender history, the origins of a gender hierarchy in which men are dominant and women are subordinate, what is normally called patriarchy. In every culture that has left written records, men have more power and access to resources than women, and this imbalance permeates every topic that will be a focus of subsequent chapters in this book – legal sanctions, intellectual structures, religious systems, economic privileges, social institutions, and cultural norms. Thus before we look at the ways these have separately interacted with gender, it will be helpful to explore various explanations that have been proposed as to the source of male dominance, for this will be the starting point of every chapter.

The Origins of Patriarchy

Searching for the origins of patriarchy first involves forgetting what biology, anthropology, psychology, and history have all revealed about the instability and ambiguity of dichotomous gender categories. Despite the presence of third and fourth genders, physical hermaphrodites, and transgendered individuals, most of the world's cultures have a system of two genders in which there are enormous differences between what it means to be a man and what it means to be a woman. This dualistic gender system has often been associated with other dichotomies, such as body/spirit, public/private, nature/culture, light/dark, up/down, outside/inside, yin/yang, right/left, sun/moon, a process we will examine more closely in chapter 4. Some of these dichotomies, such as sun/moon and light/dark, are naturally occurring and in many cultures viewed as divinely created, which has enabled people to view the male/female dichotomy also as natural or divinely ordained. This dichotomy, along with others with which it was associated, has generally been viewed as a hierarchy, with the male linked with the stronger and more positive element in other pairs (public, culture, light, right, sun, etc.) and the female with the weaker and more negative one (private, nature, dark, left, moon, etc.). The gender hierarchy has been remarkably resilient to change, surviving political and economic reforms and revolutions as well as intellectual and technological transformations. (Twentieth-century Russia is a good example of this; whether under the tsars or the communists or the post-Soviet government, women still did the shopping and the housekeeping and most of the child care, adding an unpaid "second shift" to their jobs in the paid work force; these tasks were necessary to keep society functioning, but left women no time for the things that were valued and rewarded, such as further education or political activities.) Why is this?

Answers to this question have varied. Some scholars have viewed the answer as outside of history, in innate physical or psychological differences between men and women. They accepted a genetic explanation from sociobiology of the 1960s and 1970s, which suggests that because men produce millions of sperm and women relatively few mature eggs, "genetic success" (defined as the transmission of one's genes to the next generation) means very different things for each gender. For men, it means impregnating as many women as possible while keeping other men from doing so (thus creating a propensity for violence), while for women it means caring for their offspring (thus creating a propensity for nurturing). This violence/nurturing dichotomy is often expressed in cultural rather than genetic terms, with men's competitiveness set against women's caring, though this, too, is often described explicitly or implicitly as "natural." In the 1990s evolutionary psychologists added to this line of reasoning, asserting that physical and psychological differences enhanced these genetic differences: pregnancy and lactation kept women dependent on others for food and protection, and men's greater upper-body strength allowed them to dominate once humans walked upright and used hand-held weapons. These ideas have been transmitted from scholarly to popular culture in the image of a club-wielding cave-man returning from hunting mammoths and dragging his wife off by her hair. They have also been challenged very recently by feminist evolutionary scientists, who assert that gathering was more important than hunting to prehistoric survival, that women may have depended for survival more on their own mothers and other older females than on males, and that promiscuity may actually be reproductively advantageous for females as well as males as it assures a greater likelihood of pregnancy.

Studies of primates, of human cultures that live by gathering and hunting, and of other human cultures around the world, have suggested that caring and violence are learned behaviors more than they are natural, and most historians see the roots of gender hierarchy in history rather than biology. The first scholars to consider the issue extensively were German social theorists of the nineteenth century, most prominently the scholar J. J. Bachofen. Bachofen asserted that human society had originally been a matriarchy in which mothers were all-powerful; the mother–child bond was the original source of culture, religion, and community, but gradually father–child links came to be regarded as more important, and superior (to Bachofen's eyes) patriarchal structures developed. Bachofen's ideas about primitive matriarchy were accepted by the socialist Friedrich Engels, who postulated a two-stage process from matriarchy to patriarchy. In matriarchal cultures, goods were owned in common, but with the expansion of agriculture and animal husbandry men began to claim ownership of crops, animals, and land, thus developing the notion of private property. Once men had private property, they became very concerned about passing it on to their own heirs, and attempted to control women's sexual lives to assure that offspring were legitimate. This led to the development of the nuclear family, which was followed by the development of the state, in which men's rights over women were legitimized through a variety of means, a process Engels describes as the "world historical defeat of the female sex."

The idea that human society was originally a matriarchy with female deities and female leaders was taken up by a few archeologists studying prehistoric cultures, for Europe most prominently Marija Gimbutus. Gimbutus argues that during the Neolithic period people living in

Europe and the Mediterranean area were egalitarian, peaceful, and matrifocal, honoring the earth as a mother goddess; this "Old Europe" was gradually overtaken through conquest and migration after 4000 BCE by Indo-European speaking people who originated in the steppes of Russia. These new people were militaristic, semi-nomadic, and patrilineal, and they worshipped a single male god and often followed a single male military leader. Though most archeologists dispute Gimbutus's ideas, they have been very influential among popular writers such as Merlin Stone and Riane Eisler, and among groups seeking alternative forms of spirituality; the Goddess now has a number of organizations and websites devoted to her worship, and her followers are developing new rituals and symbols that link to those of the prehistoric past.

Some scholars of Africa, most prominently Cheikh Anta Diop and Ifi Amadiume, agree with Gimbutus's critics that there is little evidence of matriarchy in Europe, but find evidence of matriarchy in ancient Africa. Diop points particularly to queenship among the ancient Egyptians, and Amadiume to matricentric household units and women's market networks. The notion that human society was originally a matriarchy has also been accepted by some historians from the People's Republic of China, who point to the development of certain characters in the Chinese writing system, ancient folk tales, and some archeological evidence. Most Chinese historians do not agree with this interpretation, however, noting that the evidence for a subordination of women is much stronger and includes some of the earliest written sources; they attribute the desire to see a matriarchy more to the acceptance of Engels' theories for ideological reasons among Marxist leaders than to strong evidence. Archeologists and historians of the early Americas have also debated the extent to which some groups may have been matriarchal, matrilineal, and matrilocal, or at least egalitarian in terms of gender, though here, again, the evidence is ambiguous.

The key problem in discussions of primitive matriarchy is the lack of written sources. Even those who argue that there was an original matriarchy agree that writing brought patriarchy, whether this was in Mesopotamia in the third millennium BCE or in North America in the eighteenth century CE, which means that earlier evidence – archeological remains, oral tradition, discussions of older traditions in later written records, literary sources such as creation stories or mythology – is fragmentary and difficult to interpret. Because of these problems, most historians avoid discussing matriarchy entirely, and many have chosen to stay away from all consideration of the origins of patriarchy, viewing the issue as too politicized and at any rate outside the time period in which they are interested.

One scholar of a later period who has not shied away from the issue is the historian Gerda Lerner, who has tipped Engels' line of causation on its head; women, she argues, *were* the first property, exchanged for their procreative power by men with other men through marriage, prostitution, and slavery. Thus patriarchy preceded other forms of hierarchy and domination such as kin networks and social classes, and women became primarily defined by their relation to men. Like Engels, Lerner links patriarchy with property ownership and political structures, but she also stresses the importance of non-material issues such as the creation of symbols and meaning through religion and philosophy. Women were excluded from direct links to the divine in Mesopotamian religion and Judaism, and defined as categorically inferior to men in Greek philosophy; thus both of the traditions generally regarded as the sources of Western culture – the Bible and Greek (particularly Aristotelian) thought – affirmed women's secondary position. Because other hierarchies such as those of hereditary aristocracy, class, or race privileged the women connected to powerful or wealthy men, women did not see themselves as part of a coherent group and often supported the institutions and intellectual structures that subordinated them.

Lerner's ideas have been challenged from a number of perspectives. Materialist historians have objected to her emphasis on ideas and symbols, and to the notion that gender hierarchies preceded those based on property ownership, while some classicists have argued that she misread ancient prostitution and other aspects of early cultures. Despite these objections, however, some of her – and Engels' – points are now widely accepted. Though it is unclear which came first, women's subordination emerged in the ancient Middle East at the same time as private ownership of property and plow agriculture, which significantly increased the food supply, but also significantly increased the resources needed to produce that food. Men generally carried out the plowing and care for animals, which led to boys being favored over girls for the work they could do for their parents while young and the support they could provide in their parents' old age; boys became the normal inheritors of family land and the rights to work communally held land.

The states that developed in the ancient Middle East, and then in the Mediterranean, India, China, and Central and South America, further heightened gender distinctions. They depended on taxes and tribute as well as slave labor for their support, and so their rulers were very interested in maintaining population levels. All of these states were dominated by hereditary aristocracies, who became concerned with maintaining the distinction between themselves and the majority of the population, and by male property owners, who wanted to be sure the children their wives bore were theirs. All of these concerns led to attempts to control women's reproduction through laws governing sexual relations and, more importantly, through marriage norms and practices which set up a very unequal relationship between spouses. In most states, laws were passed mandating that women be virgins on marriage and imposing strict punishment for a married woman's adultery; sexual relations outside of marriage on the part of husbands were not considered adultery. Concern with family honor thus became linked to women's sexuality in a way that it was not for men; men's honor revolved around their work activities and, for more prominent families, around their performance of public duties in the expanding government bureaucracies, including keeping written records.

These economic and political developments were accompanied and supported by cultural norms and religious concepts which heightened gender distinctions. In some places heavenly hierarchies came to reflect those on earth, with the gods arranged in a hierarchy dominated by a single male god, who was viewed as the primary creator of life. In others the cosmos itself was gendered, with order and harmony depending on a balance between male and female, but a balance in which male forces were the more powerful.

Most scholars thus see the development of patriarchy as a complicated process, involving everything that is normally considered part of "civilization": property ownership, plow agriculture, the bureaucratic state, writing, hereditary aristocracies, and the development of organized religion and philosophy. Many point out that cultures in which most of these did not develop, such as the !Kung of South Africa, Mbuti of Zaire, or Innu (Montagnais–Naskapi) of Labrador, appear to be (or have been) quite egalitarian, with the tasks of men and women differentiated, but equally valued. Cultures in which several of these were lacking, such as some in North America which did not have bureaucratic states or plow agriculture, were also less patriarchal than the norm. This is not universally the case, however, for there are also gathering and hunting cultures in which male dominance is extreme. There are also differences in the level of male dominance in civilizations that grew up quite near to each other, such as ancient Mesopotamia, in which systematic repression of women was severe, and ancient Egypt, in which women were treated with more respect and were more active in politics and religion.

The gender structures that developed in the ancient world or in cultures that were largely isolated were thus variable and complex, and this complexity only increased as cultures came into contact with one another. The remainder of this book is an attempt to sort through some of this complexity, to view some of the ways in which gender has interacted with other types of structures and institutions that people have created and that subsequently shaped their lives. It is based on my own research and that of many people who examine what the (incomplete) written and material record reveals about the past. Much of that record is the story of women's subordination, which may make you, as the reader, feel angry, depressed, or defensive. If you do, please remember that this is not a book about what might have been, what should be, or what could happen in the future; that I leave to philosophers, ethicists, theologians, and you.

Further Reading

Sex and gender

The best place to begin when considering the socially constructed nature of gender is still Suzanne J. Kessler and Wendy McKenna's *Gender: An Ethnomethodological Approach* (New York: Wiley, 1978). More recent works that expand on this include: Sherry B. Ortner and Harriet Whitehead, eds., *Sexual Meanings: The Cultural Construction of Gender and Sexuality* (Cambridge: Cambridge University Press, 1981); Teresa de Lauretis, *Technologies of Gender* (Bloomington: Indiana University Press, 1987); Sylvia Walby, *Theorizing Patriarchy* (Oxford: Blackwell Publishers, 1990); Judith Butler, *Gender Trouble: Feminism and the Subversion of Identity* (New York: Routledge, 1990) and *Bodies That Matter: On the Discursive Limits of Sex* (New York: Routledge, 1993); Judith Lorber, *Paradoxes of Gender* (New Haven, CT: Yale University Press, 1994). Three studies that explore the relationship between gender hierarchies and other systems of power are: R. W. Connell, *Gender and Power: Society, the Person and Sexual Politics* (Oxford: Polity Press, 1987); Jeff Hearn, *The Gender of Oppression: Men, Masculinity and the Critique of Marxism* (Brighton: Wheatsheaf, 1987); Arthur Brittan, *Masculinity and Power* (Oxford: Blackwell Publishers, 1989). Much thinking about gender is, of course, undertaken by feminist scholars in many disciplines; two recent good overviews of feminist thought are: Judith Evans, *Feminist Theory Today: An Introduction to Second-Wave Feminism* (New York: Sage, 1995) and Rosemarie Tong, *Feminist Thought: A More Comprehensive Introduction* (Boulder, CO: Westview Press, 1998). A very brief overview is: Mary Maynard, "Beyond the 'Big Three': the development of feminist theory into the 1990s," *Women's History Review* 4 (1995), 259–81.

Most of the studies noted above refer only occasionally to any period before the twentieth century. For ways to think about gender in history, start with Joan Scott's widely reprinted article, "Gender: a useful category of historical analysis," *American Historical Review* 91/5 (1986), 1,053–75. For an excellent survey of trends in women's history around the world, see: Karen Offen, Ruth Roach Pierson and Jane Rendell, eds., *Writing Women's History: International Perspectives* (Bloomington: Indiana University Press, 1990). For analyses of the development of women's and gender history, see: Judith M. Bennett, "Feminism and history," *Gender and History* 1 (1989), 251–72; Gisela Bock, "Women's history and gender history: aspects of an international debate," *Gender and History* 1 (spring 1989), 7–30; Sonya Rose, et al., "Gender history/ women's history: is feminist scholarship losing its critical edge?" *Journal of Women's History* 5 (1993), 89–128; Joan Wallach Scott, ed., *Women's Studies on the Edge*, special issue of *differences* 9/3 (1997).

Roberta L. Hall, et al., eds., *Male-Female Differences: A Bio-Cultural Perspective* (New York: Prager, 1985) includes studies by anthropologists and psychologists exploring various aspects of sex differences such as cognitive development and size, while Beth B. Hess and Myra Marx Ferree, eds., *Analyzing Gender: A Handbook of Social Science Research* (Newbury Park, CA: Sage, 1987) and Sandra Morgen, ed., *Gender and Anthropology: Critical Reviews for Research and Teaching* (Washington, DC: American Anthropological Association, 1989) provide very helpful summaries of ideas about sexual and gender differences in biology, psychology, and anthropology. Gilbert Herdt, ed., *Third Sex, Third Gender: Beyond Sexual Dimorphism in Culture and History* (New York: Zone Books, 1994) and Sabrina Petra Ramet, ed., *Gender Reversals and Gender Cultures: Anthropological and Historical Perspectives* (London: Routledge, 1996) contain essays about gender crossing, blending, inverting, and transcending in past and present, and Leslie Feinberg, *Transgender Warriors: Making History from Joan of Arc to RuPaul* (Boston: Beacon Press, 1996) provides an easy-to-read overview along with a number of interviews.

Doubts about the value of "women" as an analytical category were conveyed most forcefully in Denise Riley, *"Am I That Name?" Feminism and the Category of "Women" in History* (Minneapolis: University of Minnesota Press, 1988), though they have primarily been associated with the work of Joan Scott, such as *Gender and the Politics of History* (New York: Columbia University Press, 1988). Scott's work, with its poststructuralist emphasis on discourse, has provoked extremely hostile responses, with both sides using words like "absurd" and "nihilistic" to characterize the work of the other; this debate is summarized in a pair of brief articles by Martin Bunzl and Judith P. Zinsser, "The construction of history," *Journal of Women's History* 9/3 (1997), 119–39.

For queer theory, a good place to begin is the aptly titled book by Annamarie Jagose, *Queer Theory: An Introduction* (Washington Square, NY: New York University Press, 1996). Beyond this, some of the basic works include: Eve Sedgwick, *Epistemology of the Closet* (Berkeley: University of California Press, 1990); Julia Epstein and Kristina Straub, eds., *Body Guards: The Cultural Politics of Gender Ambiguity* (New York: Routledge, 1991); a special issue on "Queer theory: gay and lesbian sexualities," *differences* 3/2 (summer 1991); Michael Warner, ed., *Fear of a Queer Planet: Queer Politics and Social Theory* (Minneapolis: University of Minnesota Press, 1993); Peggy Phelan, *Unmarked: The Politics of Performance* (New York: Routledge, 1993). For essays linking feminist and queer theory, see Elizabeth Weed and Naomi Schor, eds., *Feminism Meets Queer Theory* (Bloomington: Indiana University Press, 1997) and for a work that focuses on history, see Scott Bravman, *Queer Fictions of the Past: History, Culture and Difference* (New York: Cambridge University Press, 1997).

There are several excellent collections of Critical Race Theory: Kimberlé Crenshaw, et al., eds., *Critical Race Theory: The Key Writings that Formed the Movement* (New York: New Press, 1995); Richard Delgado, ed., *Critical Race Theory: The Cutting Edge* (Philadelphia: Temple University Press, 1995); E. Nathaniel Gates, ed., *The Concept of "Race" in Natural and Social Science*, Critical Race Theory 1 (New York: Garland, 1997). Most of the basic works in the field are written by legal scholars such as Lani Guinier and Patricia Williams; for additional essential writings on race, see the many works by Derrick Bell, Orlando Patterson, Cornel West, and Henry Louis Gates. For the new field of critical white studies, see Ruth Frankenberg, *White Women, Race Matters: The Social Construction of Whiteness* (Minneapolis: University of Minnesota Press, 1993) and Richard Delgado and Jean Stefancic, eds., *Critical White Studies* (Philadelphia:

Temple University Press, 1997). Bill Ashcroft, Gareth Griffiths, and Helen Tiffin provide a good introductory survey of the main ideas in postcolonial theory in *The Empire Writes Back: Theory and Practice in Postcolonial Literatures* (London: Routledge, 1989); the same three scholars have also edited a large anthology of articles by many major postcolonial scholars, *The Postcolonial Studies Reader* (London: Routledge, 1995).

The work of the Subaltern Studies group may best be seen in its ongoing series of essay collections, *Subaltern Studies*, which began publication in 1982 in Delhi. Two additional important theoretical works by Indian scholars associated with Subaltern Studies are Partha Chatterjee, *Nationalist Thought and the Colonial World: A Derivative Discourse* (London: Zed Books, 1986) and Gayatri Chakravorty Spivak, *In Other Worlds: Essays in Cultural Politics* (London and New York: Metheun, 1987). Debates about issues raised by Subaltern Studies may be found in a series of articles by Gyan Prakash, Florencia Mallon, and Frederick Cooper in the *American Historical Review* 99 (1994), 1,475–545 and by Patricia Seed, Hernan Vídal, Walter D. Mignolo and Roleno Adorno in *Latin American Research Review* 26 (1991), 181–200 and 28 (1993), 113–52.

Two articles are especially helpful for understanding links between gender and race in history, and have been widely reprinted in various collections: Tessie Liu, "Teaching the differences among women from a historical perspective: rethinking race and gender as social categories," *Women's Studies International Forum* 14 (1991), 265–76; and Evelyn Brooks Higginbotham, "African-American women's history and the metalanguage of race," *Signs* 17 (1992), 251–74. The best introduction to Critical Race Feminism is Adrien Katherine Wing, ed., *Critical Race Feminism: A Reader* (New York: New York University Press, 1997). Two works that bring together feminist and postcolonial theory are Trin T. Minh-ha, *Woman, Native, Other: Writing Postcoloniality and Feminism* (Bloomington: Indiana University Press, 1989) and Anne McClintock, Aamir Mufti, and Ella Shoalt, eds., *Dangerous Liaisons: Gender, Nation and Postcolonial Perspectives* (Minneapolis: University of Minnesota Press, 1997).

The origins of patriarchy

The classic sociobiological account of human evolution is Edmund O. Wilson's *On Human Nature* (Cambridge, MA: Harvard University

Press, 1978). Recent feminist responses from evolutionary biologists and anthropologists include: Mary Zeiss Stange, *Woman the Hunter* (Boston: Beacon Press, 1997); Dianne Hales, *Just Like a Woman: How Gender Science is Redefining What Makes Us Female* (New York: Bantam, 1999).

For the earliest writers who discussed primitive matriarchy, see Johann J. Bachofen, *Myth, Religion and Mother Right: Selected Writings of J. J. Bachofen*, trans. Ralph Mannheim (Princeton, NJ: Princeton University Press, 1967) and Friedrich Engels, *The Origin of the Family, Private Property and the State*, ed. Eleanor Leacock (New York: International Publishers, 1972). Marija Gimbutus has written over twenty books, most of which include her ideas about matriarchy and the goddess; her definitive work is *The Civilization of the Goddess: The World of Old Europe* (San Francisco: Harper San Francisco, 1991). Her work has been the inspiration for Merlin Stone, *When God Was a Woman* (New York: Dial Press, 1976) and Riane Eisler, *The Chalice and the Blade: Our History, Our Future* (San Francisco: Harper and Row, 1988). It has been criticized in Lucy Goodison and Christine Morris, eds., *Ancient Goddesses* (Madison: University of Wisconsin Press, 1999) and Lynn Meskell, "Oh My Goddess!" *Archaeological Dialogues* 5/2 (1998), 126–42. For matriarchy in Africa, see the many works of Chiekh Anta Diop, especially *The Cultural Unity of Black Africa: The Domains of Matriarchy and Patriarchy in Classical Antiquity* (London: Karnak House, 1989), and Ifi Amadiume, *Re-Inventing Africa: Matriarchy, Religion, and Culture* (London: Zed Books, 1997).

Gerda Lerner's *The Creation of Patriarchy* (New York: Oxford University Press, 1986) remains the most important discussion of the origins of patriarchy by a historian. Many studies by anthropologists and archeologists have contributed to our understanding of this issue, including Joan M. Gero and Margaret W. Conkey, *Engendering Archaeology* (Oxford: Blackwell Publishers, 1991); Henrietta L. Moore, *Feminism and Anthropology* (Minneapolis: University of Minnesota Press, 1988); Micaela di Leonardo, ed., *Gender at the Crossroads of Knowledge: Feminist Anthropology in the Postmodern Era* (Berkeley: University of California Press, 1991); Dale Walde and Noreen D. Willows, eds., *The Archaeology of Gender* (Calgary: University of Calgary Archaeological Association, 1991). Irene Silverblatt, "Women in states," *Annual Review of Anthropology* 17 (1988), 427–60 surveys the literature on the relations between patriarchy and state formation.

Periodicals and electronic resources

The newest scholarship on gender in history may be found in periodicals; most of the major history journals include articles on gender with increasing regularity, and there are also several more specialized journals, including *Gender and History, Journal of Women's History, Journal of the History of Sexuality*, and *Women's History Review*. In addition, journals devoted to women's studies, men's studies, homosexuality, and cultural studies, such as *Signs, differences, Feminist Studies, Men and Masculinity*, and the *Journal of Homosexuality* often include articles with a historical focus.

Websites, electronic journals, and electronic discussion groups also provide an increasingly important venue for dissemination and discussion of research on gender. New websites appear daily and can best be discovered by Internet search engines. The electronic discussion groups appear to be more permanent; the most relevant ones for gender in history are:

H-Women (for women's history in general)
H-Frauen (for early modern women's history)
(for these, subscribe through listserv@uicvm.uic.edu)

MedFem (for medieval women in all disciplines)
(subscribe through medfem-l@u.washington.edu)

HISTSEX (for the history of sexuality)
(subscribe through http://homepages.primex.co.uk/~lesleyah)

2 The Family

As anthropologists and historians have made clear, the structure, function, and even the definition of "the family" have varied tremendously from culture to culture, and for different social groups within each culture. Some groups practiced polygamy and others monogamy; for some, the most important unit was the nuclear family of a man, a woman, and their children, while for others the extended kin network was most important; in some groups the family was primarily a unit of reproduction, while in others it was primarily a unit of production; in some groups married couples lived with the husband's family (patrilocality), in others they lived with the wife's (matrilocality or uxorilocality), and in others they set up their own household (neolocality); in some groups non-related individuals such as slaves or servants were considered part of the family, and in others they were not; in some groups adoption or godparentage created significant kinship-like ties (termed fictive or spiritual kinship), while in others only blood mattered; in some groups marital partners were chosen by parents or the family as a whole, and in others by the individuals themselves; in some groups a woman brought goods or money to her husband or husband's family on marriage (a dowry), and in others a man gave goods or money to his wife's family (brideprice); in some groups marriage was forbidden to certain segments of the population, while in others nearly everyone married; in some groups divorce was easy and in others impossible; in some groups premarital sexuality was acceptable or even expected and in others it was harshly punished; in some groups the oldest son inherited everything (primogeniture) and in others all children or at least all sons shared in inheritance (partible inheritance); in some groups marriage was early and in others it was late; in some groups people married within their group (endogamy) and in others outside of their group (exogamy); in some groups spouses were about the same age, while in others they were very different ages; in some groups contraception, abortion, and even infanticide were acceptable practices of limiting the number of children, while in others these were strictly prohibited. All of these variables interacted and often changed over time because of internal developments or contacts with other cultures.

Despite all of this variety there are certain generalizations we can make about the family in history. Though patterns and structures differed tremendously, every group had notions of proper family life which were reinforced through law codes, religious prescriptions, taboos, education, or other means. Most individuals followed these expectations, which is why we can make generalizations about issues such as those noted in the paragraph above. This tendency for families to follow certain patterns means that family history can often be portrayed in charts and graphs of quantitative measures such as average age at marriage, average number and frequency of children, rates of remarriage for widows and widowers, inheritance patterns, rates of divorce, and so on. Because family life usually involved producing and preparing the next generation, these measures are also linked to general demographic measures such as birth and death rates, population growth and decline, fertility rates, and life expectancy.

Quantitative sources also make clear that the experience of family life was gendered. Age at first marriage was often very different for men and women, as was life expectancy, rate of remarriage after widowhood or divorce, and amount of inheritance; polygamy was much more likely to involve men with multiple wives than women with multiple husbands; kin networks involving the father's family (agnatic kin) were generally more important than those involving the mother's (morganatic kin); inheritance may have been divided among children, but if one child inherited, it was almost always a son; in some cultures, such as the Bedouin of the Middle East, only the birth of a son created a true family that was counted separately. Non-quantitative sources about family life, including diaries, letters, and court records, also indicate that the experiences within the family group differed for boys and girls, men and women. Children learned (and continue to learn) what it means to be male or female first from the older people in their families, and their first experiences with gender differences were usually within the family. Gender also shaped the consequences of breaking with the accepted pattern of family life, consequences which might include social ostracism, outlawry, psychiatric counseling, imprisonment, or death.

These gender differences within the family have been augmented by gender differences in other areas that will be explored later in this book, and all of these together have operated to link women's experience more closely than men's to family life in most cultures. Because of this, stories of men's actions and accomplishments often neglect to mention even whether they were married or had children, while those of women usually discuss their family situation; for example, few biographies of the French thinker Jean-Jacques Rousseau mention that he had several children out of wedlock and put them all up for adoption, while no biography of Queen Elizabeth I of England or the American suffragist Susan B. Anthony neglects to mention that they were unmarried and childless. Family structures and relationships, marital customs and patterns, norms and traditions of family life also had a tremendous impact on men, however, and ignoring these provides an incomplete history. Because the family was the earliest form of social organization, and the first social organization children encountered, the lessons learned about gender within the family have been the most difficult for both sexes to change.

Ancient Egypt and Mesopotamia

The discussion of explanations for the origins of patriarchy in chapter 1 notes some of the ways in which gender distinctions first emerged in prehistoric family life, before the development of writing. The earliest written law codes, such as that of the Babylonian king Hammurabi (1792–1750 BCE), included many provisions regarding marriage and family life, setting out what the Babylonian elite regarded as the proper relationship between the sexes and the proper running of a household; according to its provisions, a husband could divorce his wife without returning her dowry if she "made up her mind to leave in order that she may engage in business, thus neglecting her house and humiliating her husband" and could drown her if she "had been caught lying with another man." (The code does not mention punishment for a married man who had sex with a woman not his wife.)

In both ancient Mesopotamia and ancient Egypt marriage was generally monogamous, though men could and did have more than one wife if their economic status was high enough, especially if their first wife had not had children. Rulers of Egypt in the New Kingdom (1570 BCE–1075 CE) and rulers in Mesopotamia at roughly the same time are often described as having harems of many wives and concubines, though historians are not sure when this practice began or even if it was as extensive as later commentators thought; were the many women buried in royal tombs the king's concubines, or might they have been the queen's servants? Whatever the situation for rulers and the very wealthy, most marriages were monogamous, with the prime emphasis on pro-creation and maintaining the economic and social well-being of the household. Divorce was possible, but difficult.

Marriage in the ancient world not only linked two individuals but also two families, so that the choice of a spouse was much too important a matter to be left to young people to decide. Marriages were most often arranged by one's parents, who assessed the possible marriage partners and chose someone appropriate. Arranged marriage did not preclude the possibility of spousal affection and romantic love, however. Among the tax lists, funerary inscriptions, and legal codes that are the most common records left from early civilizations, there is also some erotic love poetry. Though we have no way of knowing whether this was written as a prelude to marriage or to someone outside of marriage, we do know that husbands in New Kingdom Egypt often referred affectionately to their wives on their tomb inscriptions and that couples were portrayed arm in arm.

Portrayal of spouses side by side may seem odd given the unequal status of men and women in marriage, but it also can serve as a visual demonstration of two aspects of ancient marriage. One is that in actual practice women may have made more family decisions and controlled more of what went on in the household than the laws would indicate. Laws always depict an ideal situation, one the lawmakers hope to create, rather than reality. We know from more recent societies in which women are far more restricted than they were in ancient Mesopotamia that they actually oppose, subvert, and ignore restrictions in ways that reading the laws alone would never indicate were possible. A second aspect of ancient marriage which these statutes hint at is the fact that though in some later societies of the Middle East concern about women's honor would mean their total seclusion, this was not true in ancient Mesopotamia or Egypt. Despite the preference for male heirs, high death rates often left women sole heirs, and the good of the family and preservation of the lineage required that they have some legal rights. Thus, though they were always a tiny minority of those appearing in legal records, women did control their own property to some degree, act as independent legal persons bringing cases to court, serve as guarantors for the loans of others, and work out in public. Husbands did not assume total control of their wives' property in all cases – probably when the wife had come from a more prominent or wealthier family, and had powerful brothers or other male relatives – so that women independently bequeathed property to their sons and acted on their behalf. Women were most independent in Egypt; the Assyrians, on the other hand (one of the many empires that conquered Mesopotamia), required respectable women to wear a veil in public and forbade them to own property.

Because a woman's identity was more closely tied to her husband's than a man's to his wife's, a husband's death often brought great changes in a woman's situation. She became a widow, a word for which there is no male equivalent in many ancient languages and one of the few words in English and other modern languages in which the male, widower, is derived from the female instead of the other way around. At that point she often became more active legally, buying and selling land, making loans, and making donations to religious establishments. A widow's actions were acceptable because she was often the guardian for her children and in control of the family finances, but she was also somewhat suspect because she was not under direct male control.

The Classical Cultures of China, India, and the Mediterranean

Many of the gender patterns in family life that developed in the world's earliest civilizations carried over into the classical cultures of Eurasia, though they were often made more rigid because of the expansion of written law codes and the development of religious and philosophical systems which posited clear gender distinctions (these will be discussed in chapters 4 and 5). The family was generally regarded as the basis of society, and rights to political positions were often limited to men who were the heads of families. As in Mesopotamia and Egypt, most people married, though in some places certain marriages, such as those between slaves, between a slave and a free person, or between persons of different social classes, were prohibited. In these cases other legal forms, such as concubinage or the Roman slave "marriage" called *contubernium* were often established to legitimate sexual relations. These forms were gender-specific, for they never included one which allowed a higher-status woman to have legitimate sexual relations with a lower-status man; such relations were instead often punishable by death. Size of the household was often dependent on social status, with wealthier households containing more relatives, servants, and slaves; in some areas extended families lived in a large family compound, while in others most households were nuclear. Whatever a household's size or composition, everyone living within it, including adult children and servants, was under the authority of the male head of household. When he died, his widow often came under the authority of her eldest son or her husband's brother rather than acting independently. In some cultures she was expected to marry the brother of her dead husband − a practice called levirate marriage − particularly if her husband had not had a son; her sons by her new husband were legally regarded as belonging to her deceased first husband.

Weddings were central occasions in a family's life, with spouses chosen carefully by parents, other family members, or marriage brokers, and much of a family's resources often going to pay for the ceremony and setting up the new household. Marital agreements, especially among the well-to-do, were stipulated with contracts between the families involved, a practice that continued for centuries throughout the world, and in many areas continues today. Opportunities for divorce varied in the classical world, but in many cultures it was nearly impossible, so the choice of a spouse was undertaken very carefully after much consultation with relatives and often astrologers or other types of people who predicted the future. Weddings themselves were held on days determined to be lucky or auspicious, a determination arrived at independently for each couple.

Rituals surrounding marriage became more complex in the classical period, particularly for the wealthy. In China during the Han dynasty (202 BCE–220 CE), for example, marriages included a number of prescribed steps, of which the most important was the presentation of betrothal gifts from the groom and the groom's family to the bride and the bride's family, an occasion of conspicuous consumption for the rich and sometimes near-bankruptcy for the poor. The bride's family then often countered with a dowry, sometimes of goods purchased with the money in the betrothal gift; using a betrothal gift for family financial needs rather than reserving it for the bride was viewed as dishonorable because it made it appear that the bride had been sold. A marriage with no betrothal gift or dowry was also dishonorable, with the woman often considered a concubine rather than a wife. Once all these goods had been exchanged, the bride was taken to the ancestral home of the groom, where she was expected to obey her husband and his living relatives, and to honor his ancestors. Confucian teachings required upper-class men to carry out specific rituals honoring their ancestors and clan throughout their lives, and to have sons so that these rituals could continue. Their names were inscribed on the official family list, and women's on the list of their marital families once they had a son; women who had no sons disappeared from family memory, unless they could arrange to adopt one, perhaps from a concubine or slave of their husband. Women continued to belong to their marital families even if they were widowed; if a widow's birth family wanted her to marry again, it often had to ransom her back from her deceased husband's family, and her children by her first husband stayed with his family.

In India, Hindu ideas about the importance of family life and many children meant that all men and women were expected to marry, and that women in particular married very young; widows and women who had not had sons were excluded from wedding festivities. Parents, other relatives, or professional match-makers chose one's spouse, and anything that interfered with procreation, including exclusively homosexual attachments, was frowned upon. The domestic fire had great symbolic importance; husband and wife made regular offerings in front of it. Children, particularly boys, were shown great affection and developed close attachments to their parents, especially their mothers. These mothers often continued to live in the house of their eldest son upon widowhood, creating stresses between mothers- and daughters-in-law; cruel and angry mothers-in-law were standard figures in the stories of classical India, reflecting what was often harsh treatment of young women in real life. (In the Mediterranean and the rest of Europe, widowed mothers generally did not live with their married sons, so the spiteful old woman in stories is generally a step-mother rather than a mother-in-law.)

In the classical Mediterranean family life was shaped more by practical and secular aims than it was in China or India, which led occasionally to marital practices and family forms that differed dramatically from the more common patriarchal and patrilocal. The most dramatic example of this is the Greek city-state of Sparta, in which all activity was directed toward military ends. Citizen boys left their homes at age seven in Sparta and lived in military camps until they were thirty, eating and training with boys and men their own age; they married at about eighteen to women of roughly the same age, but saw their wives only when they sneaked out of camp. Military discipline was harsh – this is the origin of the word "spartan" – but severity was viewed as necessary to prepare men both to fight external enemies such as Athens and to control the Spartan slave and unfree farmer population, which vastly outnumbered the citizens.

In this militaristic atmosphere citizen women were remarkably free. As in all classical cultures there was an emphasis on child-bearing, but the Spartan leadership viewed maternal health as important for the bearing of healthy, strong children, and so encouraged women to participate in athletics and to eat well. With men in military service most of their lives, citizen women owned property and ran the household, and were not physically restricted or secluded. Marriage often began with a trial marriage period to make sure the couple could have children, with divorce and remarriage the normal course if they were unsuccessful. In contrast to India, despite the emphasis on procreation, homosexuality was widely accepted, with male same-sex relationships in particular viewed as militarily expedient, leading men to fight more fiercely in defense of their lovers and comrades.

The unusual gender structures of Sparta did not leave much of a legacy, however, for the dominant city-state culturally, politically, and intellectually was Athens, in which the lives of citizen women were more like those of women in China or India than like those of their neighbors in Sparta. Athenian democracy made a sharp distinction between citizen and non-citizen, with citizenship handed down from father to son, symbolized by a ceremony held on the tenth day after a child was born in which the father laid his son on the floor of the house and gave him a name; this ceremony marked a boy's legal birth. It was thus very important to Athenian citizen men that their sons be their own, so that women were increasingly secluded in special parts of the house and allowed out in public only for religious festivals, funerals, and perhaps the theater (there is a debate about this among historians). As in India, husbands were often a decade or more older than their wives, and clearly better educated, for the formal and informal institutions for learning which developed in Athens were for men only. Most men married, but being unmarried did not bar a man from political life, which was viewed as the center of human existence by many Athenians. In contrast to most classical societies, Athenians regarded the individual man, rather than the family, as the basis of the social order, and the central relationship one between a younger man and an older man who trained him in cultural and political adulthood. (Such relationships will be discussed in more detail in chapter 8.)

Classical Rome had very different norms of family life than either Sparta or Athens. The word "family" (*familia*) in ancient Rome actually meant all those under the authority of a male head of household, including non-related slaves and servants. Thus, just as slaveowners held power over their slaves, fathers held great power over their children and husbands over their wives. Somewhat contradictorily, the Romans viewed the model marriage as one in which husbands and wives were loyal to one another and shared interests, activities, and property. These notions were often expressed on family tombstones, such as the following from the first century CE: "Pythion son of Hicesius set up this common memorial to himself and to his wife Eicydilla daughter of Epicudes. He was married at eighteen and she at fifteen and for fifty years of life together they shared agreement unbroken, happy among the living and blessed among the dead." If the marriage was less than ideal, by the late Republic (first century BCE) divorce was possible at the instigation of either the husband or wife. Romans also idealized the role of the mother, viewing women as important in their children's education and thus worthy of an education themselves.

In all classical cultures philosophical and religious ideals of family life had a much greater impact on elites than on ordinary people, a situation that continued into the post-classical period when elite women were increasingly secluded within their households in China, India, and much of the Islamic world. In both the classical and post-classical periods, and, indeed, in most of the world's cultures in all periods, the vast majority of people were peasants who spent their days producing food. Almost all of them married, not because of Confucian principles or Hindu teachings or Islamic injunctions, but because marital couples and their children were the basic unit of agricultural production; procreation was an economic necessity and not simply a religious duty. Some historians speculate that peasant women were less restricted than upper-class women, or at least that their lives were more like those of the male members of their family – made equally miserable by poverty and hard work – than was the case for wealthier women. Whether any woman would have regarded this as positive, and not traded her life for the more comfortable, though more restricted, one of an aristocratic woman, is difficult to say, for we have almost no sources which give us the opinions of peasant women or men about their families until the nineteenth century.

The family patterns sketched here for classical cultures were thus class-related, and certain small groups within the huge populations of China and India also followed very different models. Among the Khasi people in northwestern India and the Musuo in southwestern China, for example, women headed the households, owned businesses, and handed down property and the family name to their daughters. These matrilineal practices have continued to today, although there is pressure to make these groups conform more closely with the rest of India and China. The irony of this is not lost on Lakyntieth Lyndoh, a Khasi businesswoman, who commented in 1996: "Why should we be in such a hurry to give up our long-fought-for rights as independent women when most other women in the world are clamoring to increase theirs?"

Africa, the Americas, and Southeast Asia

The scarcity of written sources that limits our access to peasant family life also affects our understanding of all families in Africa, the Americas, and much of Southeast Asia and the Pacific before the modern period. Historians and anthropologists use a variety of means to study kinship organizations, marital patterns, living arrangements, and other aspects of family structure: oral history and traditions, later written records, reports of outsiders, such as Muslim traders in Africa or Christian missionaries in America and the Pacific islands, direct interviews with living individuals, archeological remains, linguistic analysis of words denoting family and kin. All of these provide evidence about families in the past, but scholars also warn about their limitations; outsiders brought their own biases, archeological remains are difficult to interpret, and oral history (like all history) represents a specific perspective. What is described as "traditional" may often be quite new, for family patterns are not static. They may also be quite different in groups which are fairly close to one another geographically; if the Khasi and the Musuo were able to survive in China and India, it is no surprise that groups in areas without strong written traditions developed very diverse family forms and arrangements.

There are a few patterns found in most cultures over these huge areas, however. The "family" was often defined as a fairly wide group of relatives, and this kin group had a voice in domestic and other matters, such as who would marry and when they would do so, who would be sent to school and how long they would attend, who would have access to land or other economic resources, whose conduct was unacceptable and worthy of censure or punishment. These decisions were arrived at through a process of negotiation and discussion within the family, with the influence of each member dependent on the situation. The opinions of older family members generally carried more weight than those of the younger, the opinions of first born more than later born, and the opinions of men more than women. These two hierarchies – age and gender – interacted in complex ways dependent on the issue at hand, with older women sometimes having control of younger men on certain matters. In some cultures older women served as matchmakers, suggesting or arranging marriages.

Wealth was another hierarchy that shaped family life in these areas, as in the rest of the world. In some areas most marriages were monogamous, and in some polygyny was quite common, but even in areas where monogamy was the rule, wealthy and powerful men married more than one wife or had several secondary wives or concubines along with a principal wife, a pattern often termed "resource polygyny." Rulers of states and villages had the most wives or other types of female dependents as a sign of status, and they used marriage as a way to make or cement alliances. Marriage could also be used as a symbol of conquest; the leaders of both the Incas and the Aztecs, for example, married the daughters of rulers of the tribes they had conquered, and in seventeenth-century Virginia, the Algonkian-speaking chief Powhatan reinforced his domination of other groups by marrying women from their villages and then sending them back once they had borne him a child.

Living arrangements varied in polygynous marriages. In Africa families lived in house-compounds in which each wife had her own house; each wife also had her own cattle, fields, and property, for the notion that a wife's property actually belonged to her husband which became standard in Europe was not accepted in most of Africa. In parts of the world in which women were secluded, all wives lived within the same household, often in a special part of the house constructed for them, termed the *harim* (which means "forbidden area") or *zenana*. (See chapters 4 and 5 for longer discussions of the seclusion of women.)

Many cultures in Africa, the Americas, and the Pacific were matrilineal, with property passed down through the female line. This did not necessarily mean that women were economically or legally autonomous, but that they depended on their brothers rather than their husbands. Their brothers also depended on them, however, for many of these cultures also had systems of marriage involving a brideprice, so that a man could only marry once his sister had, using the money or goods such as land or cattle that the family had received as *her* brideprice to acquire a wife. This system encouraged close life-long relations among siblings, with women relying on their birth families for support if they came into conflict with their husbands. This was particularly true in groups that were matrilocal, such as those in eastern North America, in which husbands came to live with their wives' clans and related women lived together. Relations with one's mother's kin were thus more important than those with one's father's kin or even one's spouse, and children often regarded their mother's brothers with particular respect.

Matrilineal inheritance systems and brideprice made some family relationships stronger, but they also created tensions. In some areas men acquired wives not through providing goods to the bride's family, but by brideservice, working for their prospective father-in-law either before the marriage or in a period of trial marriage; this could easily lead to resentment. Men objected to the influence of their wives' families, and, in areas where wives moved to their husbands' households, intentionally chose wives who came from far away, which also lessened the degree to which their sons could rely on their maternal uncles. Conflict between fathers and sons was exacerbated by resource polygyny and brideprice, as families had to decide whether their resources would best be spent acquiring a first wife for a son or another wife for the father. Some scholars have seen this generational conflict as a source for harsh initiation rituals which unmarried young men often had to undergo; only those who had gone through such rituals would be allowed to marry and join the ranks of fully adult men.

Some of these cultures had bilateral inheritance. In many groups living in the Andean region, for example, lines of descent were reckoned through both sexes, with girls inheriting access to resources such as land, water, and animals through their mothers, and boys through their fathers. In other groups with bilateral inheritance, such as the Yako of Nigeria, only men inherited, but they did so from both their fathers and their mothers' brothers.

Some form of divorce or marital separation was available in most of these cultures, and in some it was quite easy for either spouse to initiate. Among matrilocal groups in North America, for example, a man who wished to divorce simply left his wife's house, while a woman put her husband's belongings outside her family's house, indicating she wished him to leave; the children in both cases stayed with the mother and her family. Among some groups divorce was frowned upon after children had been born, however, or because it would involve complicated financial transactions, such as the return of bridewealth.

Relatively easy divorce was an essential part of systems of temporary marriage that developed in some parts of Southeast Asia and the Pacific. These were cultures in which people were taught to have a strong sense of debt and obligation to their parents and family for having been given life, termed *on* in Vietnamese and *hiya* in Tagalog, the language of part of the Philippines. This concept of debt extended beyond the family to the larger political and economic realm, so that people were often enmeshed in a complex system of dependency, sometimes placing themselves or family members into slavery to another in return for support – what is often termed "debt-slavery" – or otherwise promising loyalty or service. One also gave gifts in order to have others in one's debt; gift-giving was an important way to make alliances, pacify possible enemies, and create links and networks of obligations among strangers. Often these gifts included women, for exchanging women was considered the best way to transform strangers into relatives. These unions were often accompanied by a marriage ceremony and the expectation of spousal fidelity, but they were also understood to be temporary. If the spouses disagreed with one another or the man was from elsewhere and returned to his home country, the marriage ended, just as marriages between local spouses ended if there was conflict or one spouse disappeared for a year or more. Both sides gained from such temporary marriages; the man gained a sexual and domestic partner, and the woman and her family gained prestige through their contact with an outsider and their repayment of a debt. Concepts of debt also structured marriage patterns in other ways; prospective grooms frequently carried out brideservice for their future fathers-in-law, understood as paying off their obligations.

Medieval and Early Modern Europe

Family life in Europe during the period from the Roman Empire to Columbus was shaped to a large degree by the Christian Church. Early Christian thinkers were often hostile to the family, viewing virginity as the preferred form of existence; alternatives to family life, in which men and women lived in single-sex communities dedicated to service to God, developed in most parts of Europe. In some areas these communities took in widows as well as never-married people, providing a safe and honorable place for women who chose not to marry or not to remarry, or whose families made this decision for them.

Though there were certainly many people whose families decided when and whom and if they would marry, officially the Christian Church declared that consent of the spouses was the basis of marriage; indeed, until the sixteenth century, consent of the spouses was all that was required to have a valid marriage, though by the twelfth century many church leaders also regarded marriage as a sacrament, a ceremony that provided visible evidence of God's grace, like baptism. Because of its sacramental nature, marriage was increasingly held to be indissoluble, and sexual relations outside of marriage were viewed as illicit. Thus Christian Europe banned polygamy and divorce, and attempted to prohibit any form of sexual relationship that was not marriage, such as concubinage or premarital sex, termed fornication. Women were generally expected to bring a dowry when they married, which ranged from a few household goods to a whole province in the case of the high nobility. Remarriage after the death of a spouse was acceptable for both men and women and very common, though men remarried faster than women and rural people faster than urban residents. Most issues regarding marriage and many other aspects of family life came under the jurisdiction of church courts and were regulated by an increasingly elaborate legal system termed canon law. The ideals for marriage were not followed in many instances: powerful individuals could often persuade church courts to grant annulments of marriages they needed to end (an annulment is a ruling that there never was a valid marriage in the first place, in contrast to divorce which ends an existing marriage); men, including priests and other church leaders, had concubines and mistresses; young people had sex before marriage and were forced into marriages they did not want. Nevertheless, these ideals and the institutions established to enforce them remained important shapers of men's and women's understanding of and place within the family.

Christianity provided the basic skeleton of family structure in medieval Europe, but there were also regional differences. In eastern Europe the Orthodox Christian churches gradually came to allow divorce for adultery, abuse, abandonment, impotence, and barrenness, with both spouses allowed (somewhat grudgingly) to remarry. Consent of the parents as well as the spouses was required for first marriages, especially because age of marriage was often very early – twelve to thirteen for girls, sixteen to eighteen for boys. The couple generally lived with the parents of one spouse, usually the husband, and the strongest emotional bonds were often, as in India and China, those between mothers and sons rather than spouses.

After the Ottoman Turks defeated the Byzantine Empire in the fifteenth century, a large part of eastern Europe came under Muslim rule; open intermarriage between Christians and Muslims was not permitted, though marriage after one party (usually the wife) converted was accepted. Christian courts ceased to operate, so that Christians in the vast Ottoman Empire brought cases involving marriage or other family matters to Muslim courts. This was also true for Jews in Muslim-held areas, though in general Jewish family life was regulated by Jewish laws and traditions. Jewish marriages in most parts of Europe were similar to Christian marriages in eastern Europe, with parents playing an important role and spouses both young. Jewish writers emphasized companionship and affection between spouses, however, and described the ideal marriage as one predestined in heaven. Judaism did allow divorce, which was then sometimes justified on the grounds that the spouses had obviously not been predestined for each other.

Among Christians in western Europe two rather distinct family patterns developed in the Middle Ages. In the south – as in eastern Europe and much of the rest of the world – marriage was between teenagers who lived with one set of parents for a long time, or between a man in his late twenties or thirties and a much younger woman, with households again containing several generations. In northwestern Europe historians have identified a marriage pattern unique in the world in the premodern period, with couples waiting until their mid- or late twenties to marry, long beyond the age of sexual maturity, and then immediately setting up an independent household. Husbands were likely to be only two or three years older than their wives at first marriage, and though households often contained servants, they rarely contained more than one family member who was not a part of the nuclear family. The northwestern European marriage pattern resulted largely from the idea that couples should be economically independent before they married, so that both spouses spent long periods as servants or workers in other households saving money and learning skills, or waited until their own parents had died and the family property was distributed. The most unusual features of this pattern were the late age of marriage for women and the fact that a significant number of people never married at all; demographers estimate that between 10 to 15 percent of the northwestern European population never married in fifteenth through the eighteenth centuries, and that in some places this figure may have been as high as 25 percent. Both late marriage for women and the large unmarried population were important checks on population growth, though they also worried contemporary religious and political leaders, who continued to view marital households as the basis of society. Particularly in the sixteenth century, religious reformers urged everyone to marry (Catholic reformers excepted those who lived in religious communities, but advocated marriage for everyone else) and political leaders passed laws forbidding unmarried people to live on their own.

The Colonial World

In many parts of the world the family forms that had developed before 1500 were radically altered by European exploration and colonization. Europeans brought with them not only their own religious, political, and economic structures, but also their own ideas of proper family life and the institutions designed to enforce those ideas. As in Europe, Christianity provided the official structure for family life in much of the colonial world during the sixteenth through the eighteenth centuries; polygamy was abolished, divorce made more difficult, premarital sexual activity prohibited, church courts established to handle family issues. The lives of actual families and the roles of men and women in them were often shaped more by two other factors, however. The first was the germs that Europeans brought with them, which often advanced ahead of actual colonial forces. In some cases disease wiped out entire indigenous groups, and everywhere it disrupted patterns of marriage and family life. The second was the expansion of existing ways of understanding kinship to include huge categories of people, distinguished from one another by skin tone and facial features in what came to be understood as "race."

In many cultures "blood" was a common way of marking family, clan, and eventually class differences, with those of "noble blood" prohibited from marrying commoners and taught to be concerned about their blood lines. This has been studied most extensively in Europe, but high-status people in other parts of the world were also thought to have superior blood; in parts of Indonesia, for example, nobles were referred to as "white-blooded" and their marriages limited to others with similar blood. Blood also came to be used to describe national boundaries, with those having "French blood" distinguished from those having "German blood," "English blood," or "Spanish blood." Religious beliefs were also conceptualized as blood, with people regarded as having Jewish, Muslim, or Christian blood, and after the Reformation, Protestant or Catholic blood. The most dramatic expression of this was in early modern Spain, where "purity of the blood" – having no Jewish or Muslim ancestors – became an obsession, but it was also true elsewhere. Fathers choosing a wetnurse for their children took care to make sure she was of the same denomination, lest, if he was a Catholic, her Protestant blood turn into Protestant milk and thus infect the child with heretical ideas. Children born of religiously mixed marriages were often slightly mistrusted, for one never knew whether their Protestant or Catholic blood would ultimately triumph. Describing differences as blood naturalized them, making them appear as if they were created by God in nature.

As Europeans developed colonial empires these notions of blood became a way of conceptualizing race as well as religion, class, and nation. In some cases, such as Jews or Jewish converts in Spain and the Spanish empire, or Gaelic Irish in Ireland, religious and racial differences were linked, with religious traditions being viewed as signs of barbarity and racial inferiority. Religion was also initially a marker of difference in colonial areas outside Europe, where the spread of Christianity was used as a justification for conquest and enslavement. As indigenous peoples converted, however, religion became less useful as a means of differentiation, and skin color became more important. Virginia laws regarding sexual relations, for example, distinguished between "christian" and "negroe" in 1662, but by 1691 between "white" men and women and those who were "negroe, mulatto, or Indian."

We can see the impact of both the spread of germs and new notions of race very clearly in the Spanish and Portuguese colonies of the New World. Historians estimate that the indigenous population decreased dramatically – by about 90 percent in the sixteenth century in Central America, for example – at the same time that there was large-scale immigration from Europe and the importation of huge numbers of slaves from Africa. Originally the Spanish and Portuguese Crowns hoped to keep all these groups apart, but the shortage of European and African women made this impossible, and there were sexual relationships across many lines. The children of these relationships – termed "mixed-blood" or "mestizo" – challenged existing categories, but the response of colonial society was to create an even more complex system of socio-racial categories termed *castas*, that was in theory based on place of birth, assumed race, and status of one's mother. In practice, except for individuals who had clear connections to Spain or Portugal or who lived in isolated native villages, one's *casta* was to a large extent determined by how one looked, with lighter-skinned mixed-race persons accorded a higher rank than darker, even if they were siblings. Thus many historians have termed the social structure that developed in colonial Latin America and the Caribbean a "pigmentocracy," a system based on skin color, though contemporaries always claimed that color was linked to honor and virtue so that one's social status – termed *calidad* – involved a moral as well as physical judgment. One's *casta* determined one's ability to marry or inherit, enter a convent or the priesthood or attend university; these privileges encouraged individuals to attempt to alter their *casta*, and church officials occasionally granted licenses that made darker-skinned men or women "white."

The granting of honorary whiteness and the difficulty of assigning people to *castas* – darker-skinned people were sometimes placed in a lower *casta* than their lighter-skinned siblings – points out just how subjective this entire system was, but it was the essential determinant of family life and gender norms in Latin America. For members of the white European elite, the concern about bloodlines, color, and *casta* created a pattern of intermarriage within the extended family, with older women identifying the distant cousins that were favored as spouses. Following the southern European pattern, these marriages were often between an older man and younger woman, which limited the number of potential spouses for women, and many never married; in the Portuguese colony of Bahia, for example, only 14 percent of the daughters of leading families married in the seventeenth century. Rural native people also married most often within their own group, with the extended family exerting control over choice of spouses just as it did for elite whites. For slaves, many persons of mixed race, and poor people of all types, family and property considerations did not enter into marital considerations, and in most cases people simply did not get married at all, though in many cases they did establish long-term unions regarded by their neighbors and friends as stable. The number of births out of wedlock in Latin America remained startlingly high by comparison with most of Europe (although Spain did have the highest rate of out-of-wedlock births in Europe). During the period from 1640 to 1700 in central Mexico, one-third of the births to white women were out of wedlock, along with two-thirds of those of mixed-race individuals. Both Spanish and Portuguese law made distinctions among varieties of illegitimacy, according children of parents who could have been married but were not more inheritance rights than those of parents who could not have married, such as priests' children or those born in adulterous relationships. Thus, despite Christian norms, families in Latin America were extremely diverse: elite men married, but they often had children by slaves or servants who were also part of their household; poor free people did not marry, but might live in stable nuclear households; slave unions were often temporary, and the children stayed with their mothers or became the property of their mothers' owners.

This diversity was also found elsewhere in the colonial world, with racial hierarchies and notions of gender intersecting in complex ways to shape family life. In some areas, such as the French and British colonies of North America, Africa, and Asia, marriages or other long-term unions between Europeans and indigenous peoples were much rarer than they were in Latin America, and in many places legally prohibited; the 1691 law in Virginia forbade marriage between an "English or other white man or woman" and a "negroe, mulatto, or Indian man or woman." Though such laws were usually gender-neutral, what lawmakers were most worried about was, as the preamble to the Virginia law states, "negroes, mulattoes, and Indians intermarrying with English, or other white women" and the resultant "abominable mixture and spurious issue." Such laws were passed in all of the southern states and also Pennsylvania and Massachusetts between 1700 and 1750; they were struck down by the US Supreme Court in 1967, but remained on the books in some states for decades after that. The last of such "misc-egenation" laws was rescinded by Alabama voters in a state-wide referendum in 2000. In contrast to a hierarchy of *castas*, the British North American colonies and later the United States developed a dichotomous racial system, in which one drop of "black blood" made one black.

Whether hierarchical or dichotomous, racial systems were not simply a matter of ideas or discourse. Unmarried white women who bore mixed-race children were more harshly treated than those who bore white children, while pregnancy out of wedlock was often ignored or even encouraged among non-white women, particularly if they were slaves or other types of dependents whose children would become workers; men's fathering of mixed-race children with non-white women was tolerated or even expected. In the British North American colonies and later the United States, rape of a white woman by a black man could lead to castration. European women who married indigenous men lost their legal status as "European" in many colonies, while men who married indigenous women did not. (A similar disparity became part of the citizenship laws of many countries well into the twentieth century; even today in some countries a woman automatically loses her citizenship on marrying a foreign national, while a man does not.) It may be easy for us to see the socially constructed nature of certain categories, particularly those that are readily changeable – Does one's blood become Protestant if one converts? Or one's skin tone change if one gets a license of whiteness? – and most scholars who study the human species as a whole, such as biologists and anthropologists, avoid using the word "race" completely. Despite this malleability, however, racial, national, and to some degree class and religious boundaries were not regarded as socially constructed in the colonial world, but as undergirded by even more fundamental boundaries, such as those between "godly" and "ungodly" or between "natural" and "unnatural."

Until the middle of the nineteenth century, of course, most African-Americans in North America were slaves, and only in New England were slave marriages legally recognized. As in Latin America, the family structures that developed in North America in the eighteenth and nineteenth centuries were thus class- and race-related. White families, especially in the north, tended to follow the northwestern European model, with late marriage and a high proportion of people who never married, while black families were more fluid, and often matrifocal. Government policy toward Native Americans, which removed them from their original homelands and ordered them to live on reservations, disrupted family life along with every other aspect of indigenous society, though extended kin groups retained some voice wherever they could.

The European colonies in Africa and Asia generally developed later than those in the Americas, and in many places European rule did not disrupt existing family patterns to a great extent, which continued to be shaped by Confucian, Hindu, or Islamic ideals. European men engaged in sexual relations with indigenous women, but did not regard these as marriage (though they might be viewed by local cultures as temporary marriages). Once more white women moved to the colonies, long-term interracial relationships became less common as the European communities worried about mixed-race children and what they termed "racial survival."

The growth in mining and commercial agriculture for export in colonial areas led many men to leave their families for years at a time in search of wage labor, with women at home in the villages engaged in subsistence agriculture and caring for children and the elderly; thus, like slavery, wage labor in areas which produced raw materials led to matri-focal family patterns, with closer relationships between mothers and children than between spouses. This occurred within legal structures that were often patrilineal, with formal rights to land and other property held by men who were absent; in fact, laws regarding ownership and inheritance were often *more* patrilineal under colonial rule than they had been earlier, as colonial authorities did not understand or accept existing matrilineal or bilateral systems. Thus there could be a sharp contradiction between theory and practice regarding family structure and power relationships, with men the official and legal head of the family but women actually making most of the decisions.

The Industrial and Post-industrial World

This contradiction between theory and practice in terms of the family was not found only in the colonies during the nineteenth century, but in the colonizing countries – often termed the "metropole" – and in other European and European-background countries as well. As we will dis-cuss in greater detail in chapter 3, the growth of industrialism brought new forms of work organization that had a significant effect on family life. Young women were often the first to be hired as factories opened, for they were viewed as more compliant, willing to take lower wages, and better able to carry out the repetitive tasks of tending machines. Factory work removed young women from their parental households, however, and could lead to a lessening of paternal authority once the women had their own wages. Politicians and social commentators debated the merits of this, and suggested that factory owners establish dormitories for their workers and act as substitute fathers, restricting women's leisure-time activities and socializing habits. They further recommended that, whenever possible, women work in sex-segregated workshops or at home, so that their (and their family's) honor was not threatened by contact with men who were not their relatives, and that women's wages stay low, so that they did not become too independent. Young women were encouraged to give most or all of their wages to their families, and married women encouraged to avoid work outside the household and to make their homes a "haven in the heartless world" of industrialism and business. (This advice was bolstered by the fact that until the mid-nineteenth century, the wages of married women in European countries belonged legally to their husbands.)

Social reformers and the labor organizations that developed in the nineteenth century had a different goal for men's wages, but one that was also related to family life; they increasingly advocated a "family wage," that is, wages high enough to allow married male workers to support their families so that their wives could concentrate on domestic tasks. Both middle- and working-class male leaders emphasized the propriety of a distinction between the "private" world of home and family and the "public" world of work and politics. Europeans and Americans often criticized the societies they were colonizing for requiring women to be secluded in the home, but at the same time they were creating a stronger ideal of domesticity for their own women. This ideal included an intense emphasis on the importance of children and the mother–child bond, another family trait often found in the very cultures Europeans regarded as backwards and barbaric. (We will look more closely at such ideals in chapter 4.)

The economic realities of industrialism created further ironies. At the same time that Europeans and European-background societies were placing greater emphasis on children (some historians have dubbed this the "discovery of childhood"), white children were hired in factories and mines in increasing numbers at very young ages, and black children in areas with plantation slavery worked in the fields or household as soon as they were able. Men's wages were rarely enough to support a family, but women's wages were so low in the jobs available to them that the labor of children was needed to allow working-class families to survive.

Children were also a burden on those families, however, requiring food long before they could work, and the demand for contraception grew. The same leaders who described the family as a private haven viewed birth control as a highly public issue, however, passing laws such as the Comstock Laws in the United States which prohibited the distribution of birth control devices, and arresting those, such as Marie Stopes in England and Margaret Sanger in the United States, who disseminated birth control information, especially when this was to working- or lower-class women. Religious authorities also made pronouncements on this issue; Pope Pius IX, for example, declared in 1869 that the fetus acquires a soul at conception rather than at quickening, which had been the standard opinion before that point. (Quickening is the point that a mother feels movement, usually about the third or fourth month; the word "quick" is an old word for alive, as in the phrase "the quick and the dead.") Any post-conception methods of contraception would thus be considered abortion, whereas until this point they had been viewed as contraception, a lesser sin.

Governments intervened in family life in the twentieth century far more than they had earlier, with the most extreme examples in totalitarian regimes. In Germany, Italy, and Japan in the 1930s, birth control was prohibited and large families were rewarded among groups judged to be desirable; those judged undesirable were sterilized or executed. (Sterilization of "undesirables" also occurred in the United States from the 1930s to at least the 1970s.) All three of these countries mounted propaganda campaigns setting out their view of the ideal family, which was one in which fathers ruled and wives and children obeyed. In the Soviet Union right after World War II, the government encouraged population growth by limiting access to all contraception; even after the desire for more people abated, birth control pills never became widely available, so that abortion became the standard means of birth control for most women, a practice that continued in post-Soviet Russia.

In other parts of the world as well, governments actively intervened to limit population: in India, Puerto Rico, and elsewhere the government encouraged or condoned widespread sterilization, while in China families who had more than one child were penalized by fines and the loss of access to opportunities. Though governments which introduced strict population policies tried to minimize gender differences in their effects, the value put on male children was still higher than that on female, which led in some countries to selective female infanticide, abortion of female fetuses, and better care and nutrition for infant boys. Government campaigns at the end of the twentieth century in China tried to end such practices, and observers noted that girls may become more desirable in the future because selective abortion has made them scarcer than boys.

Government policies about birth control and other aspects of family life developed as a result of the explosive population growth that began in the late nineteenth century and continued throughout the twentieth. Medical advances such as vaccinations lowered the death rate among children dramatically; in the Arab world, for example, three out of four children survived to age fifty at the end of the twentieth century, compared with one out of four at the beginning of the century. Despite government campaigns, curtailment of family size has been selective, with industrialized countries with strong systems of social support having the lowest birth rates because people did not have to rely on their children for support in old age. Birth control became culturally acceptable, more reliable, and more widely available in Europe, North America, Japan, and Australia by the 1960s, and families were smaller. By the 1980s disputes about reproductive control in these areas revolved largely around moral issues relating to abortion and medically assisted reproductive techniques such as in-vitro fertilization, surrogate motherhood, and genetic testing.

Coercive government measures provoked strong resistance in many parts of the developing world from both religious and women's organizations, and toward the end of the century aid agencies recognized that a more effective means of decreasing the birth rate was to increase the level of basic and technical education for girls and women, while providing small loans for sewing machines, farm flocks, or even cellular phones so that women could gain economic independence. Both lower birth rates and education for girls were opposed in some parts of the world for much of the twentieth century by traditional and colonial authorities, for they regarded women's proper role as tied to the household. At the end of the century, however, worldwide fertility had been lowered, from 4.97 births per woman in 1950 to 3.38 in 1990, with sterilization the most common form of birth control; in 1990, Italy had the lowest birth rate (1.3) and Rwanda the highest (8.5).

Families in many parts of the world not only saw first more and then fewer births in the twentieth century than they had earlier, they also changed shape and became more varied. In many parts of the world, such as Africa and the Caribbean, male mobility and the lack of good jobs for either women or men meant that many people did not marry until quite late in life or never married at all. The pattern of matrifocal households that had developed during the nineteenth century continued, a pattern that could also be found among many African-American households in the United States. A similar living pattern, though under very different economic circumstances, developed in post-World War II Japan, tied in some ways to earlier Japanese traditions. Japanese companies favored male workers, expecting them to work very long hours and socialize together after work, sometimes in the company of geishas; women were expected to work only until they had children and then devote themselves to their children. Thus, like many men in colonial mining or agricultural areas, men in Japan rarely saw their wives and had little role in the upbringing of their children, though almost all of them continued to marry, for marriage remained a central part of Japanese culture and was expected by Japanese companies.

Marital patterns in many parts of Africa remained polygynous, with over half the women in western Africa in the 1980s having at least one co-spouse. Urban marriages were increasingly likely to be monogamous, both because of cultural influences such as Christianity and because of economic change. Increased mobility brought a weakening of kinship and lineage ties, with older men having less power over both younger men and women than they did earlier; this allowed for greater independence in such matters as choice of spouse or job, but also left individuals, especially women, more vulnerable because they did not have a lineage to support them economically or emotionally.

In Japan, China, and the Arab world, more than 95 percent of people continued to marry at some point in their lives, but in other parts of the world, the twentieth century saw a dramatic decline in marriage rates. In both western Europe and the United States couples lived together but did not marry; in 1995 there were ten times as many couples living together without marrying in Germany than there had been in 1972. Divorce rates increased significantly in developed countries – in the United States the divorce rate in the 1990s was three times what it had been in the 1920s, with one out of every two marriages ending in divorce – and divorces were also more common elsewhere, such as the Arabic world where one out of every four marriages ended in divorce in the 1990s. The social acceptability of remarriage after divorce in many parts of the world meant that many families included the children from several different relationships, thus returning to an earlier pattern when spousal death and remarriage had created such "blended" families. To this variety were added households in which children were raised by their grandparents, by gay or lesbian couples, by adoptive parents, by single parents, and by unmarried individuals who had no intention of marrying. In some parts of the world marriage between individuals of different races and religions became increasingly common, challenging centuries-old boundaries and definitions of who was family and who was kin. This diversity of family forms was perceived by some observers as a social problem, but showed little signs of changing in the 1990s.

The diversity in the structure and function of families in the contemporary world is less than that in the past, as we have seen in this chapter, but, given greater immigration and better communications, that diversity is more widely and more intimately known and experienced. Family and kinship are not simply matters of genetic connections, but are culturally determined and given meaning by individuals and groups. It is clear from this chapter that gender differences have been a key part of family life throughout history, which has made them more resistant to change than gender differences in other realms of life, such as the workplace or the voting booth. Thus they often survived, and continue to survive, dramatic economic or political upheavals. In Russia, for example, women did almost all the domestic work before, during, and after communism; in much of Africa, kin structures were the primary shapers of marriage during the precolonial, colonial, and postcolonial eras. Gender patterns involving the family are not as unchanging as they sometimes seem to be, but we all learned these at a very early age, and they are very difficult to shake.

Further Reading

The family is a topic of great interest in sociology, anthropology, and psychology as well as history, so that there are countless studies of all aspects of contemporary family life, many of which pay specific attention to gender issues. An excellent place to begin for historical studies of the family is the two-volume collection: André Burguière, et al., eds., *A History of the Family: Volume One – Distant Worlds, Ancient Worlds* and *A History of the Family: Volume Two – The Impact of Modernity* (Cambridge, MA: Harvard University Press, 1996). For overviews with a specifically historical focus, see: James Casey, *The History of the Family* (Oxford: Blackwell Publishers, 1989); Roderick Phillips, *Putting Asunder: A History of Divorce in Western Society* (Cambridge: Cambridge University Press, 1988); G. Robina Quale, *Families in Context: A World History of Population* (New York: Greenwood Press, 1992) and *A History of Marriage Systems* (New York: Greenwood Press, 1988). The newest research may always be found in the the *Journal of Family History*, which began publication in 1976.

There are many collections which bring together issues of family life from a number of different cultures and time periods, including: Robert I. Rotberg and Theodore K. Rabb, eds., *Marriage and Fertility: Studies in Interdisciplinary History* (Princeton, NJ: Princeton University Press, 1980); Robert M. Netting, et al., eds., *Households: Comparative and Historical Studies of the Domestic Group* (Berkeley: University of California Press, 1984); Mary Jo Maynes, et al., eds., *Gender, Kinship, Power: A Comparative and Interdisciplinary History* (New York: Routledge, 1996); special issue of the *Journal of Family History* 24/3 (1999) on the history of fatherhood; special issue *of Women's History Review* 8/2 (1999) on "Revisiting mother-hood: new histories of the public and private."

The European family has received far more attention in English-language scholarship than those in other parts of the world. These include general essay collections and surveys, such as: R. B. Outhwaite, ed., *Marriage and Society: Studies in the Social History of Marriage* (London: Europa Publications, 1981); Jean Dupaquier, et al., eds., *Marriage and Remarriage in Populations of the Past* (New York: Academic Press, 1981); Peter Laslett and Richard Wall, eds., *Household and Family in Past Time* (Cambridge: Cambridge University Press, 1983); Richard Wall, Jean Robin, and Peter Laslett, eds., *Family Forms in Historic Europe* (Cambridge: Cambridge University Press, 1983); Michael Mitterauer and Reinhold Sieder, *The European Family: Patriarchy to Partnership from the Middle Ages to the Present* (Chicago: University of Chicago Press, 1983); Richard M. Smith, ed., *Land, Kinship, and Life-Cycle* (Cambridge: Cambridge University Press, 1984); John Gillis, *For Better, for Worse: British Marriages 1600 to the Present* (Oxford: Oxford University Press, 1985); Alan Macfarlane, *Marriage and Love in England: Modes of Reproduction 1300–1840* (Oxford: Blackwell Publishers, 1986); Hans Medick and David Sabean, eds., *Interest and Emotion: Essays on the Study of Family and Kinship* (Cambridge: Cambridge University Press, 1984); David Kertzer, et al., eds., *The Family in Italy from Antiquity to the Present* (New Haven, CT: Yale University Press, 1991); Mary Abbott, *Family Ties: English Families 1540–1920* (London: Routledge, 1993); Jack Goody, *The European Family: An Historico-Anthropological Essay* (Oxford: Blackwell Publishers, 2000).

For analyses of family and gender in ancient Greece, see: W. K. Lacey, *The Family in Classical Greece* (London: Camelot Press, 1968); Eva Keuls, *The Reign of the Phallus: Sexual Politics in Ancient Athens* (New York: Harper and Row, 1985); Roger Just, *Women in Athenian Law and Life* (New York: Routledge, 1989); Nancy Demand, *Birth, Death, and Motherhood in Classical Greece* (Baltimore, MD: Johns Hopkins University Press, 1994); Sarah Pomeroy, *Families in Classical and Hellenistic Greece: Representations and Realities* (Oxford: Clarendon Press, 1997). Beryl Rawson has edited three books about families in ancient Rome: *The Family in Ancient Rome: New Perspectives* (London: Croom Helm, 1986); *Marriage, Divorce and Children in Ancient Rome* (Oxford: Clarendon Press, 1991); *The Roman Family in Italy: Status, Sentiment, Space* (Oxford: Clarendon Press, 1997).

Much research on European families has focused on the medieval and early modern period, in part because scholars were earlier very concerned with the origins of the "modern" western family. See: Jack

Goody, Joan Thirsk and E. P. Thompson, eds., *Family and Inheritance: Rural Society in Western Europe, 1200–1800* (Cambridge: Cambridge University Press, 1976); James Traer, *Marriage and Family in Eighteenth Century France* (Ithaca, NY: Cornell University Press, 1980); Linda Pollock, *Forgotten Children: Parent–Child Relations from 1500 to 1900* (Cambridge: Cambridge University Press, 1983); Christiane Klapisch-Zuber, *Women, Family, and Ritual in Renaissance Italy* (Chicago: University of Chicago Press, 1985); Sherrin Marshall, *The Dutch Gentry, 1500–1650: Family, Faith and Fortune* (New York: Greenwood Press, 1987); Wally Seccombe, *A Millennium of Family Change: Feudalism to Capitalism in Northwestern Europe* (London: Verso, 1992); Anthony Molho, *Marriage Alliance in Late Medieval Florence* (Cambridge, MA: Harvard University Press, 1994); Joel Harrington, *Reordering Marriage and Society in Reformation Germany* (Cambridge: Cambridge University Press, 1995); David Herlihy, *Women, Family and Society in Medieval Europe* (Providence, RI: Berghahn Books, 1995); Margaret Hunt, *The Middling Sort: Commerce, Gender, and the Family in England, 1680–1780* (Berkeley: University of California Press, 1996); Trevor Dean and K. J. P. Lowe, eds., *Marriage in Italy, 1300–1650* (Cambridge: Cambridge University Press, 1998); Martha C. Howell, *The Marriage Exchange: Property, Social Place, and Gender in the Cities of the Low Countries, 1300–1500* (Chicago: University of Chicago Press, 1998). Two of the few studies that focus on eastern Europe are Eve Levin, *Sex and Society in the World of the Orthodox Slavs, 900–1700* (Ithaca, NY: Cornell University Press, 1989) and Christine Worobec, *Peasant Russia: Family and Community in the Post-Emancipation Period* (Princeton, NJ: Princeton University Press, 1991).

For a discussion of racial hierarchies in Latin America, the indispensable work is still Magnus Mörner, *Race Mixture in the History of Latin America* (Boston: Little, Brown, 1967). Other studies of families in Latin America and the Caribbean include: Diana Balmori, *Notable Family Networks in Latin America* (Chicago: University of Chicago Press, 1984); Patricia Seed, *To Love, Honor, and Obey in Colonial Mexico: Conflicts Over Marriage Choice, 1574–1821* (Stanford, CA: Stanford University Press, 1988); Asunción Lavrin, ed., *Sexuality and Marriage in Colonial Latin America* (Lincoln: University of Nebraska Press, 1989); Elizabeth Jelin, ed., *Family, Household, and Gender Relations in Latin America* (London: Routledge, 1991); Susan M. De Vos, *Household Composition in Latin America* (New York: Plenum Press, 1995); Christine Barrow, *Family in the Caribbean: Themes and Perspectives* (New York: Markus Weiner, 2000).

For marriage and family life in China, see: Maurice Freedman, ed., *Family and Kinship in Chinese Society* (New Haven, CT: Yale University Press, 1970); David C. Buxbaum, *Chinese Family Law and Social Change in Historical and Comparative Perspective* (Seattle: University of Washington Press, 1978); Kay Ann Johnson, *Women, the Family, and Peasant Revolution in China* (Chicago: University of Chicago Press, 1983); Lloyd Eastman, *Family, Fields, and Ancestors: Constancy and Change in China's Social and Economic History, 1550–1949* (New York: Oxford University Press, 1988); Rubie S. Watson and Patricia Buckley Ebrey, *Marriage and Inequality in Chinese Society* (Berkeley: University of California Press, 1991); Patricia Buckley Ebrey, *The Inner Quarters: Marriage and the Lives of Chinese Women in the Sung Period* (Berkeley: University of California Press, 1993). For other parts of Asia and the Pacific, see: Margaret Jolly and Martha Macintyre, *Family and Gender in the Pacific: Domestic Contradictions and the Colonial Impact* (Cambridge: Cambridge University Press, 1989); Sumiko Iwao, *The Japanese Woman: Traditional Image and Changing Reality* (Cambridge, MA: Harvard University Press, 1994); Gloria Goodwin Raheja and Ann Grodzins Gold, *Listen to the Heron's Words: Reimagining Gender and Kinship in North India* (Berkeley: University of California Press, 1994); Laurel Kendall, *Getting Married in Korea: Of Gender, Morality, and Modernity* (Berkeley: University of California Press, 1996).

For Africa, see: Christine Oppong, *Marriage among a Matilineal Elite: A Family Study of Ghanaian Civil Servants* (Cambridge: Cambridge University Press, 1974); Sarah Le Vine, *Mothers and Wives: Gusii Women of East Africa* (Chicago: University of Chicago Press, 1979); Caroline Bledsoe, *Women and Marriage in Kpelle Society* (Stanford, CA: Stanford University Press, 1980); Kristin Mann, *Marrying Well: Marriage, Status and Social Change among the Educated Elite in Colonial Lagos* (Cambridge: Cambridge University Press, 1995); Ifi Amadiume, *Male Daughters, Female Husbands: Gender and Sex in an African Society* (London: Zed Books, 1987); Barbara M. Cooper, *Marriage in Maradi, 1900–1989* (Portsmouth, NH: Heinemann, 1997); Jean Davison, *Gender, Lineage, and Ethnicity in Southern Africa* (Boulder, CO: Westview Press, 1997). For the Middle East, see: Elizabeth Warneck Fernea, ed., *Women and the Family in the Middle East: New Voices of Change* (Austin: University of Texas Press, 1985); Alan Duben and Cem Behar, *Istanbul Households: Marriage, Family, and Fertility, 1880– 1940* (Cambridge: Cambridge University Press, 1991); Margaret Meriwether, *The Kin Who Count: Family and Society in Ottoman Aleppo* (Austin: University of Texas Press,

1999); Margaret Meriwether and Judith Tucker, eds., *A Social History of Women and the Family in the Middle East* (Boulder, CO: Westview Press, 1999).

The history of the family in the United States has been very well studied, and there is an extensive bibliography in Joseph M. Hawes and Elizabeth I. Nybakken, eds., *American Families: A Research Guide and Historical Handbook* (New York: Greenwood Press, 1991). Just a few of the many recent works include: Robert V. Wells, *Revolutions in Americans' Lives: A Demographic Perspective on the History of Americans, Their Families, and Their Society* (Westport, CT: Greenwood Press, 1982); John Demos, *Past, Present, and Personal: The Family and the Life Course in American History* (New York: Oxford University Press, 1986); Steven Mintz and Susan Kellogg, *Domestic Revolutions: A Social History of American Family Life* (New York: Free Press, 1988); Helena M. Wall, *Fierce Communion: Family and Community in Early America* (Cambridge, MA: Harvard University Press, 1990); Laura McCall and Donald Yacovone, eds., *A Shared Experience: Men, Women, and the History of Gender* (New York: New York University Press, 1998). For North American ideas of race, see Winthrop Jordan, *White over Black: American Attitudes toward the Negro, 1550–1813* (Chapel Hill: University of North Carolina Press, 1968).

For studies which focus on twentieth-century issues around the world, see: Amy Swerdlow, et al., eds., *Household and Kin: Families in Flux* (Old Westbury, CT: Feminist Press, 1981); Rae Lesser Blumberg, ed., *Gender, Family and Economy: The Triple Overlap* (Newbury Park, CA: Sage, 1991); Esther Chow and Catherine Berheide, *Women, the Family and Policy: A Global Perspective* (Albany: State University of New York Press, 1994); Gordon L. Anderson, ed., *The Family in Global Transition* (St Paul, MN: Professors World Peace Academy, 1997). Daniel Bertaux and Paul Thompson, *Between Generations: Family Models, Myths, and Memories* (Oxford: Oxford University Press, 1993) and John R. Gillis, *A World of Their Own Making: Myth, Ritual and the Quest for Family Values* (New York: Basic Books, 1996) make excellent use of interviews and oral history along with other sources to explore contemporary notions (often mythological) about family history. Studies that specifically examine reproduction and contraception in the twentieth century include: Elisabeth J. Croll, Delia Davin, and Penny Kane, eds., *China's One Child Family Policy* (New York: St Martin's Press, 1985); Janet Smith, *Humanae Vitae: A Generation Later* (Washington, DC: Catholic University Press, 1991); Faye Ginsburg and Rayna Rapp, eds., *Conceiving the New World*

Order: The Global Politics of Reproduction (Berkeley: University of California Press, 1995); Gita Sen, Adrienne Germain, and Lincoln Chan, eds., *Population Policies Reconsidered: Health, Empowerment and Rights* (Cambridge, MA: Harvard University Press, 1994).

3 Economic Life

Drawing boundaries between economic issues and other realms of life may be difficult and in some cases artificial. As we saw in chapter 2, in many of the world's cultures the family or kin group was (and is) the primary unit of production and trade, growing crops or making different types of items together and then using and selling them; ownership and control of land and other forms of wealth was also a family venture. In even more of the world's cultures, families were the primary units of consumption, with the majority of goods and services purchased for the use of the whole household rather than a single individual. Economic life was also tied to religious, political, and educational institutions, which we will be examining in later chapters: religious institutions often owned large amounts of land and consumed significant amounts of goods and services; a person's or family's economic status was often more dependent on access to royal or noble favors than on anything we would recognize as labor; schooling in most – though not all – cultures was designed to improve one's own and one's family's economic well-being.

Recent scholarship on economic matters has stressed these links to other areas of life, and has also drawn attention to how "economic" is defined. Traditional studies of the economy focused primarily on production, and even the broadest usually viewed four activities – work, trade, ownership, and consumption – as the defining aspects of economic life; they are, after all, what governments tax, through income taxes, tariffs, property taxes, and sales taxes. Newer research suggests that even this broad view misses activities that have a tremendous economic impact, however. To be accurate and inclusive, an analysis of economic life in any period should include reproductive as well as productive activities; reproduction means not simply child-bearing, but the care and nurturing of all family members, activities that allowed them to take part in production or trade. This is especially true for pre-industrial or non-industrial societies in which labor for the family's own sustenance or for the market often went on in the household, with all family members taking part in both productive and reproductive labor.

Some of this broadening of the definition of "economic" has come from feminist analysis, which has made it clear that economic concepts are highly gendered. In many cultures men's tasks have been defined as "work" while women's have been defined as "assisting," "helping out," or "housework." Some tasks generally done by women, such as the care and nurturing of family members, have not been regarded as "work" at all, though they would be considered "work" if they were done for pay by individuals who were not family members. Because of this, women's activities were (and are) not counted in various statistical measurements such as the gross national product, and women were viewed as not contributing to economic development. Even when women's activities were regarded as work, they were generally not valued as highly as the tasks normally done by men, though they might have taken the same amount of time, skill, and effort. Thus economic life was profoundly shaped by notions of gender, and in most of the world's cultures sharp distinctions were drawn between men's work (which might be thought of simply as "work") and women's work. In some societies these distinctions were so strong that individuals who were morphologically male but who did tasks normally assigned to females were regarded as members of a third gender, an issue we will analyze more fully in chapter 8. These gender distinctions in work were accompanied by and related to gender distinctions in other segments of the economy, for women rarely had the same access to land, cash, or other types of wealth as did the men of their family or social group, and this, together with their lower wages, lessened their ability to purchase goods or services.

Gender hierarchies in the division of labor and other aspects of economic life were present in many of the world's earliest civilizations, and they have survived massive changes. New occupations have tended to be valued – and paid – according to whether they were done primarily by men or women. This has begun to change within the last several decades in some parts of the world, but, precisely because the economy is so linked to other realms, it is clear that changes in economic structures – and in the meaning of those structures – will continue to shape and be shaped by gender.

Foraging and Horticultural Societies

Though early human cultures are often labeled "hunting and gathering" cultures, recent archeological research indicates that both historical and contemporary hunter-gatherers actually depend much more on gathered foods than hunted meat. (This is not true for Arctic cultures where the opportunities for gathering are very limited.) This can be assessed for contemporary hunter-gatherers by observation, and for historical ones by analysis of the wear patterns on stone tools (termed "microwear analysis"), chemical analysis of human bones which reveal the relative amounts of animal and plant foods eaten (termed "stable isotopic analysis"), analysis of the food remains in fossilized human feces, and analysis of cooked and uncooked food remains, primarily bones. Such analysis indicates that the majority of hunter-gatherers' diet comes from plants, and that much of the animal protein in their diet comes from foods gathered or scavenged rather than hunted directly, for it consists of insects, shellfish, small animals caught in traps, and animals killed by other predators. Thus early human societies might be more accurately termed "gatherer-hunters" or "foragers," a term now favored by scholars.

This reanalysis of the importance of hunting has been accompanied by a refinement in the timetable of early human development. The need for hunting meat was earlier described as an impetus for bipedalism and tool manufacture – man the hunter stood up to look over the savanna in search of large game animals and then crafted stone spear points to kill those animals. It is now recognized that bipedalism predated tool manufacture by about two million years, and that along with pointed flaked stones early tools included spheroid pieces probably for grinding, cracking, or other types of plant processing. Those pointed flaked stones themselves were also not necessarily spear points, but may have been used for a wide variety of tasks such as chopping vegetables, peeling fruits or cracking open shells. Evidence of animal killing and consumption – stones and bones – survives better than that of plant consumption, and was responsible for the earlier emphasis on hunting, but more sophisticated analysis has now given a more balanced picture. The most important element of early human success was flexibility and adaptability, with gathering and hunting probably varying in their importance from year to year depending on environmental factors and the decisions of the group.

This emphasis on adaptability has led a number of archeologists and prehistorians to speculate whether women might have been more influential in developing early human culture than the "man the hunter" model suggests. If hunting was not the impetus for bipedalism, what was? Could it possibly have been the need for hominid and early human mothers to carry their babies, a task made more difficult as humans lost the body fur characteristic of other primates that allows infants to grasp their mothers? Might the first "tool" have been a sling of some sort – found in all of the world's cultures – for carrying an infant? Might early human females have developed the first tools for harvesting and processing food because they were more adept at this than human males, in the same way that female chimpanzees are more adept at fishing termites out of nests and cracking nuts? Questions such as these have also led to a broader questioning of the entire "man the hunter/woman the gatherer" dichotomy; in some of the world's cultures, such as the Agta of the Philippines, women hunt large game, and in numerous others, women are involved in some types of hunting, such as driving herds of animals toward a cliff or compound. Though most foraging societies have some type of division of labor by sex – and also by age, with children and older people responsible for different tasks than adult men or women – it is not universal, and the stone tools that remain from the Paleolithic period give no clear evidence of who used them. In the cultures in which women hunt, they either carry their children in slings or leave them with other family members, so that cultural norms, rather than biological necessity, must be seen as the basis for male hunting.

Answering questions about early tool use and the prehistoric division of labor is difficult because the sources on which to base an answer are scarce, and open to widely varying interpretations. Because direct evidence is so limited and difficult to interpret, scholars use a number of other types of sources when asking questions about the gender division of labor in prehistory: comparisons with other primates; observation of the few foraging societies left in the world; reports from ethnographers and missionaries of foraging societies in the last several centuries; written sources from cultures which existed centuries later in the same area.

Though the division of labor by sex in foraging cultures is not strict or uniform, in most of them women appear to have been primarily responsible for gathering plant products, so that they may also have been the first to plant seeds in the ground rather than simply harvesting wild grains. Early crop planters began to select the seeds they planted in order to get more productive crops, and, by observation, learned the most optimum times and places for planting. This early crop planting was done by individuals using hoes and digging sticks, and is often termed horticulture to distinguish it from the later agriculture using plows. Horticulture can be combined quite easily with gathering and hunting as plots of land are usually small; many cultures, including some of those in North America, remained mixed foragers/horticulturists for thousands of years, with base camps they returned to regularly during the growing season. In these cultures, and also in many horticultural groups in Africa, women appear to have retained control of the crops they planted, sharing them with group members or giving them as gifts. They developed means of storing and transporting the harvested seeds, including skin bags, carved wooden vessels, and pottery. Intentional crop-planting developed first in the Near East (about 8500 BCE) and slightly later in China (about 7500 BCE); it developed significantly later in central America (3500 BCE), the Andes region (3500 BCE), and eastern North America (2500 BCE). Domesticated crops spread from these areas to much of the rest of the world, though there may also have been independent domestication in west Africa, east Africa, and New Guinea.

In some parts of the world horticulture produced enough food to allow groups to settle more or less permanently in one area. Women no longer had to carry their small children with them all the time, and horticulture provided food that was soft enough for babies to eat − primarily cereals − which allowed women to wean their children at a younger age. (The primary foods of many foragers are hard for small children to eat or digest, and women in such cultures nurse their children until they are three or four. If nursing is a child's sole source of nutrition, lactation tends to suppress ovulation in the mother, so that births are more widely spaced even without other methods of birth control.) Children may have been born at more frequent intervals and infant mortality may have decreased slightly, leading to a growth in population. Though we cannot be sure about the exact mechanism for this − whether an increase in the birth rate or a decrease in the death rate was the most important factor − we do know that crop-raising villages, beginning in the Near East, began to grow quite rapidly.

The division of labor by gender is just as difficult to ascertain in early horticultural societies as it is in foraging cultures, and most scholars stress diversity over one single pattern. We can tell that many groups, such as the Linear Pottery Culture in central Europe around 5000 BCE, lived in large, rectangular longhouses that probably housed more than one set of parents and children. In the Linear Pottery Culture women appear to have been responsible for agricultural work, as querns used to mill flour have been found in female graves, whereas men hunted, because arrowheads have been found in male graves and the charred bones of wild animals found throughout the sites. We cannot know for sure about the organization of the groups living in the longhouses, but they were probably kin groups of some sort, perhaps sisters or brothers and their children. Most horticultural societies adopt living arrangements that are either matrilocal, in which husbands leave their homes to live with their wives, or patrilocal, in which wives leave their homes to live with their husbands, but we have no way of telling which was the case in the Linear Pottery Culture. It does appear that there was little differentiation in status based on sex, as there is not much difference in terms of the quantity or quality of grave goods found with men and women. There were a few domesticated animals such as cattle, sheep, and pigs, although, judging by the enclosures which were animal stalls and the number of bones, there were not many; many other horticultural societies around the world, such as those of Native Americans in what is now the eastern United States or those in western Africa, have kept no domesticated animals at all.

In areas of the world without large domesticable animals (or with animals such as the llama that could not be trained to pull a plow) crops continued to be planted with hoes and digging sticks for millennia, and crop-raising remained primarily a woman's task. Women in Africa and South America grew and processed roots and tubers, and in North America they grew corn, beans, and squash. Because of this, women in these areas occasionally inherited land or the rights to farm certain pieces of land directly, or boys inherited land through their mother's family, both of which are termed matrilineal systems of inheritance. This division of labor and these systems of inheritance were often misunderstood by cultures that came into contact or conquered horticulturists and then tried to enforce their own division of labor. In North America and Africa, for example, Europeans assumed men were the primary agricultural producers, and developed various plans to make indigenous men better farmers; they often introduced patrilineal inheritance laws at the same time. Such schemes generally failed to convince men that they should farm, though in some places male elites welcomed patrilineal inheritance.

Agricultural Societies

The division of labor by gender in foraging and horticultural societies around the world was linked in complex ways with other sources of gender distinctions, such as family structure, religion, and cultural practices, so the level of female subordination in such societies varied widely. Some of the world's most egalitarian cultures were foragers or horticulturists, as were some in which female subordination was the most extreme. This diversity was less in cultures that adopted plow agriculture, which was developed first in the Middle East beginning around 3000 BCE. As noted briefly in chapter 1, plowing was almost universally a male task, with women handling plows only in emergencies or in cultures in which men were gone for much of the growing season, such as coastal areas of Spain, Portugal, or Norway in which men left on long fishing voyages. The earliest depictions of plowing are on Mesopotamian cylinder seals, and they invariably show men with the cattle and plows. At the same time that cattle began to be raised for pulling plows and carts rather than for meat, sheep began to be raised primarily for wool. Spinning thread and weaving cloth became primarily women's work; the Egyptian Old Kingdom hieroglyph for weaving is, in fact, a seated woman with a shuttle, and a Confucian moral saying asserts that "men plow and women weave."

Though in some ways this arrangement seems complementary, with each sex doing some of the necessary tasks, in fact plow agriculture was one of the factors that increased gender hierarchy. Men's responsibility for plowing led to their being favored as inheritors of family land and the rights to farm communally held land. Plow agriculture increased the amount of food available, but also increased the amount of goods needed to produce and store that food, including animals, storage bins and containers, and wood or metal equipment. This economic gap between families that owned lands and plows and those that did not widened, and social differentiation increased. Ownership and control of property (and often of the persons who worked it) became the basis of power for political and religious elites, who developed more complex legal and normative structures to determine how resources would be owned, managed, and distributed. These elites generally became hereditary aristocracies, who sought to maintain their control of land by highlighting what made them distinctive – connections with a deity, military prowess, "natural" superiority – and to maintain the distinction between themselves and everyone else by regulating sexual relations.

We will trace the control of sexuality in more detail in chapter 8, but in terms of economic life, the laws and norms regulating social differentiation in agricultural societies often required elite women to work at tasks that would not take them beyond the household or outside of male supervision. Poor or slave women, whose sexual contacts were not of much concern to male elites, were generally expected to do whatever work was required, which in societies with large-scale slavery might be the same as that of male slaves (though slave women were often fed significantly smaller amounts of food). Even among slaves, however, and among poor free or semi-free people, women tended toward work that could be done within or close by the household, such as cooking, cloth production, and the care of children, the elderly, and small animals; men's work, such as clearing new fields and plowing, took them further away. A special program set up under the third-century BCE Indian emperor Ashoka, for example, supported poor women by paying them to spin and weave in their own homes; the most honorable among them were to bring their work into the palace at dawn so they would not be seen, with royal officials forbidden to look at their faces. Ideals of seclusion even shaped attitudes toward women whose primary work was sexual; high-status courtesans lived in *harims* or special women's quarters where they might receive training in music or other skills, while low-status women sold sex publicly in the streets.

Women's tasks were generally not valued as highly as those of men and provided little access to resources; this in turn shaped the work women could do, as they were not able to purchase more expensive tools or supplies. Spinning was thus the perfect women's occupation, for the tools required were simple and inexpensive, and it could be easily taken up or put down, and so combined with other tasks such as minding children or preparing meals. In England the female branch of a family was termed the "distaff" side, after the staff used to hold flax or wool in spinning before the invention of the spinning wheel. Among the Aztecs women spun feathers as well as cotton and maguey fiber; girls were given spindles and shuttles at their birth ceremony while boys were given a shield and four arrows, all of these symbols of the activities they would perform as adults in service to the Aztec state.

Along with gender distinctions in production there were also distinctions in trade in agricultural societies. Trade requires both access to trade goods and the ability to move about, both of which were more available

to men. Male heads of household generally had control over the products of their household, including those made or harvested by female
family members as well as slaves and servants of both genders. Because of
this and because women's ability to travel was often limited by cultural
norms about propriety and respectability, men became the primary
traders in most agricultural societies. This was particularly true for
long-distance traders, who sent or took items of great value such as
precious metals, spices, perfumes, amber, and gems, and for those who
handled large quantities of less valuable goods, such as grain, timber, and
metals. In some cultures women did trade locally, handling small retail
sales of foodstuffs and other basic commodities, though in others men
handled this small-scale distribution of goods as well.

These developments were not the same in all areas of the world,
however. In parts of Africa and Southeast Asia women were important
traders at the regional and even international level for many centuries,
handling both basic commodities such as cloth and luxuries such as
pepper or betel. In other areas the amount of total trade was very limited,
so that trade was not an avenue to wealth or power for either men or
women. Attitudes toward trade and traders also varied widely in agricultural societies, with some cultures holding individuals who made
their living this way in high esteem, and others regarding them as at
best a necessary evil.

Even in cultures in which there was a significant amount of trade, the
most important form of wealth was possession of land and the people
who worked it; this remained the case from the earliest development of
agriculture until the nineteenth century in most parts of the world and
until today in many areas. As we have seen, systems of inheritance in
plow-using cultures tended to favor sons over daughters, so that men
generally predominated in this aspect of economic life as well. Sons were
not always available, however, and many inheritance schema turned next
to brothers, nephews, grandfathers, or any other male relative. In other
cultures close relatives were favored over those more distant, even if this
meant allowing daughters to inherit. Thus the drive to keep property
within the family – however "family" was defined – resulted in women
inheriting, owning, and in some cases managing significant amounts of
wealth. (This continues today, of course; lists of the "hundred most
wealthy people" generally include some women, most of them heir-
esses.) In many instances women were simply conduits of wealth from
one generation to another or from one family to another on marriage –
the anthropologist Claude Lévi-Strauss called this "the exchange of

women" – but in others they were able to be more active, buying and selling property and, in slave societies, buying and selling people. The gender hierarchy thus intersected with the wealth hierarchy in complex ways, and in many cultures age and marital status also played a role. In many European and African cultures, for example, widows were largely able to control their own property, while unmarried sons were often under their father's control even if they were adults.

Because wealth was based primarily on the earning power of the land and people under one's control and not on one's own labor, leisure rather than work was a mark of status in many agricultural societies. In some cases, such as France in the sixteenth and seventeenth centuries, members of the hereditary aristocracy might actually be prohibited from engaging directly in business activities; nobles in France were required to live off the rents and income of their lands or lose the exemption from taxation that nobles enjoyed. In other cultures economically productive work was viewed as less important than certain types of intellectual work, such as studying sacred texts. Among Jews in Europe or upper-caste Hindus in India, for example, men were praised for devoting themselves to prayer and the study of religious writings. Even scholars have to eat, of course, which was not a problem for upper-caste Hindu men whose families were wealthy enough to support them; this was also the case with many Jewish men, and in other instances their wives worked to support them and the family. This meant that Jewish women were often more economically independent than their Christian neighbors in premodern Europe, but their activities were still not valued as highly as those of their scholarly husbands.

Foraging, horticulture, and agriculture remained the primary economic activities for most people throughout the entire history of the world, though there are only a few foraging groups in very isolated areas and slightly more horticulturists left in the world today. Just a hundred years ago their numbers were much greater, however, and at that point the vast majority of the world's people still made their living directly through plow agriculture. The social patterns set in early agricultural societies – with most of the population dependent farmers, a small group of merchants, skilled artisans, and religious leaders, and rule by a hereditary aristocracy – lasted for millennia, as did the agricultural gender division of labor. It is important to keep these continuities in mind as we look at later economic changes, for it is easy to forget how slowly economic developments altered the lives of most people. It is also important to remember that later dramatic economic changes

built on a base of gender divisions that had been in place for a very long
time.

Capitalism and Industrialism

Economic historians often joke about the phrase "the rise of capitalism,"
as it is invoked to describe and explain quite varied developments over a
long period of time; no matter where you look, capitalism always seems
to be rising, seemingly independent of human agents, sort of like bread
dough. Some of this expansionism comes from the elastic meaning of
capitalism, which generally includes private ownership of property and
the materials used to make or provide goods and services (what economists call the means of production), wage labor, well-developed financial
institutions such as banks, and large and complex forms of economic
organization. All of these were present to some degree in many agricultural societies, but they became increasingly important in Europe during
the fifteenth through the eighteenth centuries, with income derived
from capitalist business ventures eventually displacing land-holding as
the primary form of wealth. Capitalism developed first in long-distance
trade – this is often termed mercantile capitalism – then in production.
Capitalist production was initially carried out in households, but gradually workers were brought together into larger units eventually termed
factories, and by the eighteenth century these factories began to use
machines and new sources of power such as coal or water for their work,
in what is termed industrial capitalism or industrialism.

At the same time that capitalism and industrialism were developing in
Europe, Europeans were also traveling to the Americas, Asia, Australia,
and Africa to settle and conquer. These phenomena – first capitalism and
colonization, and then industrialism and imperialism – were intimately
related. (Many other factors also played a role in European colonialism
and imperialism, of course, such as religion and politics; we will discuss
these in more detail in chapters 5 and 6.) Capitalist merchants often
provided the impetus and the equipment for colonization, and many
colonies were established to be both sources of raw materials and markets
for trade goods. Consumer goods such as sugar and coffee produced in
colonial areas were handled by international traders, who also bought,
transported, and sold large numbers of slaves primarily from Africa to
produce these goods. Capitalist production began first in cloth, using
wool and linen from Europe, but by the nineteenth century cotton

grown in colonial areas (or formerly colonial areas, such as the United States) was the most important material. European cotton cloth was shipped throughout the world, clothing slaves and agricultural workers on tropical plantations, and buying consumer items from around the world.

European capitalism, including its gender patterns, grew out of the agricultural system that had developed in medieval Europe. During the Middle Ages the household became the basic unit of production in most parts of Europe, a process some social historians label the familialization of labor. The central work unit was the marital couple, joined by their children when they became old enough to work. Though in some parts of southern and eastern Europe extended families lived together, in central and northern Europe couples generally set up independent households upon marrying, making the production unit also a residential unit. Urban households often included individuals who were not family members – servants, apprentices, journeymen – but at their core in most parts of Europe was a single marital couple and its children.

During the thirteenth and fourteenth centuries urban producers of certain products began to form craft guilds in many cities to organize and regulate production; guilds set the rules by which most items were manufactured, including training requirements, quality and price levels, hours of operation, and size of shops. There were a few all-female guilds in cities with highly specialized economies such as Cologne, Paris, and Rouen, but in general the guilds were male organizations and followed the male life-cycle. One became an apprentice at puberty, became a journeyman four to ten years later, traveled around learning from a number of masters, then settled down, married, opened one's own shop and worked at the same craft full-time until one died or got too old to work any longer. This process presupposed that one would be free to travel (something that was more difficult for women than men), that on marriage one would acquire a wife as an assistant, and that pregnancy, childbirth, or child-rearing would never interfere with one's labor. Transitions between these stages were marked by ceremonies, and master-craftsmen were formally inscribed in guild registers and took part in governing the guild. Thus, though work continued to be carried out by a household unit, only the male head of that unit was recognized officially. By the late fifteenth century journeymen began to resent the power of the masters and to form their own guilds with elaborate rituals reinforcing group identity and loyalty. Because women fit into guilds primarily through their relation with a master craftsman – as his wife, daughters, or servants – and their work was not recognized formally, they did not organize separately. By the sixteenth century journeymen resented even this informal participation, and increasingly asserted that the most honorable workplace was the one in which only men worked.

All of these factors shaped the development of capitalism. Though women occasionally invested in the new joint-stock companies and other capitalist enterprises, most of the merchants and traders in the first era of mercantile capitalism were men, as were those who began to invest in capitalist forms of production. Urban investors often hired whole households, but paid wages only to the male head of household; in mining, for example, men were paid per basket for ore, but it was expected that this ore would be broken apart and washed, jobs which their wives, sisters, and children did, though they did not receive separate wages for their work. In households hired to produce cloth, women and children often spun while men wove, with the investor paying for the finished pieces. When wages were paid to individuals, ideas about the value of men's and women's labor and about the household as the proper economic unit shaped both wages and hiring practices; women's wages for manufacturing tasks were generally about one-half to two-thirds those of men for the same or similar tasks, which sometimes meant that employers preferred them. Married women's wages were also less than those of widows for the same task, a wage structure based on the idea that married women needed less because they had a husband to support them, not on an evaluation of the quality of their work.

Capitalist production challenged the monopoly of many guilds, and slowly more and more of the goods produced in Europe were made outside of guilds, but the ideas about work developed by the guilds carried over into capitalism. The most honorable trades were those in which few or no women worked, and the tasks that women did in their homes, which could be very labor-intensive and time consuming, were not considered work. Not working for wages became a mark of middle-class status, so that women often hid the work they did, such as taking in boarders, or defined it as "housekeeping."

Housekeeping itself became more elaborate, as international trade and then industrial production provided a steadily increasing amount of consumer goods to households in Europe and European households in the colonies. People purchased much more clothing, table linen, and bedding than they had before, and wealthier households now contained a vast array of new products: watches, snuff boxes, umbrellas, fans, paintings, silks and fine cottons from Asia, feathered hats, window-curtains, tea-tables, wall- and hand-mirrors, and writing desks. Most strikingly, Europeans ate very different foods – coffee, tea, and hot chocolate (prepared in public coffee-houses or their own homes), rum, and new types of fruits and vegetables. Their sugar consumption increased astronomically, from about two pounds a year in England in 1650 to almost twenty-five pounds in 1800. This new consumer culture provided opportunities for men and women to socialize in new ways, with men gathering in coffee-houses and women in the homes of their friends or relatives around a tea-pot. The increase in consumer goods also shaped the types of work available, as more shops were opened even in very small towns – an opportunity not limited to men the way work in guilds was – and wealthier households hired more – mostly female – servants to polish all that brass and wash all those windows. Domestic service became the most common form of paid work for women in western Europe in the nineteenth century and in Latin America in the twentieth.

Mercantile capitalism and the demand for consumer goods also influenced the gender division of labor in indigenous societies outside of Europe. For example, by the early seventeenth century in the eastern part of North America, native trading networks also involved Europeans, almost all of them men, who brought in goods of interest to both men and women: guns, rum, cloth, kettles, flour, needles, and tea. The Europeans were primarily interested in furs for beaver hats and other articles of clothing, which were hunted and trapped by men. This meant that men's activities often came to be more highly regarded as a source of imported goods, in contrast to earlier periods in which men's hunting and women's horticulture had been valued more equally. In the Middle East women's central role in spinning and weaving for their own families was disrupted by the large-scale importation of cheap European cloth; European demands for specialized textiles such as fine silks and carpets provided some factory jobs for women, but also for men. In colonial areas indigenous women were often hired as domestic servants in white households, which brought them into intimate contact with colonizing families; sometimes this was done forcibly, as in Australia where Aboriginal girls were seized by the government and placed in white homes as domestic servants.

The growth of industrialism has traditionally been regarded as one of the great breaks in economic history – it is one of the few economic developments that is termed a revolution – but in terms of gender arrangements the industrial economies of Europe and North America also built on earlier patterns. The separation of workplace from home made it difficult for married women to combine factory work with their family responsibilities, and factory work became the province of men, younger unmarried women, and children. Young women were often the first to be hired when factories opened, particularly in cloth production, because their work was seen as less valuable and they could be hired more cheaply. Older daughters – and less often, sons – often gave part of their wages to their parents even when they lived apart from them, so that vestiges of the household economy remained. Supervisory positions were reserved for older men, who were often expected to oversee the morals and leisure-time activities of their workers as fathers has been expected to earlier. In some heavy industries, such as steel and machine production, almost all of the workers were male; work was thus segmented by gender both within factories and across industries. In some areas segmentation by race or national origin was added to that of gender; by the 1880s in the tobacco industry of North Carolina, for example, black men handled the bales of tobacco, black women stemmed tobacco leaves, white women operated cigarette-making machines, and white men repaired machinery and supervised the entire operation.

Industrial development in the rest of the world occurred later than in Europe and North America, in the nineteenth century in much of Latin America and parts of Asia, and in other areas not until after World War II. In some ways industrialism elsewhere followed the European pattern, with women and children paid lower wages and supervisory positions going to men, but it was also shaped by local conditions and traditions. In Japan, for example, though both labor organizations and political leaders opposed women working in factories and urged them to stay home to become "good wives, wise mothers," their lower wages made them attractive to factory owners; in 1909, 62 percent of the factory labor force was female, working primarily in silk production. Some of these women had been sold by their families to factory owners, and the cloth and clothing they made earned the foreign exchange that made possible the later development of heavy industry in Japan, such as the manufacture of steel and automobiles.

Wherever and whenever it occurred, industrialism often led to the deskilling of certain occupations, in which jobs that had traditionally been done by men were made more monotonous with the addition of machinery and so were redefined and given to women, with a dramatic drop in status and pay; secretarial work, weaving, and shoemaking are prominent examples of this. Like the definition of "work," the definition of "skill" is often gendered, and women were excluded from certain jobs, such as glass-cutting, because they were judged clumsy or "unskilled," yet those same women made lace, a job which required an even higher level of dexterity and concentration than glass-cutting.

This link between gender and "skill" had actually begun in the pre-industrial period, though in these cases the addition of machinery often made jobs "male" instead of "female." Both brewing and stocking-knitting, for example, were transformed during the fifteenth and six-teenth centuries into male-dominated occupations in some parts of Europe. When knitting-frames and new brewing methods were introduced, men began to argue that they were so complicated women could never use them; in reality they made brewing and knitting faster and increased the opportunities for profit. Women were limited to small-scale brewing and knitting primarily for their own family's use. Links between gender and "skill" have continued in the post-industrial economy as well. Using a typewriter was gendered female in the early twentieth century, but working with computers has been gendered male and accompanied by an increase in pay and status. This regendering of work on a keyboard has been accomplished by associating computers with mathematics and machinery, fields viewed as masculine that girls have been discouraged from studying; advertisements in computer magazines often portray women at the keyboard only if they are emphasizing how easy a computer system is to use.

The conditions of work under early industrialism were often horrendous, with twelve-hour days and dangerous machinery and chemicals very common. Such conditions led workers to develop labor organizations that sought shorter hours and better wages and working conditions. These labor organizations varied in their gender politics. In some countries, such as Great Britain and the United States, labor unions organized primarily along craft lines, and, like the earlier craft guilds, often opposed women's labor as dishonoring or cheapening their craft. They argued in favor of a "family wage," that is, wages high enough to allow married male workers to support their families so that their wives could concentrate on domestic tasks and not work outside the home. This family wage was only an ideal, however, and most working-class women had to work at whatever was available to keep families supported, which after the invention of the sewing machine in the late nineteenth century was often piece-work for very low wages, what is often termed "sweated" labor.

In continental Europe and Latin America labor unions generally organized along industrial lines and had closer connections with socialist and other left-wing political parties. This made them slightly more open to including women members, particularly as some socialist parties, such as those in Germany and Argentina, began to advocate for women's greater political and legal rights. In general, however, labor organizations continued to be ambivalent toward women, at times encouraging their inclusion or separate women's unions, but more often opposing women's work and trivializing women's issues. Women were harder to organize than men, as their wages were often too low to pay union dues, their family responsibilities prevented their attending union meetings, and they had been socialized to view their work as temporary and not to challenge male authorities. Women made up a much smaller share of union membership than they did of the work force, though they often participated with men in strikes, demonstrations, and protests for better conditions, even if they were not members. Separate women's unions were formed in some countries, however; by 1900, for example, women's unions in the tobacco, coffee, and textile industries in Mexico and Puerto Rico were demanding recognition and the right to bargain collectively. Demands by unions combined with paternalistic ideas about women's health on the part of political authorities led to laws limiting the hours of work by women in factories; because men's hours were not similarly limited, these measures lessened women's desirability as workers.

Industrialization was a very uneven process. In some parts of the world subsistence agriculture remained the primary economic activity until well into the twentieth century, although the gender structures in many non-industrial areas were also shaped by industry and international trade. For example, international commercial networks began to shape some east African societies in the eighteenth century, with goods acquired by male hunters such as ivory and horns often allowing them to acquire still more wives and cattle. There seem to have been fewer women traders in these areas than in western Africa, although women's lives were also influenced by trade in that they were the major agricultural producers, and trade with the New World brought in new crops such as maize, cassava, and groundnuts. Some of these crops, especially cassava (also called manioc, and the source of tapioca), increased women's work load, as the roots needed to be cooked and pounded in order to make edible starch, a process which often took days. Cassava was also introduced into western Africa during this period, providing an incentive for the maintenance of polygynous households that included many women who could share the work. In the nineteenth century commercial agriculture for export and mining began in many parts of Africa, both of which employed many more men than women. Men left their villages for years at a time to grow cocoa, mine diamonds, or build railroads, leaving women to continue subsistence horticulture or agriculture. This same pattern developed in many parts of Latin America, with men migrating to large plantations, cities, or other countries in search of paid labor, and women remaining to care for children and the elderly and to engage in unpaid agricultural work.

Corporations, the State, and the Service Economy of the Twentieth Century

The twentieth century saw dramatic changes in the gender division of labor in many parts of the world, though these changes were not the same everywhere. In contrast to areas of the world which industrialized first, such as England, the United States, and Japan – where young women were the first to be hired as factories opened – the introduction of wage labor in agriculture, mining, and industry in other parts of the world in the twentieth century provided jobs initially for boys and men. Men traveled to plantations, mines, and cities, leaving women responsible for producing food largely through subsistence agriculture. Cash crops for export took the best land, so women were left with increasingly infertile land on which to support burgeoning populations. This problem was most acute in Africa, exacerbated by the fact that, as noted above, colonial governments and international development agencies assumed – based on western practices – that men were the primary agricultural producers; they thus often sought to "modernize" agriculture by teaching men new methods of farming or processing crops in cultures where these tasks had always been done by women. Only in the 1980s did the focus begin to shift somewhat to smaller-scale projects directed at women, such as small irrigation systems, improvements in stock-raising techniques, and credit associations.

In the last several decades the composition of the industrial labor force in more recently industrialized countries has shifted. By the 1980s the most profitable industries were those in electronics, clothing, chemicals, and textiles rather than heavier industries, and multinational corporations increasingly favored women – and in some areas children – as workers; by the 1990s perhaps as many as 80 percent of the workers in factories geared for world markets were young women. Particularly in east, southeast, and south Asia, young women were as likely as young men to migrate to cities in search of work, though they were more likely to send the majority of their wages home to their families. This was not the case in the Muslim countries of the Near East, however, which remained the area of the world in which women formed the smallest share of the paid labor force, generally between 2 and 10 percent. (Many of these were highly educated professionals such as teachers and health-care workers, trained to assist other women in sex-segregated settings.) Young women in Muslim countries outside the Middle East, such as Malaysia, were caught between these two systems; their labor in factories was essential to their families' survival, yet they were also criticized for flouting Muslim norms.

These shifts in the organization of production have largely resulted from the decisions of multinational corporations, but the links between gender and work in the twentieth century were also shaped to a greater extent than earlier by state policies. During World Wars I and II government propaganda campaigns in Europe and North America, combined with improved wages and facilities such as child-care centers, encouraged women to enter the paid labor force to replace men who were fighting; the granting of female suffrage in many countries right after World War I was in part thanks for women's work as nurses and munitions workers. Though the demobilization of men once the wars were over led to women being fired or encouraged to quit, the enormous losses among soldiers in the wars also made it impossible to return completely to prewar patterns. Though war-time measures such as dining halls and child-care centers were generally ended, the total percentage of women in the paid labor force did not decline substantially.

In Japan and many countries of Europe the 1920s and 1930s saw the development of authoritarian dictatorships, which transformed ideas about women's "natural" role as wives and mothers into government policies promoting maternity and limiting women's employment. Particularly during the depression of the 1930s, working women in dictatorships and democracies were denounced as taking jobs away from men, and work was celebrated in vigorous propaganda campaigns as inherently masculine; in the United States, England, and elsewhere, women could get fired if they married. Despite this rhetoric, the expanding industrial sector required ever-increasing numbers of workers, particularly as many countries mobilized for war in the late 1930s and 1940s. In Stalinist Russia and Fascist Italy the number of single and married women in the labor force increased steadily, though the Nazi regime in Germany decided to solve its need for workers by drafting forced labor from occupied countries (most of it male) rather than encouraging women to work.

Along with the policies of corporations and national governments the gender division of labor in the twentieth century was shaped by changes in communications technology and business practices that began to create a new type of economy, often termed post-industrial. In the post-industrial economy, service, sales, and information transfer played a more important role than production, with the office rather than the factory becoming the primary place of work and more formal "white-collar" clothing replacing more easily cleaned "blue-collar" clothing. In the first half of the century new types of jobs were created, such as secretaries, postal clerks, bank tellers, telegraph and telephone operators, and department store clerks, which required serving customers or assisting supervisors. These came to be viewed as especially appropriate for young women, who were hired for their appearance and pleasing demeanor as well as their abilities; in some areas women who held these positions were fired if they married or planned to marry – men in similar positions were not – or if they became too old. Open discrimination by age or marital status continued in some "female" service occupations until the 1970s, with flight attendants being the best-known example. Male managers and salesmen were celebrated for both competition and teamwork, and regarded as the brains of corporate culture, while women were its heart; women who became managers often specialized in personnel or human relations.

The growth in women's paid employment in industrialized countries that began during the 1970s was also largely concentrated in lower-paying service jobs such as office work, child-care, hairdressing and cleaning (dubbed the "pink collar ghetto"), so that women's average full-time earnings remained about two-thirds those of men. Sweden was the most egalitarian industrialized country in terms of wages in the late twentieth century, with female wages about 90 percent of male in 1985; Japan was the least, with female wages about 43 percent of male, a situation that has caused many highly educated young Japanese women to leave Japan. The growth of the service economy has also led many poorly educated women to migrate in search of domestic or other types of work, especially from poorer states such as the Philippines or Sri Lanka to Europe, North America, or oil-rich Middle Eastern states.

The post-industrial work force is much more decentralized than that of the industrial economy, for computer and communications technology allows many employees to work from their own homes rather than in factories. Like the domestic production of much earlier centuries, such work is often paid by the piece rather than the hour, which allows for greater flexibility but also greater exploitation, as there is no limitation of the work day and benefits such as health-care are often not included. Because it can be combined with minding children and cooking, home production is often favored by women; in areas of the world such as India or the Arab countries where women are secluded, such work may be undertaken without disturbing religious or cultural norms. A few of those who work at home are highly educated and highly paid "tele-commuters" in the burgeoning information industry, but most home labor involves routine data processing and other forms of computerized office work, or more traditional jobs such as making lace or gloves or shoes; along with the computer, the sewing machine continues to be an effective tool of decentralization.

Work at home, whether using a sewing machine or a computer, is sometimes included in official statistics, but often it is not, and it shades into what economists term the "informal," "underground," or "gray-market" economy. Gray-market transactions (called such to differentiate them from actually illegal black market transactions), such as the small-scale selling of commodities and services, often by street vendors, were intentionally unrecorded to avoid taxes and do not form part of official statistical measures, but are the only way people survived in some areas in the twentieth century. Such work "off the books" was an important part of the economies of many developing countries and even some in Europe; estimates from Italy judge that the unrecorded exchange of goods and services probably equaled that of the official economy after World War II. Women often predominated in the informal economy, selling commodities and services – including sex – on a small scale as they had for centuries; such work provided women with a decent income, though in many it barely sustained them and their families. In some cases such work, particularly in the sex trade, was essentially slave labor; in 2000, for example, the CIA estimated that perhaps 50,000 women and children were being brought into the US each year under false pretenses from countries such as Thailand, Mexico, and Russia, and forced to work as prostitutes or servants. Labor that had never been paid or counted – such as that on family land holdings – must be added to this intentionally unrecorded labor to get a true picture of the work situation; in the same Muslim countries where women formed less than 10 percent of the paid labor force in the 1990s, for example, they are estimated to have performed 50 to 75 percent of the unpaid agricultural labor.

Evaluating the gender division of labor in the twentieth century must also take unpaid work within the household into account. Even in areas in which women made up more than half of the full-time labor force outside the household, such as the Soviet Union, women continued to do almost all of the household tasks. In the Soviet Union and communist eastern Europe shortages in foodstuffs and household goods such as soap meant that women had to spend hours each day (after their paid workday was done) standing in lines. Because of this "second shift" women were not free to attend Communist Party meetings or do extra work on the job in order to be promoted; in the 1970s, though women made up over 50 percent of the paid work force in the Soviet Union, only 0.5 percent of managers and directors were women. This situation did not change when communism ended in eastern Europe in 1989, though more women had time to spend in lines because they were more likely than men to be unemployed. The time needed to obtain basic consumer goods was much shorter in western Europe, so that the second shift was less onerous, but it was no less gender specific; even in relatively egalitarian Sweden, women who worked full time spent at least twice as long on household tasks as men, and even longer if there were children in the house. This situation led some European feminists in the 1970s to advocate "wages for housework," while others opposed this idea as reinforcing an unfair gender division of labor.

Despite the fact that we recognize economic life involves more than work, this chapter, like the vast majority of studies of gender and the economy, has focused primarily on work, perhaps because work is the most universal economic activity, or the one laden with the most meaning. As we have seen, though the gender division of labor is variable and changing, it has always been present; when English peasants in the fourteenth century wished to describe the lack of social differentiation based on wealth and class at the beginning of human history, they still envisioned gender differences, singing: "When Adam delved and Eve span, who was then the gentleman?" It is difficult to predict how current economic trends, such as the introduction of market economies in the former Soviet bloc and in China, or government-directed restructuring in developing countries designed to lessen their foreign debt obligations and achieve higher rates of economic growth, will shape the gender division of labor and access to wealth. In the 1980s and 1990s these trends generally provided more opportunities for men than for women, with economists and policy-makers around the world noting a "feminization of poverty," as social programs were cut back and women were more likely to be unemployed or underemployed. This was accompanied, however, by steadily increasing numbers of women in traditionally male occupations in many countries, and steadily – though more slowly – increasing numbers of women in highly paid professional and management positions. In addition, the increasingly global nature of business led men's work in many areas to become "feminized," that is, not bound by long-term contracts or providing much job security. Whether the interactions of these and other changes will eventually end the gender division of labor, or at least make it less significant for large numbers of people throughout the world, remains to be seen.

Further Reading

Examinations of the role of gender in economic life were initially conceptualized primarily as studies of women's work, and this focus has continued in much research; until very recently most studies of men's work did not recognize their subjects as men or use gender as a tool of analysis, so they have not been included here. In terms of theoretical underpinnings, the feminist critique of Marxist analysis, which began during the 1970s, is particularly important, especially in its explorations of the relations between gender and class hierarchies in economic matters. See, for example, Roberta Hamilton, *The Liberation of Women: A Study of Patriarchy and Capitalism* (London: George Allen and Unwin, 1978); Heide Hartmann, "The unhappy marriage of Marxism and feminism: towards a more progressive union," *Capital and Class* 8 (1979), 1–33 and "The family as the locus of gender, class and political struggle: the example of housework," *Signs* 6 (1981), 366–94; Joan Kelly, "The doubled vision of feminist theory" in her *Women, History and Theory* (Chicago: University of Chicago Press, 1984), pp. 51–64. More recent considerations of these issues include: Wally Seccombe, *A Millennium of Family Change: Feudalism to Capitalism in Northwestern Europe* (London: Verso, 1992); Leonore Davidoff, *Worlds Between:*

Historical Perspectives on Gender and Class (New York: Routledge, 1995); Mary Murray, *The Law of the Father: Patriarchy in the Transition from Feudalism to Capitalism* (London: Routledge, 1995); Harriet Bradley, *Men's Work, Women's Work: A Sociological History of the Sexual Division of Labour in Employment* (Oxford: Blackwell Publishers, 1989); Marilyn Waring, *Counting for Nothing: What Men Value and What Women are Worth*, 2nd edn (Toronto: University of Toronto Press, 2000). A brief general history of gender and industrialization is Louise A. Tilly's *Industrialization and Gender Inequality* (Washington, DC: American Historical Association, 1993).

As with so many of the issues in this book, the scholarship available in English on women's work in Europe and the United States outweighs that available for the rest of the world. Some general overviews of Europe include: Louise A. Tilly and Joan W. Scott, *Women, Work and Family*, 2nd edn (New York: Metheun, 1987); Pat Hudson and W. R. Lee, eds., *Women's Work and the Family Economy in Historical Perspective* (Manchester: Manchester University Press, 1990); Deborah Simonton, *A History of European Women's Work: 1700 to the Present* (London: Routledge, 1998). For the medieval period, see: Martha Howell, *Women, Production and Patriarchy in Late Medieval Cities* (Chicago: University of Chicago Press, 1986); David Herlihy, *Opera Muliebria: Women and Work in Medieval Europe* (New York: McGraw Hill, 1990); Judith Bennett, *Ale, Beer, and Brewsters in England: Women's Work in a Changing World, 1300–1600* (New York: Oxford University Press, 1996). For the early modern period, see: Barbara Hanawalt, ed., *Women and Work in Preindustrial Europe* (Bloomington: Indiana University Press, 1982); Lindsey Charles and Lorna Duffin, eds., *Women and Work in Pre-Industrial England* (London, Croom Helm, 1985); Merry E. Wiesner, *Working Women in Renaissance Germany* (New Brunswick, NJ: Rutgers University Press, 1986); Bridget Hill, *Women, Work and Sexual Politics in Eighteenth-century England* (Oxford: Blackwell Publishers, 1989); Daryl Hafter, ed., *European Women and Preindustrial Craft* (Bloomington: Indiana University Press, 1995); Pamela Sharpe, *Adapting to Capitalism: Working Women in the English Economy 1700–1850* (New York: St Martin's Press, 1996). For women's work in the industrial revolution in Europe, see: Joanna Bourke, *Husbandry and Housewifery: Women, Economic Change and Housework in Ireland, 1890–1914* (Oxford: Clarendon Press, 1993); Deborah Valenze, *The First Industrial Woman* (New York: Oxford University Press, 1995). For women's work in twentieth-century western Europe, see: Jane Jenson, ed., *The Feminization of the Labour*

Force (Cambridge: Polity Press, 1988); Jane Lewis, *Britain Since 1945: Women, Work and the State in the Postwar Years* (Oxford: Blackwell Publishers, 1992); Annie Phizacklea and Carol Wolkowitz, *Homeworking Women: Gender, Racism and Class at Work* (London: Sage, 1995).

Women's work in eastern Europe and Russia before, during, and after communism has been the focus of a number of studies. See: Barbara Alpern Engel, *Between the Fields and the City: Women, Work and Family in Russia, 1861–1914* (Cambridge: Cambridge University Press, 1994); Barbara Einhorn, *Women and Market Societies* (Aldershot: Edward Elgar, 1995); Rachel Alsop, *Reversal of Fortunes? Women, Work, and Change in Eastern Germany* (Oxford: Berghahn, 1998); Jane McDermid and Anna Hillyar, *Women and Work in Russia, 1880–1930: A Study in Continuity through Change* (London: Longman, 1998).

For studies of the gender division of labor in modern Europe that do not focus primarily on women's work, see: Francesca Bettio, *The Sexual Division of Labor: The Italian Case* (Oxford: Oxford University Press, 1988); Sonya Rose, *Limited Livelihoods: Gender and Class in Nineteenth Century England* (Berkeley: University of California Press, 1992); Hettie Pott-Butler, *Facts and Fairy Tales about Female Labor, Family, and Fertility: A Seven-Country Comparison, 1850–1990* (Amsterdam: Amsterdam University Press, 1993); Diane Sainsbury, ed., *Gendering Welfare States* (London: Sage, 1994); Tessia P. Liu, *The Weaver's Knot: The Contradictions of Class Struggle and Family Solidarity in Western France, 1750–1914* (Ithaca, NY: Cornell University Press, 1994); Laura L. Frader and Sonya O. Rose, *Gender and Class in Modern Europe* (Ithaca, NY: Cornell University Press, 1996); Francisca de Haan, *Gender and the Politics of Office Work: The Netherlands 1860–1940* (Amsterdam: Amsterdam University Press, 1998).

There are, not surprisingly, more studies of gender and work in the United States than of any other single country. Several good overviews of women's work are: Barbara Mayer Wertheimer, *We Were There: The Story of Working Women in America* (New York: Pantheon, 1977); Claudia Dale Golden, *Understanding the Gender Gap: An Economic History of American Women* (New York: Oxford University Press, 1990); Rosalyn Baxandall and Linda Gordon, eds., *America's Working Women: A Documentary History, 1600 to the Present*, 2nd edn (New York: Norton, 1999); Sharlene Hesse-Biber and Gregg Carter, *Working Women in America: Split Dreams* (New York: Oxford University Press, 2000). For more specialized studies, see: Margery Davies, *Woman's Place at the Typewriter: Office Work and Office Workers, 1870–1930* (Philadelphia:

Temple University Press, 1982); Susan Lehrer, *Origins of Protective Labor Legislation for Women, 1905–1925* (Albany: State University of New York Press, 1987); Eileen Boris and Cynthia R. Daniels, eds., *Homework: Historical and Contemporary Studies on Paid Labor at Home* (Urbana: University of Illinois Press, 1989); Ronald C. Kent, et al., eds., *Culture, Gender, Race, and US Labor History* (Westport, CT: Greenwood Press, 1993); Sharon Hartman Strom, *Beyond the Typewriter: Gender, Class, and the Origins of Modern American Office Work, 1900–1930* (Urbana: University of Illinois Press, 1992); Jacquelyn Dowd Hall et al., *Like a Family: The Making of a Southern Cotton Mill World* (Chapel Hill: University of North Carolina Press, 1995); Leslie A. Schwalm, *A Hard Fight for We: Women's Transition from Slavery to Freedom in South Carolina* (Champaign: University of Illinois Press, 1997); Ruth Oldenziel, *Making Technology Masculine: Men, Women and Modern Machines in America, 1870–1945* (Amsterdam: Amsterdam University Press, 1999); Ruth Milkman, *Gender at Work: The Dynamics of Job Segregation by Sex during World War II* (Urbana: University of Illinois Press, 1987); Angel Kwolek-Folland, *Engendering Business: Men and Women in the Corporate Office 1870–1930* (Baltimore, MD: Johns Hopkins University Press, 1994).

The gender politics of the labor movement in Europe and North America have been analyzed in: Philip S. Foner, *Women and the American Labor Movement: From Colonial Times to the Eve of World War I* (New York: Free Press, 1979); Marjorie Griffen Cohen, *Women's Work, Markets, and Economic Development in Nineteenth-century Ontario* (Toronto: University of Toronto Press, 1988); Lourdes Beneria and Martha Roldan, *The Crossroads of Class and Gender: Industrial Homework, Subcontracting, and Household Dynamics in Mexico City* (Chicago: University of Chicago Press, 1987); Ava Baron, ed., *Work Engendered: Toward a New History of American Labor* (Ithaca, NY: Cornell University Press, 1991); Mary Davis, *Comrade or Brother: A History of the British Labour Movement, 1789–1951* (London: Pluto Press, 1993); Laura Lee Downs, *Manufacturing Inequality: Gender Division in the French and British Metalworking Industries, 1914–1939* (Ithaca, NY: Cornell University Press, 1995); Ulla Wikander, Alice Kessler-Harris, and Jane Lewis, eds., *Protecting Women: Labor Legislation in Europe, the United States and Australia* (Urbana: University of Illinois Press, 1995); Kathleen Canning, *Languages of Labor and Gender: Female Factory Work in Germany, 1850–1914* (Ithaca, NY: Cornell University Press, 1996); Anna Clark, *The Struggle for the Breeches: Gender and the Making of the British Working Class* (Berkeley: University of California Press, 1996); Linda Kealey, *Enlisting Women for the Cause: Women, Labour, and the Left in Canada, 1890–1920* (Toronto: University of Toronto Press, 1998); Nan Enstad, *Ladies of Labor, Girls of Adventure: Working Women, Popular Culture, and Labor Politics at the Turn of the Twentieth Century* (New York: Columbia University Press, 1999).

Issues surrounding gender and work have also been studied extensively in east Asia, particularly in the modern period. For China, see: Emily Honig, *Sisters and Strangers: Women in the Shanghai Cotton Mills, 1919–1949* (Stanford, CA: Stanford University Press, 1986); Tamara Jacke, *Women's Work in Rural China: Change and Continuity in an Era of Reform* (Cambridge: Cambridge University Press, 1997); Francesca Bray, *Technologies and Gender: Fabrics of Power in Late Imperial China* (Berkeley: University of California Press, 1997); Ching Kwan Lee, *Gender and the South China Miracle: Two Worlds of Factory Women* (Berkeley: University of California Press, 1998); Lynda S. Bell, *One Industry, Two Chinas: Silk Filatures and Peasant-family Production in Wuxi County, 1865–1937* (Stanford, CA: Stanford University Press, 1999). For Japan, see: E. Patricia Tsurumi, *Factory Girls: Women in the Thread Mills of Meiji Japan* (Princeton, NJ: Princeton University Press, 1990); Dorinne K. Kondo, *Crafting Selves: Power, Gender, and Discourses of Identity in a Japanese Workplace* (Chicago: University of Chicago Press, 1990); Jeannie Lo, *Office Ladies, Factory Women: Life and Work at a Japanese Company* (Armonk, NY: M. E. Sharpe, 1990); Gail Lee Bernstein, *Recreating Japanese Women* (Berkeley: University of California Press, 1991); Janet Hunter, ed., *Japanese Women Working* (London: Routledge, 1993); Mary C. Brinton, *Women and the Economic Miracle: Gender and Work in Postwar Japan* (Berkeley: University of California Press, 1993); Anne Allison, *Nightwork: Sexuality, Pleasure, and Corporate Masculinity in a Tokyo Hostess Club* (Chicago: University of Chicago Press, 1994); Hitomi Tonomura, Anne Walthall, and Wakita Haruko, eds., *Women and Class in Japanese History* (Ann Arbor: University of Michigan Press, 1998). For Korea, see: Seung-Kyung Kim, *Class Struggle or Family Struggle? The Lives of Women Factory Workers in South Korea* (Cambridge: Cambridge University Press, 1997).

South and Southeast Asia have not received as much attention as other areas, but there are several good collections and studies of specific situations, including: Ursula Sharma, *Women, Work, and Property in North-West India* (London: Tavistock, 1986); Maria Mies, *The Lace Makers of Narsapur: Indian Housewives Produce for the World Market* (London: Zed Books, 1982); Aihwa Ong, *Spirits of Resistance and Capitalist Discipline: Factory Women in Malaysia* (Albany: State University of New York Press, 1987); Alison Murray, *No Money No Honey: A Study of Street*

Traders and Prostitutes in Jakarta (New York: Oxford University Press, 1991); E. U. Eviota, *The Political Economy of Gender: Women and the Sexual Division of Labor in the Philippines* (London: Zed Books, 1992); Diane L. Wolf, *Factory Daughters: Gender, Household Dynamics, and Rural Industrialization in Java* (Berkeley: University of California Press, 1992); Saraswati Raju and Deipica Bagchi, eds., *Women and Work in South Asia: Regional Patterns and Perspectives* (London: Routledge, 1993); Wazir Jahan Karim, ed., *"Male" and "Female" in Developing Southeast Asia* (Oxford: Berg Publishers, 1995); Samita Sen, *Women and Labour in Late Colonial India: The Bengal Jute Industry* (Cambridge: Cambridge University Press, 1999).

Much of the scholarship on Africa, Latin America, and some parts of Asia has focused on issues surrounding women and development; for an extensive bibliography, see Parvin Ghorayshi, *Women and Work in Developing Countries: An Annotated Bibliography* (Westport, CT: Greenwood Press, 1994). Several good general studies and collections of articles are: Haleh Afshar, ed., *Women, Work, and Ideology in the Third World* (New York: Tavistock, 1985) and *Women, Development and Survival in the Third World* (London: Longman, 1991); Swasti Mitter, *Common Fate, Common Bond: Women in the Global Economy* (London: Pluto Press, 1986); Janet Momsen and Vivian Kinnaird, eds., *Gender and Development in Africa, Asia, and Latin America* (London: Routledge, 1993); Nahid Aslanbeigui, et al., eds., *Women in the Age of Economic Transformation: Gender Impact of Reforms in Post-Socialist and Developing Countries* (London: Routledge, 1994); Maithreyi Krishnaraj, et al., eds., *Gender, Population, and Development* (Oxford: Oxford University Press, 1998). For studies that focus on very recent developments, but still include a historical perspective, see: Daphne Spain, *Gendered Spaces* (Chapel Hill: University of North Carolina Press, 1992); Joan Smith and Immanuel Wallerstein, *Creating and Transforming Households in the World Economy* (Cambridge: Cambridge University Press, 1992); Belinda Probert and Bruce W. Wilson, eds., *Pink Collar Blues: Work, Gender, and Technology* (Melbourne: Melbourne University Press, 1993); Gloria T. Emeagwali, ed., *Women Pay the Price: Structural Adjustment in Africa and the Caribbean* (Trenton, NJ: Africa World Press, 1994); Noeleen Heyzer, et al., eds., *The Trade in Domestic Workers: Causes, Mechanisms and Consequences of International Migration* (London: Zed Books, 1994); Angélique Janssens, ed., *The Rise and Decline of the Male Breadwinner Family?* (New York: Cambridge University Press, 1998); special issue of *Journal of Women's History*, 11/4 (2000), "Marginalizing economies: work, poverty, and policy."

For specific studies of Latin America, see: Florence E. Babb, *Between Field and Cooking Pot: The Political Economy of Marketwomen in Peru* (Austin: University of Texas Press, 1989); Joel Wolfe, *Working Women, Working Men: São Paulo and the Rise of Brazil's Industrial Working Class, 1900–1955* (Durham, NC: Duke University Press, 1993); Ann Zulawski, *They Eat from Their Labor: Work and Social Change in Colonial Bolivia* (Pittsburgh: Pittsburgh University Press, 1995); Christine E. Bose and Edna Acosta-Belén, eds., *Women in the Latin American Development Process* (Philadelphia: Temple University Press, 1995); Altagracia Ortiz, ed., *Puerto Rican Women and Work: Bridges in Transnational Labor* (Philadelphia: Temple University Press, 1996); Daniel James and John D. French, eds., *The Gendered Worlds of Latin American Women Workers: From Household and Factory to the Union Hall and Ballot Box* (Durham, NC: Duke University Press, 1997); Sarah Hamilton, *The Two-Headed Household: Gender and Rural Development in the Ecuadorean Andes* (Pittsburgh, PA: University of Pittsburgh Press, 1998); Altha J. Cravey, *Women and Work in Mexico's Maquiladoras* (Lanham, MD: Rowman and Littlefield, 1998); Félix V. Matos Rodrigues and Linda C. Delgado, *Puerto Rican Women's History: New Perspectives* (Armonk, NY: M. E. Sharpe, 1998).

For Africa, see: Niara Sudarkasa, *Where Women Work: A Study of Yoruba Women in the Marketplace and in the Home* (Ann Arbor: University of Michigan Press, 1973); Colin Murray, *Families Divided: The Impact of Migrant Labor in Lesotho* (Cambridge: Cambridge University Press, 1981); Edna Bay, ed., *Women and Work in Africa* (Boulder, CO: Westview Press, 1982); Regina Smith Oboler, *Women, Power, and Economic Change: The Nandi of Kenya* (Stanford, CA: Stanford University Press, 1985); Jane L. Parpart and Sharon Stichter, eds., *Patriarchy and Class: African Women in the Home and the Workforce* (Boulder, CO: Westview Press, 1988); Karen Hansen, *Distant Companions: Servants and Employers in Zambia, 1900–1985* (Ithaca, NY: Cornell University Press, 1989); Jane L. Parpart and Gloria A. Nikoi, eds., *Women and Development in Africa: Comparative Perspectives* (Lanham, MD: University Press of America, 1989); Claire Robertson, *Sharing the Same Bowl: A Socioeconomic History of Women and Class in Accra, Ghana* (Ann Arbor: University of Michigan Press, 1990) and *Trouble Showed the Way: Women, Men and Trade in the Nairobi Area, 1890–1990* (Bloomington: Indiana University Press, 1997); special issue of *Signs*, 16/4 (1991) on "Women, family, state, and economy in Africa"; Iris Berger, *Threads of Solidarity: Women in South African Industry, 1900–1980* (Bloomington: Indiana University

Press, 1992); Elizabeth Schmidt, *Peasants, Traders and Wives* (Portsmouth, NH: Heinemann, 1992); Gracia Clark, *Onions Are My Husband: Survival and Accumulation by West African Market Women* (Chicago: University of Chicago Press, 1994); Bessie House-Midamba and Felix K. Ekechi, eds., *African Market Women and Economic Power: The Role of Women in African Economic Development* (Westport, CT: Greenwood Press, 1995); Kathleen Sheldon, ed., *Courtyards, Markets, City Streets: Urban Women in Africa* (Boulder, CO: Westview Press, 1996); Claire Robertson and Martin A. Klein, eds., *Women and Slavery in Africa* (Portsmouth, NH: Heinemann, 1997).

Studies of women's work in the Near East have largely focused on the impact of modernization and the growth of Islamic fundamentalism. See: Munira A. Fakhro, *Women at Work in the Gulf: A Case Study of Bahrain* (London: Kegan Paul International, 1990); Arlene Elowe Macleod, *Accommodating Protest: Working Women, the New Veiling, and Change in Cairo* (New York: Columbia University Press, 1991).

There has been far less research on aspects of economic life other than work, but there are beginning to be a few studies of how such issues as property ownership and consumption intersect with gender. For the former, see: Vanessa Maher, *Women and Property in Morocco: Their Changing Relation to the Process of Stratification in the Middle East* (Cambridge: Cambridge University Press, 1974); Susan Staves, *Married Women's Separate Property in England, 1660–1833* (Cambridge, MA; Harvard University Press, 1990); William C. Jordan, *Women and Credit in Pre-industrial and Developing Societies* (Philadelphia: University of Pennsylvania Press, 1993); Bina Agarwal, *A Field of One's Own: Gender and Land Rights in South Asia* (Cambridge: Cambridge University Press, 1994); John Brewer and Susan Staves, eds., *Early Modern Conceptions of Property* (London: Routledge, 1995); Amy Louise Erickson, *Women and Property in Early Modern England* (London: Routledge, 1995); Jill Liddington, *Female Fortune: Land, Gender and Authority* (London: Pandora, 1996); Kathryn Bernhardt, *Women and Property in China, 960–1949* (Stanford, CA: Stanford University Press, 1999). For consumption, see: Carole Shammas, *The Pre-industrial Consumer in England and America* (Oxford: Clarendon Press, 1990); John Brewer and Roy Porter, eds., *Consumption and the World of Goods* (London: Routledge, 1993); Timothy Burke, *Lifebuoy Men, Lux Women: Consumption, Commodification, and Cleanliness in Modern Zimbabwe* (Durham, NC: Duke University Press, 1996); Susan B. Hanley, *Everyday Things in Premodern Japan: The Hidden Legacy of Material Culture* (Berkeley: University of California Press, 1997);

Suzanne Brenner, *The Domestication of Desire: Women, Wealth, and Modernity in Java* (Princeton, NJ: Princeton University Press, 1998); Marcia Pointon, *Strategies for Showing: Women, Possession, and Representation in English Visual Culture 1665–1800* (Oxford: Oxford University Press, 1998); Roger Horowitz and Arwen Mohun, eds., *His and Hers: Gender, Consumption and Technology* (Charlottesville: University Press of Virginia, 1998).

4 Ideas, Ideals, Norms, and Laws

In many ways the topics covered in this chapter are the easiest ones to research when looking at gender, at least for those cultures that had written records. Among the earliest of the world's written records, whether in Mesopotamia, Egypt, China, or elsewhere, were laws specifying how husbands and wives were to treat each other, religious literature setting out the proper conduct for men and women, or stories and myths that described relations between men and women, or gods and goddesses. Slightly later came more formal considerations of the nature of women and men, and speculations – couched in the language of religion, medicine, or philosophy – about the reasons for the differences between them. Early visual sources also provide extensive evidence about ideals and norms, as the individuals depicted often represented idealized heroes, gods, and goddesses rather than actual men and women. Because of the relative availability of materials, much of the earliest work in women's history focused on ideas about women or laws regarding women, and for some of the world's early cultures this is as far as the written historical record can take us. The code of the Babylonian king Hammurabi, for example, dating from roughly 1750 BCE, includes many laws that regulate marriage and divorce, but we have no way of knowing the extent to which these were enforced, or the degree to which, as is common with law codes, they were only selectively enforced.

Intellectual constructs regarding gender and the formal laws that resulted from them both underlay and grew out of everything else considered in this book – work, politics, education, religion, sexuality, even the family – for one of the key insights of gender history is how closely notions of gender are interwoven with other aspects of life. We have already traced this in regard to the family and work, and the later chapters will focus on other areas of life such as religion and politics. Thus to avoid too much overlap, this chapter will be organized differently. Instead of highlighting change over time and cultural differences, it will explore the ways in which certain key concepts emerged in a number of cultures, and then shaped the informal norms and more formalized laws regulating the lives of women and men. This is not to say that these concepts were the same everywhere or that they did not change over time, but that certain ideas have been particularly influential in many cultures, ideas that have come from a range of different sources.

It is important to keep in mind that though ideas, norms, and laws shaped many aspects of gender, they were not the same as lived experience; they represent the way people conceptualized their world, hoped things would be, or tried to make them. Sometimes historians have confused these realms, a problem that occurs not only in considerations of gender, but also in discussions of other historical issues; laws about tax collection have sometimes been read as if they described actual revenue streams, for example, or regulations about guilds or labor unions as if they described the actual workplace. Normative sources about gender are particularly easy to misread in this way, as writers often used phrases such as "women are . . ." or "marriage is . . ." or "fathers are . . ." and may have thought they were describing an objective reality rather than an idealized one. Particularly influential ideas and opinions were also often no longer recognized as such, but came to be regarded as religious truth or scientific fact. Ideals, particularly those for women, were often viewed as descriptions of historical individuals, and laws were developed that attempted to recreate this golden age. The character traits set out in the first century BCE in the biographies of ideal women written by Chinese philosopher Liu Hsiang, for example, later became the basis for social and legal restrictions.

It is also important to remember that normative and intellectual records contain the ideas of only a small share of any population, skewed in most cultures toward elite men. Their ideas were the most significant, because they led to the formal laws and institutions that structured societies, but not everyone necessarily agreed with the powerful and prominent. Some historians argue that women (and in some cases other subordinate groups) had a separate value system in many societies, a special women's culture and counter-discourse shared among themselves and transmitted orally. Through this culture they communicated ideas about matters particularly important to them, such as methods of birth control or the treatment of illnesses common in women. This notion of a hidden women's culture is very attractive to many contemporary women, who may tie it to a search for non-patriarchal religious traditions; its oral and secret nature makes it impossible either to verify or disprove its existence.

A few sources from women or non-elite men have survived from many of the world's cultures, but they may be even more unrepresentative than those from elite men because of their singular status. We can compare the thoughts of Plato and Aristotle on the nature of women, for example, and set them within the context of laws and norms in Athens drawn up by male political leaders, but for the ideas of ancient Greek women, we have only a few poems by Sappho and even fewer fragments from a handful of other Greek female poets. These come from areas outside Athens about which we know far less, so that along with being rare, they are much more difficult to contextualize than Athenian works; there are no works by Athenian women at all, however, so Sappho becomes representative for all Greek women over several centuries.

Another interpretive problem arises when we turn to works that are clearly fictional to learn about notions of gender in any culture. Most of what was recorded as "history" until the last several centuries was the story of rulers and battles; information about gender was sometimes embedded in these accounts, but it was never very extensive. These same cultures have left fascinating sources that focus on the relations between men and women, but these are fictional stories which were often first told orally, then repeated with many variations, and eventually written down. They can tell us a great deal about the values of a culture, but their message can also be mixed or ambiguous, for they are designed both to teach a lesson and to entertain, and thus may both reinforce and subvert the values of the society in which they were produced. In the Arabic story collection *1001 Nights*, for example, the women are veiled and women who are not loyal to their husbands are always punished, but the main character, Shahrazad, is highly educated and saves herself from death by telling her royal husband amusing stories for 1001 nights and thus changes his negative opinion of women. Some scholars read this as demonstrating that Arabian women could really be powerful and independent despite limitations, while others stress that Shahrazad is a fictional character meant to amuse people with her boldness and not a model for real women. Such differences of opinion lead some historians to reject fiction completely as a historical source, but because the information it contains often cannot be found in official histories or anywhere else, most scholars – particularly those of premodern societies in which all sources are scarce – use it carefully.

Ideas about women and men in any culture are not only expressed in works focusing specifically on gender issues, laws regulating marriage or other sorts of male/female interactions, or fictional descriptions of men and women, of course, but in nearly everything produced by that culture. Notions of gender are often so self-evident to people that they make little comment about them directly and do not recognize where they have obtained their ideas. The process through which ideas about gender became informal norms and conventions and then more formal rules and laws also differed widely around the world. In many cultures the development of writing made gender structures more rigid and the differences between men and women greater, but some oral traditions were also extremely harsh and inegalitarian. You will need to keep this diversity among groups, along with the diversity within groups that I have just highlighted, in the back of your mind as you read this chapter, for there will always be a counter-example from somewhere in the world to each of its generalizations.

There has been a strong emphasis on difference in women's studies and gender scholarship over the last several decades to counteract earlier totalizing narratives and stress the specific point of view, social background, and intellectual context of any author or thinker. This chapter thus goes against that trend somewhat, but I think it is also important at times to highlight similarities, parallels, and continuities. The chapter looks at five areas where these have emerged: ideas about the nature and proper roles of men and women (what is often termed masculinity and femininity or manhood and womanhood); male/female-related binaries, including nature/culture, public/private, inner/outer, order/disorder, rational/passionate; norms and laws regarding motherhood and fatherhood; ideas and laws prescribing male dominance and female subservience and dependence; ideas and laws promoting gender egalitarianism.

The Nature and Roles of Men and Women

Until the development of women's history, the subjects of most historical studies were men, and the actions and thoughts of men were what made it into the historical record. One would think, then, that it would be easier to discover ideas about manhood than womanhood, but the opposite is, in fact, the case. Educated men – the authors of most historical sources until very recently – saw women as an undifferentiated group about which they could easily make pronouncements and generalizations. They have thought and written about women since the beginning of recorded history, trying to determine what makes them different from men and creating ideals for female behavior and appearance. When they turned their attention to their own sex, however, they viewed men as too divided by differences of age, wealth, education, social standing, ability, and other factors to fall into a single category. As recent French feminist theorists have put it, men saw women as a group as the Other, an object for their analyses, but saw themselves as the One, about whom generalizations which extended to the whole sex were either impossible or unnecessary.

The differences among men have often provided ways of conceptualizing societies and social or economic groups. In medieval Europe, for example, society was thought of as divided into three groups: those who fought (nobles), those who prayed (clergy), and those who worked (peasants). Women were in some ways part of all of these groups, though they were not technically members of the clergy and they generally did not fight, so that they did not fit this conceptualization exactly. They also did not fit later Marxist distinctions between working class and middle class very well either; married women in many European countries did not own any property independently, so had no direct control of the "means of production" so important in Marxist concepts of capitalism. Such differentiation among men was not limited to works of social or economic theory, but was often reflected (and reinforced) by activities, ceremonies, and practices. In early modern European cities, for example, residents might celebrate a visit by a ruler or a religious holiday with a procession, in which the men of the town marched in groups according to their political positions or occupations; women, if they marched at all, generally did so as an undifferentiated group at the end. Those who sought to overcome social and status differences also spoke of bringing together different groups of men; Thomas Jefferson's words in the American Declaration of Independence expresses this as "all men are created equal," and seventeenth-century English writers wanting to encompass all of society described their audience as "all men and both sexes." (It is clear from Jefferson's own writings and from this latter phrase that "all men" did not mean women in seventeenth- and eighteenth-century political theory, just as it is clear from other of Jefferson's writings that he did not really mean "all men" when he used that phrase.)

Differences among men were also expressed as conceptual schema of the stages of life, which were marked by physical and emotional maturing and then increasing and decreasing involvement in the world of work and public affairs. The number of these stages was often correlated with other intellectual constructs or natural objects such as the seasons, the signs of the zodiac, or the planets, but most of these discussions did not mention women at all. This was also the case with one conceptual schema in which men *were* usually considered as an undifferentiated group, the Great Chain of Being, in which all of creation from the rocks to God was linked in a single chain. A few discussions of the Great Chain of Being did include women, though they always placed women lower than men, between men and higher animals.

Highlighting the differences among men allows a thinker to neglect or downplay the differences between men and women, and to ignore the ways that gender has affected the lives of men. In nineteenth-century Europe and North America, for example, women were often described as "the Sex," as if men did not have any. This sense that one group is an unmarked or default category (i.e. that in the case of gender one is always talking about a man unless noted otherwise, as in "woman doctor") has also been noted by scholars of other subordinate groups. In terms of race, whiteness is the unmarked category, appearing much less often in discussions of an individual or group than does blackness. These tendencies, along with the tendency of labor history to focus on men, were brought together in the line heard frequently about a decade ago: "Women have more gender, blacks have more race, but men have more class."

The highlighting of women's gender in both original sources and secondary analyses means that there have been many more studies investigating ideas about women in specific thinkers or societies than ideas about men that recognize men as gendered beings. Thus books with titles like *Woman in Western Philosophy* do analyze gender, while those with titles like *Man in Western Philosophy* generally do not. This usage of "man" was initially defended as gender-neutral, but has since been recognized as gender-oblivious, and investigations of ideas about men as men generally use the term masculinity or manhood. Because differences among men are so pronounced in the sources, and because diversity of experience is such a strong emphasis in current gender history, these studies often use the plural "masculinities." For some reason "femininity" has never been used very much in historical analyses, and "femininities" not at all, perhaps because we still view femininity as more restrictive and less open to variation than masculinity.

Though studies of ideas about men have only recently been labeled as such — rather than as studies of a gender-neutral "man" or simply as "intellectual history" or "philosophy" — the fact that the male experience has been normative has also skewed the way that women have been viewed. This can be seen most dramatically in scientific and medical works, particularly those in the western tradition that originated with Greek thinkers. Greek philosophers and scientists differed among themselves as to the reasons for gender differences and the role of each sex in conception and reproduction, but the most powerful voices, particularly Aristotle, argued for what the historian Thomas Laqueur has labeled the "one-sex model." In this model, both men and women were viewed along the same line, with women seen as imperfect and misbegotten men whose lack of body heat had kept their sex organs inside rather than pushing them out as they were in the more perfect male; as late as the anatomies of Vesalius in the sixteenth century, female sex organs were depicted as the male turned inside out. In western medical theory, heat was the most powerful force in the body; women's lack of heat was seen as the reason they menstruated (men "burned up" unneeded blood internally) and did not go bald (men "burned up" their hair from the inside). Females were born when something was less than perfect during conception and pregnancy, but could occasionally become male later in life through strenuous exercise or unusual heat; males never became female, however, for nature, according to Aristotle, always strives for perfection. Because both women and men were located along the same continuum, certain women could be more "manly" than some men, and exhibit the qualities that were expected of men such as authority or self-control.

Similar ideas developed in India, though with a more religious cast. In later Vedic literature the idea developed that all fetuses are male until malignant spirits turn some of them into females. Male-producing ceremonies were introduced (which are sometimes still performed), held during the third month of pregnancy.

The one-sex model was opposed in Europe by another view, deriving from the Greek physician Galen and becoming more common after 1600, which held that men and women were equally perfect in their sex, distinct and complementary. In some parts of the world, such as several indigenous North American groups, a stress on the complementarity of the sexes led to fairly egalitarian economic and social arrangements, but in Europe this led instead to the idea that gender differences pervaded every aspect of human experience, biological, intellectual and moral. This occurred at the same time that physicians and scientists began exploring the reasons for differences among humans, and, not surprisingly, shaped the results of their experiments and measurements. Male brains were discovered to be larger than female, male bones to be stronger. When it was pointed out that female brains were actually larger in proportion to body size, female brains were determined to be more child-like, for children's brains are proportionately larger still. In the nineteenth century new fields of knowledge such as psychology and anthropology often gave professionals and officials new languages to describe and discuss gender distinctions. They located gender differences much more clearly in the body than had earlier thinkers, for whom the differences between men and women derived primarily from their social role or place in a divinely created order.

Ideas about gender differences based in the body were interwoven with those about racial differences as European countries developed colonial empires: white women were viewed as most likely to incorporate female qualities viewed as positive, such as piety and purity, while non-white (especially black) women were seen as incorporating negative female traits, such as disobedience and sensuality. White men, in this view, were more rational because of their sex *and* their race, while non-white men were more likely to demonstrate negative or ambiguous male qualities such as anger or physical prowess. The relations between gender and racial – and also class – hierarchies were worrisome, however. It was clear to most Europeans who stood at the top of the hierarchy – white men – and who at the bottom – non-white women – but the middle was more ambiguous. Were hierarchies of race easier to overcome than those based on gender, i.e. was it easier for a woman to be "manly" or for a non-white man? If social class could outweigh gender as a determinant of social role for a woman like Queen Elizabeth, could gender outweigh race for a man like Shakespeare's Othello?

To address such questions, by the eighteenth century medical and scientific measurements were applied to ethnic and racial differences as well as those of gender, and it was "proven" that various groups had smaller brains or other markers of inferiority. Emile Durkheim, often referred to as the "father of sociology," linked racial and gender measurements by noting that "although the average cranium of Parisian men ranks among the greatest known crania, the average of Parisian women ranks among the smallest observed, even below the crania of the Chinese, and hardly above those of the women of New Caledonia." Such dichotomous crania were, in Durkheim's view, a sign of French superiority, for they marked the greatest gender distinctions. Debates about gender, race, and class differences continued well into the twentieth century, with arguments for both inequality and equality couched in scientific language and the body used as evidence.

Though science was used in many eras to make discussions of the nature of men and women appear objective and irrefutable, it is clear that basic ideas about gender are influenced by political factors. For example, ideas about manhood became more closely linked to war in Japan during the Tokugawa period (1603–1867) because of the civil wars which immediately preceded this era; those civil wars made a "code of the warrior" the ideal for upper-class men, in which dying for one's leader was highly praised. These links to politics may shape something as basic as the words one uses. In China, for example, the words used for female persons in the twentieth century had (and have) political implications and purposes. The most common word in imperial China was *funü*, which originally implied "female family member" and linked women with their kin groups. In the 1920s Chinese middle-class intellectuals adopted the word *nuxing* to signify a more "modern" type of woman, more sexualized and commercial and less linked to her family. In their rejection of middle-class values the communists went back to *funü*, but reinterpreted it to link women with the state rather than the family. In the post-Mao period some writers have gone back to *nuxing* to downplay the association between women and the state, and others have adopted *nuren*, a word influenced by social science terminology which downplays the link with both family and state. There is thus no word for female person in Chinese that does not have some political and social implications.

Many scholars have noted similar situations, though perhaps less dramatic, in other cultures and languages, noting that when people use the word "woman" or "women" categorically in descriptions and generalizations ("women are . . .") they are only rarely really thinking about all women. They often cite the words ascribed to the African-American ex-slave and abolitionist Sojourner Truth (*c.*1797–1883), who is reported to have responded at a women's rights convention to the notion that women were too weak to vote by pointing out the hard physical labor she had carried out throughout her life and asking "Ar'n't I a woman?" The historian Nell Irvin Painter has demonstrated that though Truth did make many speeches and published pamphlets in favor of women's rights and abolition, this phrase was added in a later account of her speech by the woman chairing the convention. The phrase is so effective at highlighting ways in which the category and even the word "woman" are socially constructed and linked to power relationships, however, that it is hard to stop using it.

"Man" and even "person" are similarly variable, particularly when used in formal legal documents. Jurists in sixteenth-century Europe debated whether the laws regarding homicide applied equally to men and women, leading one to remark "a woman, categorically speaking, is not a human being." Laws extending voting rights to broader groups of men in the nineteenth century began to add the word "male" for the first time because women had attempted to interpret the existing word "person" to include women and to vote as long as they had the required amount of property.

Binaries

Though we can recognize the historical and social nature of the categories "woman" and "man," and are often fascinated by individuals who do not fit in these categories, for most of the world's cultures woman/man is a fundamental binary and, as noted briefly in chapter 1, is often linked with other dichotomous conceptualizations. Some linguistic and sociological theorists argue, in fact, that gender opposition is the root of the very common tendency to divide things into binary oppositions, viewing this almost as "natural" because it is found in so many cultures. In some cases these conceptualizations are complementary, with "male" and "female" categories regarded as equally important; in others, the categories are clearly hierarchical, with "male" categories always valued more highly than "female." In others, the categories may vary in their asymmetry, with certain "male" categories viewed as more important than "female" and certain categories as equal. Cultures vary in the sharpness of their dichotomies, with the categories sometimes sharply divided and sometimes interpenetrable; some scholars see western binaries as more dichotomous than those in non-western cultures, though anthropologists point out that sharp social binaries – which they term moieties – were also widely present in indigenous South America and Oceania. Cultures also vary in the degree to which differences are enforced; in some areas male/female distinctions are quite loose, while in others men or women risk severe punishment or death simply by being present in a space assigned to the other sex. People, especially women, may vary in their association with certain categories throughout the life-cycle; post-menopausal women sometimes come to be associated with conceptual categories and work or ritual activities usually viewed as "male," and very old people with qualities usually regarded as female, such as dependence.

One of the dichotomies frequently associated with gender is that of the household and the world beyond the household. This is described in different ways in different places: in China as a split between inner and outer (*nei-wai*), in ancient Greece as a split between public and domestic, among the Bun people of Papua New Guinea as a split between internal and external. This division is most often described as one between public and private, and much of the earliest work in women's history explored the ways in which men in many cultures have been associated with the public world of work, politics, and culture and women with the private world of home and family. These studies traced the differing degrees of separation between public and private, generally viewing points at which the household and the political realm were less separated, such as the early Middle Ages in Europe or colonial North America, as times of greater gender egalitarianism, and those at which they were more separated, such as Song China or the nineteenth-century US, as points of greater hierarchy.

Feminist political theory and activism often argued that the public and the private were never really separate (an idea captured in the slogan "the personal is political"), and historians have more recently explored the various ways these arenas have been linked. They have also pointed out that though men are usually associated with the public realm, with a common ideal for men being one of active participation in all aspects of public life, in some instances this was not the case. In classical India and in Judaism for much of its history, the ideal for men was one of renunciation of worldly things for a life that concentrated on study and piety. In Judaism this ideal often meant that women were quite active in the "public" realm of work and trade to support the family, though this was not the case in classical India, where the work to support scholarly men was carried out by lower-caste men rather than the scholar's wife and daughters.

Another oppositional pair is that of nature/culture. In a very influential essay the anthropologist Sherry Ortner asked "Is female to male as nature is to culture?" She gathered together examples from many geographic areas of ways in which women's physiology, social role, and psyche are viewed as closer to nature than men's, and in which women are viewed as intermediaries between nature and culture, responsible for transforming natural products into food and clothing for their household, and for the early stages of transforming "uncivilized" children into members of society. The links between women and nature have also been explored by historians of science, who point out that nature is often described as female, and that exploring nature or carrying out scientific research is often described in terms of masculine sexual conquest or domination.

As with the dichotomy between public and private, counter-examples to the woman/nature vs. man/culture linkage exist, such as the mythical American West, where "cultured" women tamed "natural" men when they brought in schools and churches, or Nazi Germany, where women were praised as the bearers of culture and morality. There are also nature/culture divisions that are not especially gendered, such as the sharp contrast in many west African societies between a cultivated area associated with humans – in which all human activities, including sex and burial, had to take place – and the non-cultivated bush. Ortner herself has modified her conceptualization somewhat, though she still asserts that the opposition between human agency (culture) and processes that proceed in the world apart from that agency (nature) is a central question for all societies, and in most of them gender provides a "powerful language" for talking about this opposition.

The nature/culture dichotomy is often related to one of order/disorder, though the way these correspond may be different, with nature sometimes representing order and sometimes disorder. This linkage is itself gendered: when nature is conceptualized as orderly, as in Confucian understandings of the cosmic order, it is usually linked to male superiority; when it is regarded as disorderly and capricious, it is linked to women. The order/disorder dichotomy is sometimes expressed in psychic terms, as an opposition between the rational and the emotional or passionate, with men generally representing the rational and women the emotional. As noted above, this gender dichotomy was often qualified by class and racial hierarchies which limited the capacity for reason to one type of man, with certain types of men, like women, seen as closer to nature and less rational.

Along with binaries that split men and women, there were also binary categorizations within each sex that shaped ideas about gender and the norms and laws that resulted from them. One of these was that of purity and impurity. Women in many cultures were regarded as impure or polluting during their menstrual periods and during or after childbirth, and many taboos or actual laws limited women's activities or contacts with others during these times. Women were sometimes secluded or sent to special places during menstruation and childbirth, and then went through rituals that reincorporated them into the community once this period was over. Menstrual and childbirth taboos have generally been regarded as representing a negative view of women, judging them as unclean or dangerously powerful simply as the result of natural bodily processes. This may have been the opinion of educated or prominent men, but both historians and anthropologists have discovered that women often developed their own meanings for such rituals. They regarded menstrual huts as special women's communities, and demanded rituals of purification after childbirth (often termed "churching" in Christian areas), sometimes despite men's efforts to end such rituals. Contemporary women have, in fact, devised new rituals to celebrate certain bodily events such as menarche (first menstruation) and meno-pause, arguing that in earlier societies these were important and positive markers of life changes.

Men also went through periods of purity and impurity in many cultures which shaped their abilities to undertake certain activities, particularly religious ones. Very often this was related to a discharge of bodily fluids or sexual activity, but in some religious traditions any contact with women also made male religious personnel impure.

Purity and impurity are closely related to one of the most studied cultural dichotomies, that of honor and dishonor or honor and shame. Honor is a highly gendered quality, with male honor generally associated with action of some type, while female honor is associated with inaction. In most of the world's cultures a woman's honor was tied to sexual purity – indeed that was often the only thing determining whether a woman was considered honorable or not – so that it was to be preserved, but could not be regained once lost. Women were thus divided into two categories on the basis of sexual honor, sometimes labeled "the virgin" and "the whore." Men's honor was more variable, and generally had to be won and then defended. Men gained honor by protecting their families, demonstrating physical prowess, exercising authority, and showing courage, and also by defending the sexual purity of female relatives, a facet of male honor especially important in Mediterranean cultures and their outgrowths in Latin America. Class and other types of social divisions sometimes created very different standards of male honor, with qualities such as honesty, financial stability, and trustworthi-ness increasingly important for bourgeois notions of male honor, for example, in contrast to aristocratic ideals centered on military activities.

Honor was very often shared among the members of one's family or clan group, so that the actions of any member reflected on the others. Loss of honor in some societies resulted in legal punishments, as did charging someone with being dishonorable if those charges proved to be untrue. Even more often, however, honor was affirmed or disputed through popular rituals – waving bloody sheets the morning after a wedding (which still continues in some areas) or throwing rotten food at husbands suspected of being cuckolds.

Along with purity and honor, physical attractiveness is another dichotomous category that has been intimately shaped by, and in turn shapes, ideas and norms of gender. What characteristics make a woman or man attractive are, of course, highly variable both among cultures and among sub-groups within a culture; some people would argue that beauty is so subjective that it is truly "in the eye of the beholder" and cannot be discussed at a more general level. This argument appears to be countered by the remarkable lengths to which people have gone throughout history to make themselves appear more desirable to themselves and others, or to look more like a more acceptable group. Cosmetics were common in many of the world's earliest societies, and products that were thought to increase beauty or sexual appeal were traded across vast distances because they could bring a high profit. Cosmetics have been enhanced more recently by cosmetic surgery, with both of these in the modern world more often associated with women than with men, though this is changing. Particularly for women, purity, honor, and beauty have been linked in various ways; the directors of women's protective shelters in early modern Italy, for example, explicitly limited the women they took in to those who were attractive, for, in their minds, ugly women did not need to fear a loss of honor and so did not merit protection.

Motherhood and Fatherhood

Just as it is easier to find information about women as a conceptual and legal category than about men, it is easier to find information about mothers and motherhood than about fathers. Many psychological theorists view one's relation with one's mother as the central factor in early psychological development, with some arguing that this is not culturally specific but innate. (Psychology has been criticized as a field, of course, for just this type of assertion.) Whether one accepts this view or not, the fact that women can become mothers has certainly shaped many of the laws and norms regulating women's activities and behavior; what is usually referred to as the "sexual double standard" could more accurately be labeled the "parenthood double standard." (A phrase that might also be used to describe the realities of parenting in many households.)

Though the possibility of motherhood has led to restrictions on women, motherhood has also been a source of great power, a much stronger and more positive role for a woman than being a wife. Many of the world's religious traditions, including Hinduism, Confucianism, and Islam, view strong relations between mothers and sons as ideal, and interviews with contemporary people in societies as disparate as Jamaica, the Solomon Islands, and Japan have found that mothers are viewed as central to people's lives while fathers are perceived as indifferent or distant. The power associated with the role of mothers has also been disturbing, however. Legal sources often refer to "wife of so-and-so" rather than "mother of so-and-so" even in cases involving a woman's relations with her own children, thus emphasizing a clearly dependent relationship rather than the one in which the woman has power over others. Stories and myths from many areas revolve around bad mothers, though because criticizing mothers directly is often viewed as unacceptable, the evil character is generally a step-mother or mother-in-law. Sometimes these myths affect the way real women are treated; in the witch trials of early modern Europe, for example, witches were often portrayed as bad mothers, killing or injuring children instead of nurturing them.

Nazi Germany and other European Fascist regimes in the twentieth century provide excellent examples of the ambiguities of motherhood, and also of the ways in which motherhood has been used and manipulated symbolically. Nazi Germany itself was extolled as the "fatherland" and Nazi leaders used hyper-masculine imagery; their pro-natalist movements were directed at fathers, not mothers, so as not to appear to grant women authority. "Motherhood" was celebrated in the abstract and medals awarded to women of the approved racial groups who had many children, but the power of husbands over their wives was also strengthened through various legal changes. Authoritarian regimes in Italy and Spain also passed pro-natalist measures such as maternity or paternity bonuses and issued extensive propaganda seeking to make motherhood women's only calling. The actual impact of these measures on birth rates and women's employment rates was limited, however, and the regimes themselves toned them down by the 1940s when they needed women's labor to carry out the war effort.

Similar disjunctures between the rhetoric and reality of motherhood can be found in many other places. Nineteenth-century Britain is often viewed as a high point of emphasis on maternity and domesticity for women; on closer investigation this turns out to have been an ideal limited only to middle-class women. In a country with two million nannies, few upper-class women actually mothered (or were expected to mother) their own children, and few lower- or working-class women had the leisure to spend much time on child care. In colonial and more recent Latin America women were encouraged to follow an ideal of seclusion, modesty, and devotion to their families termed *marianismo* after the Virgin Mary, the mother of Jesus, but their poverty made this impossible for most women. Official propaganda in Stalinist Soviet Union exalted motherhood as a patriotic duty and used motherhood as a metaphor for nationhood, but women were also expected to have full-time jobs and earlier institutions that had made their mothering easier – such as communal kitchens – were no longer supported by the state.

The rhetoric of motherhood itself has also been used in very different ways. Most often it has been used to urge women to stay out of the workplace and concentrate on family concerns, to become, as conservative Japanese authors recommended, "good wives, wise mothers." Nineteenth-century reformers often used motherhood to argue for an expansion of women's public role, however, stressing that education would make women better mothers. They asserted that having the vote would allow mothers to assure the well-being of their families and children, and to clean up corrupt politics in the same way that they cleaned up their households. Since the 1960s women in Latin America have protested various military dictatorships abducting and murdering their sons and husbands through public protests; the most famous of these, the "Mothers of the Plaza de Mayo" in Argentina, gathered weekly wearing white headscarves embroidered with the names of the "disappeared" and painting their silhouettes on walls.

Fatherhood has also been linked to politics and the exercise of power in both real and metaphorical terms. The words for "father" and "leader" are etymologically related in many languages, and the male originators of institutions and structures were often labeled "fathers" – the Church Fathers, the Founding Fathers. Hereditary monarchs such as kings, emperors, and tsars were praised as the fathers of their people and used paternal language in their attempts to build or maintain their own power. They employed ideologies of kinship to mask their control over others, and hoped such language would encourage respect and obedience. Paternal rhetoric was also used, however, to criticize leaders for not living up to what was expected of a good father and could, in fact, become part of the language of revolution. Criticism of the French kings in the period leading up to the French Revolution often described them as bad fathers, not caring properly for their people; in the case of Louis XVI, the last king, he was also seen as too influenced by his queen Marie Antoinette, the archetypal bad mother whose lack of concern for her subjects was expressed in her (probably invented) comment to hungry people clamoring for bread: "let them eat cake."

In most conceptualizations of the stages of life for a man, fatherhood did not mark a clear break the way motherhood did for a woman, but in many societies it did bring real differences. In some Muslim areas, a man gained (and continues to gain) a new name once his first son was born – usually beginning with "abu" meaning protector of or father of – and no longer uses his original first name. In some parts of the world a husband restricted his ordinary activities while his wife was pregnant or giving birth, or even mimicked her pregnancy with special clothing or rituals, practices labeled "couvade." Certain positions of authority in groups and institutions in many cultures were limited to men who were fathers, for this was both a sign of their potency and their stake in the future. Fatherhood played a particularly strong role in areas where society was conceptualized as an amalgam of families or households rather than as individuals, for the adult male head of household was both in charge of the smallest political unit and the representative of that unit to the wider world.

Ideologies, Norms, and Laws Prescribing Gender Inequity

As noted in chapter 1, and as you have or will see in every other chapter in this book, the historical record provides countless examples of calls for male dominance and female dependence or other types of gender inequity. Religious literature urged women to be subservient, and described the divine plan as one of gender inequality. Medical and philosophical works noted that women were physically, mentally, and morally weaker than men, clearly in need of male guidance and protection. Popular rituals and norms transmitted orally from generation to generation established sharp gender boundaries, generally limiting the ability of women to move or act and criticizing or punishing those who did. The gender inequity in most written norms and laws has been so striking, in fact, that much early women's history involved pointing out ways in which women transcended, subverted, or ignored such restrictions, and attempting to convince readers that the situation for women was not as dreadful as the laws made it seem.

Many of the customs and norms now perceived as the most extreme involved the restriction of women's mobility, generally justified as a way of protecting women from the unwanted sexual advances of men. Of these, the Chinese practice of footbinding has received the most attention, a practice that began in the period about 1000 and was firmly entrenched among the elite and middle classes in northern China by about 1200. In order to bind a girl's feet, her toes are forced down and under her heel until the bones in the arch eventually break; this generally began when she was about six, though a woman's feet needed to remain bound all her life to maintain their desirable small size. Explanations of footbinding involve a wide range of factors: male fantasies that eroticized small feet and a mincing walk; a change in the ideal of masculinity in Song China from warrior to scholar, which meant that the ideal woman had to be even *more* sedentary and refined; women's internalization of neo-Confucian notions of the importance of self-sacrifice and discipline (for it was mothers who generally bound their daughters' feet); a desire to hide the actual importance of women's labor by families eager to prove they were rising socially and economically; Chinese sexual ideas which linked bound feet with improved reproductive capacity and stronger infants, which might in turn lead to lower infant mortality. Whatever the reasons for its initial adoption, footbinding was tenacious in northern China; some families were still binding their daughters' feet in the 1930s, though government officials, missionaries, and eventually the communist leadership under Mao Zedong worked to end the practice. Footbinding was not accepted by other east Asian societies, though the importation of Confucian ideas from China later restricted women's capacities to perform ceremonies of ancestor worship and to inherit family land in Korea and Vietnam.

Footbinding tied women physically to the household and thus kept them out of public view, as did other practices found in a great many cultures around the world. In many areas women have been secluded by law or custom, either in particular parts of the house – the *gyneceum* in ancient Athens or the *harim* in the Ottoman Empire – or by veiling. The first records of veiling come from the ancient Near East in about 3000 BCE, where the links between this practice and household seclusion were already recognized, for the ancient Akkadian word for veiling is the same as that for shutting a door. However it was accomplished, secluding women generally involved or at least began with the elites in any society, for the vast majority of cultures could not afford to lose the labor power of half of their workers; slave and peasant women were generally not secluded, and their activities made the enclosure of elite women possible. Sometimes seclusion was more clearly an issue of status than gender. In the Ottoman Empire, for example, elite males rarely left their households, conducting their business through agents and obtaining their education through tutors; as the pinnacle of Ottoman society, the sultan never left his palace, but required all those who had business with him to meet him there. (This is another example of the complex interplay between "public" and "private.")

Other than very elite men in some cultures, however, and one or two groups around the world such as the Tuareg of northern Africa in which men were veiled, attempts to restrict visual and physical contact between men and women have led to the seclusion of women. As we will see in chapters 5 and 6, women in some areas have developed their own interpretation and understanding of the meaning of veiling, viewing it as empowerment rather than restriction and a means of asserting cultural or national identity. This is a good example of the way in which practices originally based on one idea about the nature of men and women can be reinterpreted when the social or political context changes, or be understood differently by various individuals or groups.

Many cultures that did not practice seclusion or veiling developed norms of conduct for women that were demonstrations of their dependent status. Women in some parts of India were expected to adopt a deferential posture when speaking with men, and in Japan were expected to drop their eyes when in public to avoid making eye contact with men. Restrictive norms have often been justified with reference to "tradition," but may, in fact, have been recent innovations. In India, for example, the British government expanded upper-caste Brahminic customs into Hindu law, which put greater limitations on the mobility and independence of lower-caste married women than they had experienced earlier. The 1898 Civil Code in Japan limited women's civil rights sharply, denying them existence as legal persons and requiring inheritance to pass through the male line, a break with earlier customs.

Women's lack of legal status as persons was actually a common feature in many of the world's written law codes, which have sometimes regarded women as a form of property. In most cultures until the nineteenth or twentieth centuries (or until today), marriage explicitly established a relationship of husbandly authority and wifely obedience. This relationship was often enshrined or symbolized in wedding ceremonies in which the wife vowed to obey her husband, or put a body part such as a hand, foot, or head, under the husband's foot or within his hands. In European and North American law the relationship of marriage was described as "coverture," a permanent relationship in which the husband's authority was absolute and the wife was not a legal person. This relationship began to be modified in many countries in the nineteenth century with laws that, for example, allowed married women to have control over their own wages, but as late as 1981 in France, men were still the official "heads of family" and it was illegal for a married woman to sell any of her own property without her husband's permission.

Ideologies of Egalitarianism

Norms and laws that restricted women's activities or placed them in a position subservient to men were numbingly common throughout the world, which can make studying women's or gender history often seem quite depressing. Along with individuals and groups that ignored or overcame these restrictions through their actions, however, there have also been many that developed ideas supporting greater gender egalitarianism or otherwise enhancing the situation of women; since the mid-nineteenth century these ideas have slowly been translated into legal changes. Such ideas have generally been labeled "feminism," a word developed first in French in the 1890s, though there are great disagreements about the limits, meaning, and implications of this word.

Individuals and groups have questioned or rejected gender hierarchy for centuries, and much early research within women's history involved finding and celebrating "feminist foremothers." The works of women such as Christine de Pizan, a fifteenth-century French author who challenged misogyny and extolled the achievements of women, were reissued and translated, and the writings of other feminists – most, though not all of them women – were discovered and analyzed. These investigations generally focused first on white European or American women whose ideas led to the nineteenth-century women's rights movements (which will be discussed more fully in chapter 6) and they often stressed commonalities among feminists across time and cultures. This research was an integral part of the second-wave women's movement that began during the late 1960s, in which raising the consciousness of women about gender inequities frequently involved a study of the past.

Though early researchers argued that "sisterhood is global," by the early 1980s both the feminist movement and historians of women were criticized for concentrating too much on the experiences of white western women and not recognizing racial and ethnic diversity or the power of colonialism in shaping women's lives. This led some advocates of women's rights to develop other words to describe themselves, such as "womanist," while others noted that feminism should always be used in the plural to emphasize its diversity. That diversity, they noted, was even present within white European feminism; English (and American) feminists emphasized equality of individual rights, while continental Europeans emphasized the equally important responsibilities of women and men. In both the past and the present, feminists have often been involved with other movements advocating social change, such as social-ism, anti-colonialism, or the civil rights movement, and have developed very diverse ideas about the intersection among their various aims. The variety within both historical and contemporary feminism makes it a difficult word to define to everyone's satisfaction, with the ideas of some types of feminists regarded by others as not especially positive for women. Some eco-feminists, for example, view women as more caring and environmentally conscious because they have the possibility of motherhood, while others see such ideas as dangerously close to the old notion that "biology is destiny," which has often been harmful to women.

The diversity within feminism has allowed its opponents to highlight the ideas and activities of more flamboyant groups, such as those women who allegedly burned their bras at a Miss America competition. (This story was, in fact, invented by a reporter, but it has had a very long life.) Such characterizations have led some who oppose gender inequity to reject the label "feminist" while still advocating women's rights, a posi-tion expressed in the phrase "I'm not a feminist, but . . . ."

However they have chosen to label their ideas, over the last century and a half many people have worked to transform ideals of greater gender equity into laws; these have allowed women to keep their wages and own property, vote and hold office, obtain divorce on an equal basis with men, and receive equal pay for equal work. Such laws sometimes resulted from social change or changes in widely held atti-tudes, but they more often anticipated widespread social change and were the result of changes in ideas among elites. Laws were passed against veiling in Turkey in the 1920s and Iran in the 1930s, for example, because the leadership of these countries came to view unveiled women as a symbol of modernity, not because of popular pressure. Sometimes laws were passed as a result of conquest or colonialism. The British in India, for example, passed various measures designed to end practices they saw as backward, and the Soviets forced through laws against veiling and polygamy when they took over Islamic areas in central Asia.

When the impetus for legal change came from outside an area, laws were very difficult to enforce. The 1931 Civil Code in China, for example, outlawed arranged marriages and concubinage, but it was not followed in rural areas for decades. Though such lack of compliance comes in some instances from entrenched norms of gender hierarchy, in other places laws were (and are) ignored because women did not view them as beneficial. The 1956 Hindu Succession Act in India, for example, theoretically gave women equal rights to the inheritance of any property their parents themselves had acquired. Its provisions have been scarcely followed, and women have not taken cases to court to assert their rights to property. This is not because they do not know about the law, are too passive, or are too guided by older notions of propriety, but because they seek to optimize their own economic and emotional needs and promote family stability and affections. When they do seek their rights in the courts, the decisions follow the law, but are often expressed in terms of older customary provisions regarding the protection of women and not the newer language of rights.

Sometimes the introduction of new norms can have contradictory results. In post-Soviet Russia, increased interaction with the West has led to greater awareness of egalitarian ideals and practices, but also greater sexism, especially in terms of pornography and the exploitation of the female body in advertising and popular culture that had been forbidden in restrictive and puritanical Soviet culture.

In many parts of the world the emphasis on the individual in Anglo-American feminism is seen as misguided or even destructive; advocates for women, such as the scholar Ifi Amadiume in Nigeria, point to high levels of poverty and isolation among western women, especially after divorce. Activists for women's causes in these areas express their goals in terms of the needs of women and men rather than their rights, and stress the benefits gained by the family and community when women are given greater opportunities. Because of these differences in emphasis, international measures promoting greater gender equality are always worded very carefully. The 1979 United Nations Convention on the

Elimination of All Forms of Discrimination Against Women (CEDAW) did describe discrimination against women as a violation of "the principles of equality of rights and respect for human dignity," but it was also careful to stress the effects of such discrimination on families, society, women's countries, and all humanity, and not simply on the women as individuals. (As of 2000, CEDAW has been ratified by 163 countries, with 22 countries remaining to ratify, including the United States; some of those that have ratified have exempted customary, family, and religious law, however, which lessens its impact considerably.)

As we enter the new millennium, ideas, norms, and laws regarding gender appear by some measures to be very resistant to change: a majority of people in India approve parent-controlled marriages; a majority of people in South America have negative views of women taking jobs outside the home; a majority of people (and judges) in North America and Europe regard mothers as "naturally" better parents than fathers, and the list could go on and on. Laws that proclaim equality between men and women are supported in the abstract, but are often not enforced, and may even be counteracted by other laws – especially those regarding marriage, divorce, and inheritance – which have a much greater impact in terms of day-to-day opportunities than general statements. On some issues it is clearly easier to make laws than to change long-standing attitudes and ideas about the proper roles and nature of women and men. The desirability of change in something as basic to one's under-standing of the world as gender is also not always clear; some studies of psychological and physical health indicate, for example, that people with firmer and more conservative notions of gender are healthier than those who are more open to change, for change brings uncertainty, which can lead to stress. Thus in times of rapid change, people may hang on to more traditional notions of gender as an anchor of stability.

If one takes a long view, however, even in areas where traditions are very strong, there are clear signs of change; though laws prohibiting gender discrimination are not always enforced, they are at least part of most constitutions and legal codes developed in the twentieth century, which would have been unthinkable (or regarded as laughable) several centuries earlier. In the industrialized world, though young women hesitate to call themselves feminists, many of the demands of the feminist movement are now accepted as self-evident, at least in theory: equal pay for equal work, access to education, legal equality for women and men. Grassroots women's groups in many parts of the world are using local and village courts to curtail domestic violence, and exploring religious and cultural traditions for teachings that support greater opportunities for women. They have made it clear that many sources of ideas and norms are ambiguous, and that what really matters is how prescriptive statements play out in the real world.

Further Reading

It is hard to know where to begin with suggestions, for the amount of materials is vast. For general overviews of certain issues, see Katherine Rogers, *The Troublesome Helpmate: A History of Misogyny in Literature* (Seattle: University of Washington Press, 1966); Peggy Reeves Sanday, *Female Power and Male Dominance: On the Origins of Sexual Inequality* (Cambridge: Cambridge University Press, 1981); Jo Murphy-Lawless, *Reading Birth and Death: History of Obstetric Thinking* (Bloomington: Indiana University Press, 1998); Joan Landes, ed., *Feminism, The Public and the Private* (Oxford: Oxford University Press, 1998). Interesting comments on recent changes in gender norms are provided in Sylvia Chant and Cathy McIlwaine, *Three Generations, Two Genders, One World: Women and Men in a Changing Century* (London: Zed Books, 1998).

Analyses of ideas in Asia include: Leigh Minturn, *Sita's Daughters: Coming out of Purdah: The Rajput Women of Khalapur Revisited* (New York: Oxford University Press, 1993); Lisa Raphals, *Sharing the Light: Representations of Women and Virtue in Early China* (Albany: State University Press of New York Press, 1998); Sherry J. Mou, ed., *Presence and Presentation: Women in the Chinese Literati Tradition* (New York: St Martin's Press, 1998); Lisa Rafel, *Other Modernities: Gendered Yearnings in China After Socialism* (Berkeley: University of California Press, 1999); Charlotte Furth, *A Flourishing Yin: Gender in China's Medical History, 960–1665* (Berkeley: University of California Press, 1999).

More specific discussions of ideas about manhood and womanhood in Europe include: Julian Pitt-Rivers, *The Fate of Schechem or the Politics of Sex: Essays in the Anthropology of the Mediterranean* (Cambridge: Cambridge University Press, 1977); Susan Miller Okin, *Women in Western Political Thought* (Princeton, NJ: Princeton University Press, 1979); Arlene Saxonhouse, *Women in the History of Political Thought from the Greeks to Machiavelli* (New York: Praeger, 1985); Constance Jordan, *Renaissance Feminism: Literary Texts and Political Models* (Ithaca, NY:

Cornell University Press, 1990); Michael Roper and J. Tosh, eds., *Manful Assertions: Masculinities in Britain since 1800* (London: Routledge, 1991); Joy Wiltenburg, *Disorderly Women and Female Power in the Street Literature of Early Modern England and Germany* (Charlottesville: University Press of Virginia, 1992); Elaine Fantham, et al., *Women in the Classical World: Image and Text* (New York: Oxford University Press, 1994); Margaret Somerville, *Sex and Subjection: Attitudes to Women in Early-Modern Society* (London: Arnold, 1995); Kim F. Hall, *Things of Darkness: Economies of Race and Gender in Early Modern England* (Ithaca, NY: Cornell University Press, 1995); Sally-Ann Kitts, *The Debate on the Nature, Role, and Influence of Woman in Eighteenth-Century Spain* (New York: Mellen, 1995); Helena Goscilo, *Dehexing Sex: Russian Womanhood During and After Glasnost* (Ann Arbor: University of Michigan Press, 1996); Victoria Lorée Enders and Pamela Beth Radcliff, eds., *Constructing Spanish Womanhood: Female Identity in Modern Spain* (Syracuse: State University of New York Press, 1999).

Discussions of the United States include: Gail Bederman, *Manliness and Civilization: A Cultural History of Gender and Race in the United States, 1880–1917* (Chicago: University of Chicago Press, 1995); Theda Purdue, *Cherokee Women: Gender and Culture Change, 1700–1835* (Lincoln: University of Nebraska Press, 1998); Darlene Clark Hine and Earnestine Jenkins, eds., *A Question of Manhood: A Reader in US Black Men's History and Masculinity* (Bloomington: Indiana University Press, 1999). Studies of other parts of the Americas include: Hilary M. Beckles, *Centering Woman: Gender Relations in Caribbean Slave Society* (New York: Markus Weiner, 1998); Irene Silverblatt, *Moon, Sun, and Witches: Gender Ideologies and Class in Inca and Colonial Peru* (Princeton, NJ: Princeton University Press, 1987). For other parts of the world, see: Denise O'Brien and Sharon W. Tiffany, *Rethinking Women's Roles: Perspectives from the Pacific* (Berkeley: University of California Press, 1984); Karen Armstrong, *Shifting Ground and Cultural Bodies: Postcolonial Gender Relations in Africa and India* (New York: University Press of America, 1999).

Works that look at law as well as ideas include: Mary Ann Glendon, *The Transformation of Family Law: State, Law, and Family in the United States and Western Europe* (Chicago: University of Chicago Press, 1989); Thomas Kuehn, *Law, Family, and Women: Toward a Legal Anthropology of Renaissance Italy* (Chicago: University of Chicago Press, 1992); Laura Gowing, *Domestic Dangers: Women, Words, and Sex in Early Modern London* (Oxford: Clarendon Press, 1996); Judith Baer, *Women in American Law: The Struggle toward Equality from the New Deal to the Present*, 2nd.

edn (New York: Holmes and Meier, 1996); Karen J. Maschke, *Women and the American Legal Order* (New York: Garland, 1997); Srimati Basu, *She Comes to Take Her Rights: Indian Women, Property, and Propriety* (Albany: State University of New York Press, 1999); Erin P. Moore, *Gender, Law, and Resistance in India* (Tucson: University of Arizona Press, 1998); Tim Stretton, *Women Waging Law in Elizabethan England* (Cambridge: Cambridge University Press, 1998); Nancy Levit, *The Gender Line: Men, Women, and the Law* (New York: New York University Press, 1998); Henrik Hartog, *Man and Wife in America* (Cambridge, MA: Harvard University Press, 1999).

Specific discussions about the links between gender and nature include: Annette Kolodny, *The Lay of the Land: Metaphor as Experience and History in American Life and Letters* (Chapel Hill: University of North Carolina Press, 1975) and *The Land Before Her: Fantasy and Experience of the American Frontiers, 1630–1860* (Chapel Hill: University of North Carolina Press, 1984); Carolyn Merchant, *The Death of Nature: Women, Ecology and the Scientific Revolution* (New York: Harper and Row, 1980) and *Ecological Revolutions: Nature, Gender, and Science in New England* (Chapel Hill: University of North Carolina Press, 1989); Londa Schiebinger, *Nature's Body: Gender in the Making of Modern Science* (Boston: Beacon Books, 1993); Vera Norwood, *Made From This Earth: American Women and Nature* (Chapel Hill: University of North Carolina Press, 1995); Sherry Ortner, *The Politics and Erotics of Culture* (Boston: Beacon Books, 1996).

More general analyses of the role of gender in science historically include: Thomas Laqueur, *Making Sex: Body and Gender from the Greeks to Freud* (Cambridge, MA: Harvard University Press, 1990); Ornelia Moscucci, *The Science of Women: Gynecology and Gender in England, 1800–1929* (Cambridge: Cambridge University Press, 1990); David Noble, *A World Without Women: The Clerical Culture of Western Science* (New York: Alfred A. Knopf, 1992); Joan Cadden, *Meanings of Sex Differences in the Middle Ages: Medicine, Science, and Culture* (Cambridge: Cambridge University Press, 1993); Barbara Laslett, et al., eds., *Gender and Scientific Authority* (Chicago: University of Chicago Press, 1996); Londa Schiebinger, *The Mind Has No Sex? Women in the Origins of Modern Science* (Cambridge, MA: Harvard University Press, 1989) and *Has Feminism Changed Science?* (Cambridge, MA: Harvard University Press, 1999); Clara Pinto-Correla, *The Ovary of Eve: Egg and Sperm and Preformation* (Chicago: University of Chicago Press, 1997). A good overview of ideas about menstruation is provided in Janice Delaney, Mary

Jane Lupton, and Emily Toth, *The Curse: A Cultural History of Menstruation* (Urbana: University of Illinois Press, 1988), and of contraception in Lara Marks, *Sexual Chemistry: An International History of the Pill* (New Haven, CT: Yale University Press, 2001).

Studies of the social construction of beauty and its links to gender include: Susan R. Bordo, *Unbearable Weight: Feminism, Western Culture, and the Body* (Berkeley: University of California Press, 1993); Sander Gilman, *Making the Body Beautiful: A Cultural History of Aesthetic Surgery* (Princeton, NJ: Princeton University Press, 1999).

For discussions of motherhood and fatherhood, see: Clarissa W. Alkinson, *The Oldest Vocation: Christian Motherhood in the Middle Ages* (Ithaca, NY: Cornell University Press, 1991); Ann Taylor Allen, *Feminism and Motherhood in Germany, 1800–1914* (New Brunswick, NJ: Rutgers University Press, 1991); Robert L. Griswold, *Fatherhood in America: A History* (New York: Basic Books, 1993); Rima D. Apple and Janet Golden, eds., *Mothers and Motherhood: Readings in American History* (Columbus: Ohio State University Press, 1997); Ralph LaRossa, *The Modernization of Fatherhood: A Social and Political History* (Chicago: University of Chicago Press, 1997); Heléna Ragoné and France Winddance Twine, eds., *Ideologies and Technologies of Motherhood: Race, Class, Sexuality, and Nationalism* (New York: Routledge, 2000).

Almost every book in this list, as well as most of those suggested in the other chapters, refers to ideologies prescribing difference or inequality. For twentieth-century examples of this carried to the extreme, see: Claudia Koonz, *Mothers in the Fatherland: Women, the Family, and Nazi Politics* (New York: St Martin's Press, 1987); Victoria de Grazia, *How Fascism Ruled Women: Italy 1922–1945* (Berkeley: University of California Press, 1992); Melanie Hawthorne, *Gender and Fascism in Modern France* (Hanover, NH: New England University Press, 1997).

Studies of egalitarian ideologies, including feminism, are numerous, and becoming more international in their scope. See: Sharon L. Sievers, *Flowers in Salt: The Beginnings of Feminist Consciousness in Modern Japan* (Stanford, CA: Stanford University Press, 1983); Nancie Caraway, *Segregated Sisterhood: Racism and the Politics of American Feminism* (Knoxville: University of Tennessee Press, 1991); Linda Kaufmann, *American Feminist Thought at Century's End: A Reader* (Cambridge, MA: Harvard University Press, 1993); Chilla Bulbeck, *Re-Orienting Western Feminisms: Women's Diversity in a Postcolonial World* (Cambridge: Cambridge University Press, 1998); Eileen Janes Yeo, *Radical Femininity: Women's Self-Representation in the Public Sphere* (London: Manchester University Press,

1998); Rosemary Du Plessis and Lynne Alice, *Feminist Thought in Aotearoa/New Zealand: Differences and Connections* (Auckland: Oxford University Press, 1998); Sandra Kemp and Judith Squires, *Feminisms* (Oxford: Oxford University Press, 1998); special issue of *Gender and History*, "Feminisms and internationalism" 10: 3 (1998); Karen Offen, *European Feminisms, 1700–1950: A Political History* (Stanford, CA: Stanford University Press, 2000); Patricia Hill Collins, *Black Feminist Thought: Knowledge, Consciousness and the Politics of Empowerment*, 2nd edn (New York: Routledge, 2000); Bonnie Smith, ed., *Global Feminisms since 1945: Rewriting Histories* (New York: Routledge, 2000). For studies of women's rights movements around the world see the list of further reading in chapter 6.

5 Religion

Every culture appears to have developed ideas about supernatural forces that controlled some aspects of the natural world and the place of humans in it. These supernatural forces often determined basic rules for human existence, which were revealed through human agents who were especially adept at or trained in knowing the will of the supernatural forces. Breaking these rules could lead to chaos in society, so many cultures established structures to teach and enforce them, and to shape the relationship between people and the supernatural. These structures take a bewildering variety of forms: some of them focus on ancestors or spirits, while others have clear notions of multiple gods or a single god; some of them have sacred texts, while others are passed down orally; some of them require exclusive allegiance, while others allow adherents to follow other belief systems as well; some of them are linked to political or kin structures, while others are voluntary groups which may set their members against existing political or kin structures. Though some scholars make distinctions and label some beliefs and practices "cults" or "magic," it is more useful to take a broader view and consider them all as religious traditions. ("Religion" sometimes has a negative connotation for contemporary people, who describe themselves as "spiritual, but not religious" and do not belong to any formal religious institution; such spirituality often draws on many religious traditions, however, and so is included here.)

The world's religions may have been (and continue to be) extremely varied in their concepts of and approaches to the supernatural and divine, but all of them are gendered, that is, they have created and maintained differences between what it means to be male and female. Conversely, religious ideas are influenced by gender structures arising from other parts of the culture, such as the family or the state. Religious traditions have been used both to strengthen and to question existing gender structures, providing ideas about hierarchy as well as complementarity and equality. Though religious leaders have attempted to create and enforce uniformity through specific religious texts, patterns of worship, clerical personnel, court systems, and alliances with political leaders, individuals have often chosen to interpret supernatural instructions and divine will regarding gender differently, creating variety not only among religions but within them. Because ideas about gender and religious beliefs are very often at the heart of people's systems of values, such variety has created tremendous conflicts, and continues to do so in many parts of the world today.

Animism, Shamanism, and Paganism

Religious beliefs clearly predate writing, and both archeological evidence and studies of more recent non-literate cultures around the world indicate that concepts of the supernatural pervaded all aspects of life: hunting, planting, sexual intercourse, birth, death, and natural occurrences such as eclipses, comets, or rainbows, all had religious meaning. Special rituals attached to these events involved men and women, but generally not on an equal basis; some rituals excluded women, while others excluded men. In some cultures certain rituals appear to have been conducted by individuals of an indeterminate or mixed gender, such as two-spirit people in North America, the *hijras* in India, or the *bissu* in Indonesia. Along with rituals, certain objects came to have a religious function; they were worn, carried, or viewed, and often represented men or women, or male or female spirits and divinities, engaged in various activities.

Interpreting archeological evidence about the earliest human belief systems is often very difficult. For example, small stone statues of women with enlarged breasts dating from the Paleolithic period (roughly 40,000–8,000 BCE) have been found in many parts of Europe. Such statues, dubbed "Venus figures," provoke more questions than answers. Are they aids to fertility, carried around by women hoping to have a child – or perhaps hoping not to have another – and then discarded in the household debris where they have been most commonly found? Are they fertility goddesses, evidence of people's beliefs in a powerful female deity? If they are, did this translate into power and authority for real women? (They are one of the sources Marija Gimbutus uses for her theory of matriarchy discussed in chapter 1, though her detractors note that images of individual women or female deities are often found in cultures that deny women official religious or other types of authority; the Blessed Virgin Mary, for example, has been one of the most common images in Christianity since the fifth century, though women have until very recently been excluded from the priesthood in all Christian denominations.) Or do such images represent the objectification and subordination of women, a conclusion drawn from the fact that many of them have no facial features, with some little more than sticks with breasts, reminding one of the numerous images of large-breasted women in certain contemporary magazines? If they do, were they carried around by men? Might they have represented different things to different people? Like so much Paleolithic evidence, Venus figures provide tantalizing evidence about early human cultures, but evidence that is not easy to interpret

Understanding the gender implications of post-Paleolithic religions that have been transmitted largely through oral tradition may also be quite difficult. Such religions are often labeled shamanism, tribal religions, paganism, traditional religions, or animism, and generally center on spirits that link the natural and supernatural worlds. Such spirits may appear as ghosts, be heard as voices, be felt as a power, or make their wishes known in other ways, with certain individuals especially skilled at communicating with them. The rituals and medicines through which they operated were often a closely guarded secret, passed down orally from one individual to another, so that it is difficult to gain information about them. Much of our information comes from outsiders who were (and are) hostile to animistic religions, and whose own ideas about gender influenced what they saw and reported. Thus European missionaries and officials in nineteenth-century Africa, for example, paid more attention to traditional religious activities carried out by men and neglected those carried out by women because they assumed male activities were more important, just as they were in their own Christianity. It may also be misleading to assume that religious activities carried out today or in the recent past are the same as those from centuries or even decades ago. Tradition is far less static than we often think, with new ideas or activities described as "traditional" in order to give them validity and authority. The *zar* cult in North Africa and the Middle East, for example, in which spirits known as *zar* make women ill and can only be tamed by female healers, developed first in the eighteenth century and continues to be very forceful over a wide area today; though it is often labeled "traditional," it grew as a form of religious practice for women only at about the same time that Islam began to provide more public worship opportunities for men, and some analysts see the two as clearly related.

Despite great variety, traditional religions often exhibit certain similarities in terms of gender, particularly in contrast to text-based religions. The power to communicate with and influence the spirits is generally regarded as a natural gift rather than something obtained through formal education or a position in a hierarchy, so that women as well as men in many cultures acted (and continue to act) as spirit mediums, shamans, healers, or other types of religious specialists. People judged religious rituals by how well they worked to solve problems or maintain the normal order, and often consulted a number of religious specialists if they had special needs or requests, rather than staying with one individual or one sex. Sometimes spiritual power was even unwanted or opposed by the individual to whom it came, with the spirits causing demonic possession, visions, or illness over which the shaman had little control. The connection with the spirit world usually gave shamans the ability to do good or evil, with their evil activities labeled black magic or witchcraft. Often their powers were related to gender-specific areas of life, such as menstruation, childbirth, coming of age in men and women, or certain work activities, but some shamans were so powerful that they transcended gender roles and could influence the entire spirit world.

The more gender-egalitarian nature of animism has made it popular within the last several decades among people who view most text-based religions as hopelessly patriarchal. They have drawn eclectically from a number of sources – among them Native American and African religions, the pagan deities of Europe (especially the Great Goddess), non-diabolic witchcraft, psychological theory – to create new types of rituals and organizations, often labeled neo-pagan or New Age. Some of these groups are explicitly feminist or womanist (a movement which developed among black women), interpreting ambiguous feminine imagery from many traditions in ways that empower women, and many emphasize environmentalism and ongoing revelation or communication with the dead.

In some instances the followers of shamans regarded their power as offering protection from material as well as spiritual dangers. In 1987, for example, Alice Lakwena, a religious leader called the Messiah by her followers, raised an army called the "Holy Spirit Mobile Forces" which opposed the National Resistance Army of Uganda armed mainly with charms of snake bone, beeswax, and shea nut oil provided by Lakwena. They believed these charms would turn into weapons or provide protection against bullets, following a long line of groups in many religious traditions that have regarded spiritual armor as more important than physical. Because her followers saw her as divinely inspired, the fact that Lakwena was a woman did not affect their loyalty to her, a situation that also shaped people's responses to the fifteenth-century French mystic and military leader Joan of Arc. Spiritual or divine inspiration could be a source of power for women even in religions with strong formal patriarchal hierarchies, though this was often regarded skeptically or with hostility by those with official religious positions; both Alice Lakwena and Joan of Arc were charged with witchcraft by men who opposed their power.

Written Religions in the Ancient Near East

Many of the earliest human records are religious in nature, providing accounts of how the world began, describing the exploits of the gods, and setting up rules for human society. The writing systems of Mesopotamia and Egypt, the first cultures to develop writing, were extremely complex and took many years to learn, so that the ability to write was limited to a very small group of individuals. These individuals often came to have religious authority, and writing was regarded as in some ways a religious activity, recording the deeds of the gods and setting down prayers and hymns. In the cities of Mesopotamia the temple was also the economic authority, keeping tax records and organizing work along with developing religious institutions; one performed one's religious duties in Mesopotamia through labor as well as honoring the gods. The gods in Mesopotamia and Egypt included both male and female figures, as well as deities that were a combination of human and animal, but the religious personnel were predominantly male.

Some scholars interpret archeological evidence from the Near East as suggesting that sometime before the development of writing, animistic beliefs in many spirits were replaced by a religion centering on a mother goddess who gave birth to the world. By the time religious documents were written down, however – beginning in the fourth millennium BCE – this account of creation had generally changed to one which emphasized the role of a male deity. In Babylon this god was Marduk, who created the world by ripping open the body of Tiamat, a goddess with whom Marduk engaged in battle; Babylonian midwives were instructed to retell the story of Marduk to women in labor. For the ancient Israelites this god was Yahweh – or in the Anglicized version, Jehovah – who created the world out of nothing, simply by the power of his own will. This creator god was to be served by male priests who staffed temples and other religious institutions, with women's religious activities taking place at home.

Though the religion of the Israelites – Judaism – was similar to those of other Near Eastern groups in its male god and priests, in other ways it was very different. Yahweh is a single god, not surrounded by lesser gods and goddesses; there is thus no female divinity, though occasionally aspects of God are described in feminine terms, such as Sophia, the wisdom of God. Though Yahweh is conceptualized as masculine, he did not have sexual relations like Mesopotamian, Egyptian, or Greek male deities did, so that his masculinity was spiritualized, and human sexual relations were a source of ritual impurity. Despite this, sex itself was basically good because it was part of Yahweh's creation, and the bearing of children was seen in some ways as a religious function. In the codes of conduct written down in the Hebrew Bible or Tanakh – which Christians adopted and later termed the Old Testament to parallel specific Christian writings termed the New Testament – sex between a married woman and a man not her husband was termed an "abomination," as were incest, bestiality, and sex between men. Men were free to have sexual relations with concubines, servants, and slaves, along with their wives, though a woman's having many lovers – the usual word in English translations of Hebrew scripture is "harlotry" – was often used as a metaphor for the Jewish people's turning away from their single god to worship numerous other deities (e.g. Leviticus 20: 5–6; Jeremiah 3). The possibility of divorce was also gender-specific: a man could divorce his wife unilaterally (though community norms frowned on divorce for frivolous reasons) while a wife could not divorce her husband, even for desertion. In general Judaism frowned on celibacy – "chastity" is defined in Jewish law as refraining from illicit sexual activities, not from sex itself – and almost all major Jewish thinkers and rabbis were married.

Religious leaders were important in Judaism, but not as important as the written texts which they interpreted; these texts came to be regarded as the word of Yahweh and thus had a status other writings did not. The most important task for observant Jews was studying religious texts, an activity limited to men until the twentieth century. Women were obliged to provide for men's physical needs so that they could study, which often meant that Jewish women were more active economically than their contemporaries of other religions; their religious rituals tended to center on the home, while men's centered on the temple. This reverence for a particular text or group of texts was passed down from Judaism to the other western monotheistic religions which grew from it, Christianity and Islam, which gave (and give) the statements about gender in these texts particular power. Those statements have been interpreted in various ways, however, and since the 1970s some branches of Judaism have accepted female rabbis and teachers, changed the language of services somewhat, and developed new rituals. Women are increasingly active as interpreters of religious texts in the more liberal branches of Judaism, and there is enormous variation within contemporary Judaism in terms of gender roles.

Confucianism and Taoism

China and India developed writing systems shortly after the ancient Near East, and ideas about the relationship between gender and the social order are also central in these. In China the philosophical system known as Confucianism was theoretically begun by Confucius in the fifth century BCE, but built on earlier Chinese ideas and traditions and continued to develop and change for many centuries; it became the predominant intellectual force in China by the time of the Han dynasty (c.200 BCE–c.200 CE) and continues to have strong influence today. Confucianism is often termed a religion but it does not include specific notions of the deity that adherents must accept; instead at its core is a series of ideas about the cosmic order and the parallel human order. The cosmic order is based on the relationship between Heaven and Earth, a hierarchical one in which Heaven (normally capitalized in Confucianism in the same way that God and Allah are capitalized in Christianity and Islam) is the superior, creative element and Earth the inferior receptive one; both elements are necessary, however, and harmony and order depend on the balance between the two. This balance came to be expressed also as the balance between yin and yang, with yin representing that which was dark, moist, earthly, receptive, yielding, and female and yang that which was light, dry, active, strong, heavenly, and male.

Proper human relationships were those which were modeled on those of the Heaven and Earth, hierarchical and orderly. One of these was the relationship between a man and a woman, especially one which created human life, which was viewed as fundamentally good in Confucianism. This relationship created the family, which was thus regarded as sacred; there were no priests or special houses of worship in Confucianism, so the most important religious rituals were domestic ones. All aspects of family relationships had proper etiquette and rituals attached, which became more elaborate over the centuries and were recorded in books forming the basis of Confucian teachings, the Five Classics (of which the oldest and best known is the I Ching, or Book of Changes); these teachings formed the basic moral precepts in which children and adults were socialized for centuries in China, and continued to be important even for those who accepted another religious system, such as Taoism, Buddhism, or even Christianity.

Women's position corresponded to that of Earth in the cosmic order, and women were expected to be subordinate and deferent; these expectations were codified as the "three obediences" to which women were subject: to her father as a daughter, to her husband as a wife, and to her son as a widow. (A few contemporary Confucian intellectuals view the three obediences as originating outside Confucian teachings, but for millennia they have been generally regarded as a central part of Confucian ideology for women.) The Chinese character for "wife" showed a woman with a broom, and the ultimate goal for women was to be regarded as a "Treasure of the House"; the ultimate goal for men was to become a sage, a highly educated and wise individual who, in Confucius's words, "seeks also to enlarge others," that is to serve the broader political order.

Though the three obediences would seem to place women clearly under the authority of men, Confucianism also stressed filial piety, which meant honoring one's mother as well as one's father, and a clear hierarchy of age; both of these mitigated the gender hierarchy somewhat. In addition, ancestor worship, though carried out largely by men, honored female ancestors – at least those who had given birth to sons – along with male. The yin–yang relationship is hierarchical, but both parts are essential to cosmic order, and, as the symbol was elaborated, both parts contain the embryo of the other.

The yin–yang symbol and its notions of male–female complementarity were also part of the other major philosophical–religious system of classical China, Taoism. Like Confucianism, Taoism is viewed as the creation of one man, Lao-tzu, a contemporary of Confucius, but actually builds on earlier Chinese traditions, in this case widespread beliefs about spirits and magic; some Taoism is more philosophical and scholarly, and some more religious and spiritual. In Taoism, following nature is seen as the way to happiness, with passivity and motherly love often described as ideals; the way of nature, called the Tao, is often described as the womb of creation, and other feminine imagery occurs regularly in Taoist poetry, as does androgynous imagery which talks about balancing masculine and feminine qualities. Sexuality and the body are viewed positively, with no taboos attached to either menstrual blood or semen, and rituals developed which included sexual techniques as part of meditation for both men and women; sexual handbooks were frequently part of a bride's trousseau on marriage. Taoism encompassed a huge range of practices and beliefs and incorporated many rituals and ideas from Chinese folk religion, such as shamanism, divination, astrology, and exorcism, which caused it to be generally denigrated by official historians, who were mainly Confucian. There appear to have been a number of women among its leaders and those who attained the highest levels of meditation, which may also explain why it was frowned upon by court chroniclers.

It may be wrong to separate Confucianism and Taoism, for they shared many ideas and many people followed both of them; in terms of gender structures, it may be best to see them as two ends of a spectrum, with Confucianism emphasizing the hierarchy in male–female relationships, and Taoism the complementarity. Both of them viewed the family and children as central to human life, so that religions which viewed celibacy and chastity as positive were regarded with some suspicion.

Hinduism and Buddhism

In India as well as China gender structures developed in the classical era which lasted for millennia, and which were shaped to a great degree by religious and intellectual systems. In the Brahminic system, which combined with older and local religious and spiritual ideas to form the complex religion termed Hinduism, the four purposes of life are held to be piety (*dharma*), prosperity (*artha*), pleasure (*kama*), and liberation (*moksha*). The family was viewed as the central setting for the accomplishment of the first three of these goals, and the three purposes of marriage – religious duties, progeny, and sexual pleasure – derived directly from them. Marriage made one fully adult, and all men and women were expected to marry.

Because Hinduism is a synthesis of many traditions it often contains conflicting ideas about gender hierarchy, with some structures and ideas clearly placing women in an inferior position, others stressing the complementarity of men and women, and others valorizing women and the feminine. The normal life-cycle of a person from one of the upper castes, particularly from the highest caste, the Brahmins, marked women as inferior. When a boy in one of the three upper castes reached the age of about eight or twelve, he went through a ceremony giving him the sacred thread to wear over his shoulders, marking him as one of the "twice born." (This ceremony is still of great significance for orthodox Hindus.) With this, especially if he was a Brahmin, he began a period of study during which he memorized sacred texts and learned rituals, often studying with an individual teacher, or guru, or at one of the Brahminic universities that were established during the classical period. At the end of this, generally when he was in his twenties, came another ceremony indicating his adult status. At this point he was expected to marry quickly, taking a wife chosen for him by his family or a matchmaker who was often much younger than he was. They began having children as soon as possible – ten was regarded as ideal – and he joined, or if his father had died, led, the religious rituals which linked him with past and future male members of his family. After his own children had reached adulthood, he might choose a life as a monk or ascetic, leaving his wife to concentrate on spiritual concerns. On death, if he had lived his life according to proper moral precepts, he would be rewarded with a favorable rebirth, or perhaps achieve or attain *moksha*, the state of liberation, bliss, and awareness which freed him from the cycle of birth and death.

By contrast, a girl in the upper castes did not receive a sacred thread, nor go through a period of studying sacred texts. During the Vedic age (1200–600 BCE) women appear to have been able to study and a few highly educated women are mentioned in the Upanishads, such as the philosopher Gargi who engaged in a debate about the True Self. In later centuries service to her husband was to replace education for a Brahmin woman, so that while her brothers were off studying a Brahmin girl learned housekeeping and domestic religious rituals. Her entry into adulthood was marked by marriage, not by a separate ceremony, which generally occurred at a much younger age than that of her brothers – her teens or even earlier. She then went to live with her husband's family, and heard the names of his ancestors, not hers, recited in religious ceremonies; if she were a Brahmin she was instructed to worship her husband as if he were a god, making and serving him all of his food so that it was pure enough, entertaining him and demonstrating her devotion.

At the end of her life she could expect a period of widowhood, which might be quite long given the disparity in normal ages at marriage for men and women, a dismal time during which she was considered inauspicious, i.e. unlucky, and so not welcome at family festivities or rituals. (During the course of her marriage, she probably performed special rituals designed to prolong the life of her husband, as well as those during the third month of each pregnancy to secure the birth of a son.) Becoming a monk or an ascetic was not an option, for such individuals lived and traveled alone, which was seen as inappropriate for women. Like the male members of her family, after death she could hope for a favorable rebirth, which might include being reborn as a man. As in China, women's life-cycle was described as a series of relationships of obedience. One of the articles of the Laws of Manu, compiled between 200 and 400 CE, states: "In childhood a female must be subject to her father, in youth to her husband, and when her lord is dead, to her sons; a woman must never be independent." Restrictions on widows became harsher in the period after about 1000 CE, a bleak situation still faced by many widows and currently criticized by women's rights advocates in India. Among some sub-castes in particular regions of India, the practice of *sati*, a widow's self-immolation on her husband's funeral pyre, became a praiseworthy alternative to dismal widowhood. The origins of *sati* (which means "good wife") are unclear and hotly debated, and it was rarely a common practice, though occasional reports of voluntary and involuntary *sati* continue today. Reports of the killing of young wives because their families are slow or remiss in making dowry payments are more numerous, and dowry deaths, along with the status of widows, are a central concern of Indian feminists.

In many ways women clearly have a secondary status within Hinduism, but there are also traditions that stress the power of women. Many of the Hindu deities are goddesses, who range from beneficent life-givers like Devi or Ganga, to faithful spouses like Parvati or Radha, to fierce destroyers like Kali or Durga, and may have been viewed as empowering by women. Women also performed religious rituals either on their own or with their husbands, the latter particularly important during the Vedic period when the most important rituals required the participation of a married couple. Beginning in the eighth century CE women were active in the *bhakti* movements; these were popular devotional movements which stressed intense mystical experiences focusing on a single god rather than asceticism or scholarship and which became the most widespread form of Hinduism because they were open to everyone, regardless of caste.

Buddhism rejected certain aspects of Hindu teachings about men and women, but it also accepted others; like Hinduism, it incorporated many ideas and traditions, some of them contradictory, and later split into different branches with different emphases. Buddhism originated in the teachings of the Indian prince Siddhartha Gautama (566–486 BCE), called the Buddha ("awakened one"), who taught that the best way of life is one of moderation and meditation, a rejection of worldly concerns and a search for enlightenment. In theory, the Buddhist path to enlightenment (*nirvana* or *nibbana*) is open to all regardless of sex or caste; one needs simply to rid oneself of all desires, which may be accomplished progressively through a series of deaths and rebirths. Gender differences are part of the world which keeps one from enlightenment and not part of the true nature of existence. Such egalitarianism conflicted with other teachings, however, for women were also viewed as a dangerous threat to men's achieving enlightenment and in some writings were regarded as not capable of achieving enlightenment unless they first became men. Many Buddhist texts view the feminine as horrific, encouraging those who would achieve enlightenment to meditate on images of women's diseased, dying, or dead bodies in order to cultivate detachment from desire.

The conflict between these two notions emerged during the Buddha's lifetime. The Buddha taught that renouncing the world in favor of the life of a monk or nun made one spiritually superior, and women wanted him to form an order of nuns to offer women the same opportunities for withdrawal from the world that his order of monks (the *sangha*) had done for men. According to Buddhist tradition, the Buddha hesitated a long time, and finally established an order for nuns, but gave them special rules which stressed their subordinate status to monks and placed them clearly under male control. Despite these restrictions, women eagerly joined this new type of religious life, and during the first centuries of Buddhism nuns often sponsored large building projects and made donations for spiritual causes.

Buddhism spread in all directions from northern India and split into a number of sects. In the first century CE a series of movements arose centered around new scriptures; they called themselves the Mahayana ("Greater Vehicle"); these became predominant in Tibet, China, Korea,

Vietnam, and Japan. (Buddhism disappeared in its homeland of India after about 1200 CE as people returned to Hinduism or adopted Islam.) In Mahayana Buddhism the ultimate religious ideal is to become a buddha, and multiple buddhas can exist at one time. Those on the Buddhist path are termed *bodhisattvas*, who were also expected to help others on their own paths. In the other major division of Buddhism, Theravada ("Way of the Elders") also known as Hinayana ("Lesser Vehicle"), which centered in Sri Lanka and most of Southeast Asia, only one buddha could appear in a cosmic age, so the ultimate religious ideal is the *arhat*, an individual who achieves full enlightenment and is thus freed from material existence and reincarnation. Women and men could become both *arhats* and *bodhisattvas*, some of whom are regarded as celestial beings rather than historical persons and are themselves worshipped. Some Mahayana texts suggest, however, that women must be reborn as men before they can become buddhas, and Hinayana Buddhists believe that one of the predictions of future buddhahood – a very rare event – is male sex.

Despite the popularity of some female *bodhisattvas* such as Kuan Yin in China, human women who chose a life of religious devotion as nuns were often regarded with suspicion. The ideal woman in Buddhism – both historically and in sacred texts – was more often a lay woman who supported a community of monks or who assisted men in their spiritual progress. By about the fifth century CE in India, nuns appear to have become much poorer and less popular, with the communities of monks who were regarded as spiritually superior receiving more support. In China nuns were quite influential during the earliest centuries of the spread of Buddhism, before it was fully established, and Chinese women later established convents in Taiwan, Korea, Japan, and Vietnam. (In fact, convents which trace their history back to Chinese nuns, including several in the United States today, are the only orthodox lineage of fully ordained nuns left in Buddhism.) Convents later lost popularity, however, and the biographies written later about prominent early nuns – a collection called *Lives of the Eminent Nuns* was edited as early as 516 CE – also transformed them into women who fit better with Confucian ideals. Along with skills in meditation and teaching prized by Buddhists, the Chinese nuns were always portrayed as showing filial piety toward their parents, with their celibacy viewed as a special divine gift, not something which most women could or should emulate. *Lives of the Eminent Nuns* was written by a male monk, as were most of the other major Buddhist works of history and doctrine, and some scholars have noted that because of its authorship the written record has probably downplayed the role of women and lay people in the development and dissemination of Buddhist teachings. Some contemporary Buddhists are attempting to separate the more egalitarian teachings from their generally misogynist monastic overlay, both to develop a more accurate view of Buddhism in the past and to make their own spiritual lives in the present more satisfying.

Developing new emphases within Buddhism is a well-established pattern. The Chan school of Buddhist thought developed first in sixth-century China and later spread (as Zen) to Japan, while Vajrayana or Tantric Buddhism developed in fifth-century north India and later spread to Tibet. Chan (Zen) Buddhism – which has become increasingly popular in western cultures since the 1960s – centers on intense meditation under the close guidance of a master teacher, of which a few have been or are currently women. Vajrayana Buddhism (of which the followers of the Dalai Lama are the best-known practitioners) also emphasizes meditation and a close teacher–pupil relationship, and it has elaborate esoteric rituals which are often filled with sexual imagery and practices. Both Zen and Tantra hold out the possibility of full enlightenment – described as achieving Buddhahood – in this body and this life for both men and women, without the need for cycles of reincarnation. It has always been easier for men to reject the expected path of marriage and family in order to seek such enlightenment, however, and male teachers continue to predominate in both groups.

Christianity

The mixed messages about the relative value of men and women found in Buddhism may also be found in Christianity, which is based on the teachings of Jesus of Nazareth, called the Christ (a Greek translation of the Hebrew word Messiah meaning "anointed one"), who was apparently executed by the Romans about 30 CE and is believed by Christians to have been resurrected from the dead three days later. Jesus's teachings and life story are recorded in the first four books of the New Testament, called the Gospels, written several decades after his death. Women figure prominently in the Gospels, listening to and speaking with Jesus; in two of the Gospels (Mark and Matthew) they are the first to see Jesus after his resurrection and were told to give the good news (which is what the word "Gospel" means) to his other followers.

Women took an active role in the spread of Christianity, preaching, acting as missionaries, and being martyred alongside men. Early Christians expected Jesus to return to Earth again very soon, and so taught that one should concentrate on this Second Coming. Because of this, marriage and normal family life should be abandoned, and Christians should depend on their new spiritual family of co-believers; early Christians often met in people's homes and called each other brother and sister, a metaphorical use of family terms that was new to the Roman Empire in which Christianity developed. This made Christians seem dangerous to many Romans, especially when becoming Christian actually led some young people to avoid marriage, viewed by Romans as the foundation of society and the proper patriarchal order.

Not all Christian teachings about gender were radical, however. Many of Jesus's early followers, particularly the Apostle Paul whose letters make up a major part of the New Testament, had ambivalent ideas about women's proper role in the church, and began in the first century CE to place restrictions on female believers. Paul and later writers forbade women to preach, and women were gradually excluded from holding official positions within Christianity. Both Jewish and classical Mediterranean culture viewed female subordination as natural and proper, so that in limiting the activities of female believers Christianity was following well-established patterns, in the same way that it patterned its official hierarchy after that of the Roman Empire.

Some of Christianity's most radical teachings about gender also came to have negative consequences for women. In its first centuries, some women embraced the ideal of virginity and either singly or in communities declared themselves "virgins in the service of Christ." This was threatening to most church leaders, who termed such women, at best, "brides of Christ," that is, in a dependent relationship with a man. Some of these leaders also advocated a life of virginity for men, but this led to a strong streak of misogyny in their writings, for they saw women and female sexuality as the chief obstacles to this preferred existence; because they wrote far more than women and their writings were preserved, their opinions came to be much more influential than those of the women who chose virginity. The most important theologian in the western Christian Church, St Augustine, linked sexuality clearly with sin by viewing sexual desire as the result of disobedience to divine instructions by Adam and Eve, the first humans. The tendency to sin was passed down, in Augustine's opinion, through sexual intercourse, so that even infants were tainted with this Original Sin. Christian scripture offered positive comments about marriage and procreation – Jesus himself had blessed a wedding with a miracle – so that Augustine could not reject them completely, but he and later Christian writers clearly regarded virginity as the preferred state of existence and particularly condemned any sexual activity which could not lead to children, such as homosexual acts or masturbation.

Christianity became the official religion of the Roman Empire in the fourth century, and gradually spread throughout all of Europe and the Mediterranean. As was the case with Buddhism, women were often active in spreading Christian ideas, especially within their own families, and women's monastic communities were under the leadership of female abbesses; Jesus's mother Mary became an important figure of devotion, as did female as well as male saints. Outside of women's monasteries, however, all Christian officials were men, who were increasingly expected to follow a distinctive life-pattern, though this differed slightly in the two branches of the Christian Church, the Orthodox Church of eastern Europe and the Roman (Catholic) Church of western Europe. In eastern Europe married men could become priests, though a man who was unmarried when ordained as a priest was expected to remain unmarried and married priests could not move up the church hierarchy and become bishops. In the twelfth century, church councils in the Roman Church forbade all priests to marry and declared marriages which did exist invalid, driving priests' wives and children from their homes; at the same time it condemned homosexual activities more sharply. The policy of clerical celibacy proved difficult to enforce, and for centuries priests and higher officials simply took concubines. (Though in doing this they were technically "celibate," a word that actually means "not married" rather than "chaste.")

In the thirteenth century, church councils expanded the power of priests, decreeing that they had the power to absolve sins through confession and to change bread and wine into the body and blood of Christ to be consumed by believers during the Eucharist, the central ritual of Christianity (a transformation termed "transubstantiation"). Thus priests, who were all male, had powers that no woman (or non-ordained man, including kings) had, a situation that continues today within Roman Catholicism. The special powers of the priest make the conflict over the ordination of women especially heated within Roman Catholicism, with many observers predicting that the Catholic Church will admit married men as priests long before it accepts women.

Clerical celibacy was rejected by the religious leaders in western Europe who broke with the Catholic Church in the sixteenth century and eventually formed their own churches, later labeled Protestant. Protestant denominations – Lutheran, Anglican, Presbyterian, Calvinist, and later Methodist and many others – differed on many points of doctrine, but they agreed that the clergy should be married heads of household and that monastic life had no value. Thus there was no separate religious vocation open to women, who were urged to express their devotion within the family as "helpmeet" to their husband and guide to their children. Protestantism proclaimed family life as the ideal for all men and women, and unmarried people of both sexes were increasingly suspect. This ideal was communicated to people through sermons and printed books (the printing press was invented in Germany shortly before the Protestant Reformation), and the Catholic Church responded by promoting its own pro-marriage literature, some of which predated the Protestant Reformation. Scholars differ sharply about the impact of Protestantism; some see it as elevating the status of most women in its praise of marriage, others see it as limiting women by denying them the opportunity for education and independence in monasteries and stressing wifely obedience, and still others see it as having little impact, with its stress on marriage a response to economic and social changes that had already occurred, and not a cause of those changes.

At about the same time as the Protestant Reformation, European Christians – both Protestants and Catholics – became increasingly concerned about witches in their midst. They combined traditional ideas about witchcraft found in almost all cultures – that witches are individuals who use their connection with the spirit world to do harm – with specifically Christian ideas – that witches are individuals who make pacts with the Devil and do his bidding. Especially in central and northern Europe this combination led to the interrogation and trial of many people, and the execution of perhaps 50,000 to 100,000 individuals. Though the gender balance varied in different parts of Europe, in Europe as a whole about 80 percent of those questioned, tried, and executed for witchcraft after 1500 were women. The reasons for this are complex: women were viewed as weaker and so more likely to give in to the Devil's charms or use scolding and cursing to get what they wanted; they had more contact with areas of life in which bad things happened unexpectedly, such as preparing food or caring for new mothers, children, and animals; they were associated with nature, disorder, and the body, all of which were linked with the demonic. Europeans took their notions of witchcraft with them to the New World; a few people, most of them women, were executed for witchcraft in the European colonies in North America, and in the Andean region of South America older native women who had fled to mountainous areas and refused to become Christians were charged with witchcraft and idolatry. Some European thinkers even blamed witchcraft on the explorations, asserting that demons had decided to return to Europe from the Americas once Christian missionaries were there, and so were possessing and seducing many more people than they had in the Middle Ages.

Since the sixteenth century Protestantism has continued to splinter into more and more groups, with extremely diverse ideas about gender. Some of these, such as the Quakers, allowed women to preach as early as the seventeenth century, while others, such as the Amish and the Wisconsin synod Lutherans, continue to view patriarchal leadership as essential. Some Protestant groups developed radically different family forms and sexual patterns: Moravians determined marital partners by a lottery, Shakers saw complete chastity as a way to make men and women equal, Mormons (whose religion is based on the Bible along with other texts) practiced polygamy. In the twentieth century many Protestants termed themselves "fundamentalists," downplaying more complicated issues of doctrine and largely supporting a conservative social agenda. In the United States this came to focus in the 1980s on the issues of abortion, gay rights, prayer in schools and what were labeled "traditional family values." Fundamentalist groups often broke from the Protestant denominations that had developed in previous centuries to form non-denominational community churches, though some denominations, such as the Baptists, were also largely fundamentalist. At the same time, some Protestant denominations, or individual churches within them, became increasingly liberal on gender issues, allowing not only women but also actively practicing homosexuals as clergy. At the end of the century many seminaries in the United States were training more women than men to be pastors, and it is difficult to predict how this will affect Christianity in future.

The Protestant Reformation occurred concurrently with the beginning of European colonization, which took Christianity around the world. Indeed, the conversion of indigenous people was one of the primary justifications for conquering new territories. Christian officials tried to impose European gender patterns – monogamous marriage, male-headed households, limited (or no) divorce – but where these conflicted with existing patterns they were often modified and what emerged was a blend of indigenous and imported practices. In some areas, such as the Andes of South America and the Philippines, women had been important leaders in animistic religions, and they were stronger opponents of conversion than were men; this pattern was enhanced by male missionaries' focus on boys and young men in their initial conversion efforts. In other areas women became fervent Christians, confessing and doing penance for their sins so intensively they harmed their health, and using priests and church courts to oppose their husbands or other male family members.

Most scholars of colonization and imperialism view the activities of Christian authorities and missionaries as leading to a sharpened gender hierarchy, for religious leaders paid little attention to women's activities and either misunderstood or opposed women's power. They were also complicit in the establishment and maintenance of the racial hierarchies we traced in chapter 2, regulating marriage and other types of sexual activities so as to maintain boundaries. In the immediate postcolonial period Christianity was often rejected as a remnant of the colonial past, but this began to change in the late twentieth century, and the formerly colonial world now has the fastest-growing Christian churches, many of them non-denominational and fundamentalist rather than more traditional Catholic or Protestant; in 2000, nearly two-thirds of the world's Christians live outside Europe and North America. These churches are appealing to people whose cultural values are shaped by animism, Hinduism, Buddhism, and various other religions, and the norms they are establishing in regard to gender also draw on many traditions, with churches often deciding individually how they will handle issues such as polygamy, child marriage, remarriage of widows, and other issues in which local traditions conflict with traditional Christian teachings. Because Christianity is declining in importance in western society – except for the United States – it is clear that what is regarded as "traditional" in Christianity may also change, and that because of migration, these debates will be played out not only in the former colonies, but in Europe and North America as well.

Islam

If the interplay between gender and religion is an issue in contemporary Christianity, it is even more of an issue in contemporary Islam, and all sides draw on history to buttress their position. The debates always go back to the very beginning of Islam, which was founded in Arabia by the religious reformer and visionary Muhammad (c.570–632 CE). Muhammad's revelations were written down by his followers during his lifetime, and shortly thereafter organized into an authoritative text, the Qur'an, regarded by Muslims as the direct words of God to his Prophet Muhammad and therefore especially revered. (These revelations were in Arabic; if Muslims use translations in other languages, they do so alongside the original Arabic.) At the same time, other sayings and accounts of Muhammad which gave advice on matters which went beyond the Qur'an were collected into books termed *Hadith*, which are second only to the Qur'an in authority. In these works marriage is recommended for everyone, heterosexual sex is approved for both procreation and pleasure, and homosexual acts are condemned; the emphasis on marriage has meant that unmarried men are not accepted as teachers, judges, or religious leaders in traditional Muslim societies, and that men who are attracted to other men often marry and have children as well.

Many scholars note that the Qur'an holds men and women to be fully equal in God's eyes; both are capable of going to heaven and responsible to carry out the duties of believers for themselves. They argue that restrictions on women under Islam came from pre-Muslim practices and are thus not essential to the faith; men veiled their wives on marriage, for example, as early as the third millennium BCE in the Tigris and Euphrates valleys (present-day Iraq). They note that Muhammad's first wife, Khadijah, convinced him to take his religious visions seriously; she was never veiled and the Prophet did not marry other wives until after her death. Other scholars point out that the Qur'an does make clear distinctions between men and women; it allows men to have up to four wives and to divorce a wife quite easily, sets a daughter's share of inheritance at half that of a son's, and orders that the Prophet's later wives be secluded.

Debates about how to interpret the Qur'an are extremely important in Islam because of the book's special stature, but gender structures also have other bases, including religious law – the *shari'a* – which is regarded as having divine authority. Though women played a major role in the early development of Islam – as they had in Christianity – and appear to have prayed and attended religious ceremonies in public, after the first generation the seclusion of women became an official part of the *shari'a*. Men are to fulfill their religious obligations publicly, at mosques and other communal gatherings, and women in the home, though they generally have access to a separate section of the mosque unless they are ritually unclean (because of menstruation or childbirth). The *shari'a* views marriage as a reciprocal relationship in which the husband provides support in exchange for the wife's obedience; this support is to continue – at least in theory – even if he divorces her. Along with the *shari'a*, the words of religious leaders – termed mullahs or imams – carried (and continue to carry) great weight, particularly among the branch of Islam termed Shi'ite, which regards Muhammad's cousin and son-in-law Ali to have been designated by the Prophet as the first such divinely inspired imam. The statements of a mullah on such issues as proper clothing for women, the treatment of law-breakers, or the guardianship of children after divorce often shaped gender on a day-to-day basis more than the words of the Qur'an or the *shari'a* on which they are based.

Islam spread quickly throughout northern Africa and the Near East in the century after Muhammad, and then more slowly to other parts of Asia, Africa, and Europe. Intermarriage between Arab traders and local women was often essential to its growth, with women providing access to economic and political power through their kin networks and serving as brokers between indigenous and imported cultures. Islamic law and practices mixed with existing traditions, creating a broad range of marital practices, rituals, and norms of behavior for men and women. A few cultures, such as the Tuareg in western Sudan, adopted Islam without veiling women, but in general by the fourteenth century Muslim women were veiled. By this time as well the tradition developed that mentioning a woman's name dishonored her, so that men referred to their own wives simply as "my home" or "the weak one." In India both Islam and a stricter Hinduism favored the seclusion of women – termed purdah – although the strictness and exact rules of this varied according to social status and location; wealthy urban women were generally the most secluded, while poor rural women – the vast majority of the population – worked alongside male family members.

Recent research has indicated, however, that even wealthy women may have been more active economically and legally than the rules of seclusion suggested, particularly in the large area controlled by the Ottoman Turks who conquered Arab lands and much of southeastern Europe in the early sixteenth century. Islamic law grants women less inheritance than their brothers, but this remains theirs and does not pass to their husbands upon marriage as it did in most Christian societies until the mid-nineteenth century. Thus wealthy Muslim women often used their money to establish schools, hospitals, or mosques, invested it in business activities, or passed it on to their female relatives. In addition, women of the lower classes often developed their own rituals within a Muslim framework centered on the home; Iranian Shi'ite women, for example, practiced a food ritual called *Sofreh* designed to establish connections with Muhammad's daughter Fatima and other female saints. (Saints in Islam do not go through a formal process of canonization as they do in Christianity, but are recognized because of miraculous deeds or post-mortem communications with the living; some saints are venerated over a wide area and others only locally.) In some areas, such as in China during the Qing dynasty (1644–1911), Muslim women even had their own mosques and female religious leaders.

Women often combined (and continue to combine) animistic and Muslim beliefs in rituals to ward off evil spirits and invoke the assistance of both good spirits and Muslim saints; religious officials denigrate such practices and periodically attempt to prohibit them, but both men and women who consider themselves good Muslims believe firmly in their efficacy. For many centuries women and men have also been attracted to Sufism, a mystical movement within Islam that emphasizes direct union with God.

During the nineteenth and twentieth centuries the Muslim world was part of the process of colonialism and anti-colonialism which will be discussed in more detail in chapter 5. Particularly in countries such as Egypt and Turkey intent on modernization, men and women debated the extent to which the *shari'a* could be reformed to allow greater gender equality in such issues as divorce and inheritance, or whether women's liberation inevitably meant a weakening of Islam. In some countries reform-minded women, usually of the urban middle classes, adopted western dress and began to attend universities in the early twentieth century; both women and men were active as demonstrators, organizers, and even fighters in the twentieth-century nationalist movements in the Islamic world and a few legal reforms were enacted. During the 1970s and 1980s many of these reforms were revoked as more conservative religious leaders gained power in many Muslim countries, most prominently Iran. This movement of fundamentalist activism within Islam has made a conservative view of gender the primary symbol of Islamic purity against western cultural imperialism and commercialism; it has proven attractive to women as well as men who view it as providing them with greater security and affirming their social, moral, and religious values. Muslim women in many parts of the world have adopted the veil or other types of covering dress as a way to work or travel outside the home without being subject to male harassment. They regard Muslim dress as a means of empowering themselves, while others – both Muslims and non-Muslims – have viewed it as a clear example of women's oppression. As with other types of religious symbols involving gender, the veil clearly has multiple meanings that vary with the individual and with the political setting.

In addition to the religious traditions discussed here, there have been and continue to be many others around the world: state religions that no longer exist, such as those of the Aztecs, Incas, or Romans; state religions that continue to exist, such as Shinto in Japan; Indian religions that developed concurrently with or as an outgrowth of Hinduism, such as those of the Sikhs and Jains; religions that seek to unite all world religions, such as Bahaism; religions that center on more recent charismatic leaders and their ideas, such as the Mormons, Christian Scientists, or Unification Church. Originally many of these religions were highly localized, but with steadily increasing migration of people throughout the world, adherents now often live next door to one another. Some of these smaller religions and many groups within the major world religions discussed in this chapter are also very successful in their conversion efforts. In contrast to native language, skin color, or ethnic background, religious adherence is to some degree changeable and chosen, with converts often the most vocal advocates for their new faith. Thus the contemporary religious picture is very complex, with variety and conflicts within groups and among them, some of which are the basis for civil wars and other types of violence.

Every religious tradition has ideas about proper gender relations and the relative value of the devotion and worship of male and female adherents; every one stipulates or suggests rules for the way men and women are to act. In many, however, these messages are contradictory and ambiguous, with adherents often able to find support for their own views within them. Thus within most religions there is a fundamentalist wing, advocating stronger gender distinctions and hierarchy, and a more liberal wing, advocating greater gender egalitarianism. At the end of the twentieth century fundamentalism was more politically and socially powerful within Christianity, Hinduism, and Islam, but the gender implications of this fundamentalism also evoked strong criticism and more liberal adherents of these faiths searched their texts and traditions for less restrictive messages. The ultimate outcome of these developments is, of course, uncertain, but it is clear that religion will continue to be one of the strongest shapers of gender structures in the future, as it was in the past.

Further Reading

Collections of articles are a good place to begin, for they allow us to look more closely at a religious tradition and to make comparisons. Arvind Sharma has edited four excellent collections – *Women in World Religions*, *Religion and Women*, *Today's Woman in World Religions*, and *Feminism and World Religions* (Albany: State University of New York Press, 1987, 1993, 1994, 1999) – which cover women's role in many of the world's religions in both past and present; many of the essays are written by scholars from within the tradition they discuss. This is also true of Arlene Swidler, ed., *Homosexuality and World Religions* (Valley Forge, PA: Trinity Press International, 1993). Other useful collections include: Rosemary Radford Ruether and Rosemary Skinner Keller, eds., *Women and Religion in America*, 2 vols., (San Francisco: Harper and Row, 1981 and 1983); Pat Holden, ed., *Women's Religious Experience* (London: Croom Helm, 1983); Yvonne Yazbeck Haddad and Ellison Banks Findly, eds., *Women, Religion and Social Change* (Albany: State University of New York Press, 1985); Clarissa W. Atkinson, et al., eds., *Immaculate and Powerful: The Female in Sacred Image and Social Reality* (Boston: Beacon Press, 1985); Caroline Walker Bynum, et al., eds., *Gender and Religion: On the Complexity of Symbols* (Boston: Beacon Press, 1986); Denise Carmody, *Women and World Religions* (Englewood Cliffs, NJ: Prentice-Hall, 1989); Ursula King, ed., *Feminist Theology from the Third World: A Reader* (Maryknoll, NY: Orbis, 1994); Stephen B. Boyd, et al., eds., *Redeeming Men: Religion and Masculinities* (Louisville, KY: Westminster/ John Knox Press, 1996); Karen L. King, ed., *Women in Goddess Traditions* (Minneapolis, MN: Fortress Press, 1997); Gary David Comstock and Susan E. Henking, eds., *Que(e)rying Religion: A Critical Anthology* (New York: Continuum, 1997); Nancy A. Falk and Rita M. Gross, *Unspoken Worlds: Women's Religious Lives in Non-Western Cultures*, 2nd edn (San Francisco: Wadsworth, 1999). Susan Starr Sered's *Priestess, Mother, Sacred Sister: Religions Dominated By Women* (New York: Oxford University Press, 1994) is a fascinating study of twelve religions currently being practiced that are dominated by women, some of which are over a thousand years old. Serenity Young, ed., *An Anthology of Sacred Texts*

By and About Women (New York: Crossroad, 1993) is a wonderful collection of sources, covering everything from ancient paganism to contemporary voodoo, with long selections from the major text-based religions; another fine source book is Shawn Madigan, *Mystics, Visionaries and Prophets: A Historical Anthology of Women's Spiritual Writings* (Philadelphia, PA: Fortress Press, 1998). David Leeming and Jake Page, *God: Myths of the Male Divine* and *Goddess: Myths of the Female Divine* (Oxford: Oxford University Press, 1996) are two brief overviews of stories about divine figures from prehistory to the present. The *Journal of Feminist Studies in Religion*, which began publication in 1984, always contains the most current research, as does the series *Gender in World Religions* published by the McGill University faculty of religious studies; there are also many websites which discuss gender and religion, though their focus is usually contemporary rather than historical.

Animism

References to discussions of Paleolithic animism may be found in the works discussing the goddess in chapter 1. Studies of gender in more recent shamanistic religions include: Sheila Walker, *Ceremonial Spirit Possession in Africa and Afro-America* (Leiden: E. J. Brill, 1972); Erika Bourguignon, ed., *A World of Women* (New York: Praeger, 1980); Bruce Lincoln, *Emerging from the Chrysalis: Studies in Rituals of Women's Initiation* (Cambridge, MA: Harvard University Press, 1981); Diane Bell, *Daughters of the Dreaming* (Sydney: George Allen and Unwin, 1983); Rosan A. Jordan and Susan J. Kalcik, eds., *Women's Folklore, Women's Culture* (Philadelphia: University of Pennsylvania Press, 1985); Laurel Kendall, *Shamans, Housewives, and Other Restless Spirits: Women in Korean Ritual Life* (Honolulu: University of Hawaii Press, 1985); Gillian Bennett, *Traditions of Belief: Women and the Supernatural* (Harmondsworth: Penguin Books, 1987); I. M. Lewis, *Ecstatic Religion: An Anthropological Study of Spirit Possession and Shamanism*, 2nd edn (Harmondsworth: Penguin Books, 1989); Carol Shepherd McClain, ed., *Women as Healers: Cross-cultural Perspectives* (New Brunswick, NJ: Rutgers University Press, 1989); Janice Boddy, *Wombs and Alien Spirits: Women, Men, and the Zar Cult in Northern Sudan* (Madison: University of Wisconsin Press, 1989); Marla N. Powers, *Oglala Women: Myth, Ritual, and Reality* (Chicago: University of Chicago Press, 1996); Susan Starr Sered, *Women of the Sacred Groves: Divine Priestesses of Okinawa* (New York: Oxford University Press, 1999). For an analysis of Alice Lakwena's movement, see: Heike Behrend, *Alice Lakwena and the Holy Spirits: War in Northern Uganda, 1985–1996* (Athens: Ohio University Press, 2000). For a study of the interaction between animism and Christianity, see Ramón A. Gutiérrez, *When Jesus Came, the Corn Mothers Went Away: Marriage, Sexuality, and Power in New Mexico, 1500–1846* (Stanford, CA: Stanford University Press, 1991).

Contemporary animism and paganism have been explored in: Margot Adler, *Drawing Down the Moon: Witches, Druids, Goddess-Worshippers and Other Pagans in America Today*, 2nd edn (Boston: Beacon Press, 1986); Paula Gunn Allen, *The Sacred Hoop: Recovering the Feminine in American Indian Traditions* (Boston: Beacon Press, 1986); Judith Plaskow and Carol P. Christ, eds.,*Weaving the Vision: New Patterns in Feminist Spirituality* (New York: Harper and Row, 1989) and *Womanspirit Rising: A Feminist Reader in Religion*, 2nd edn (New York: Harper and Row, 1991).

Near Eastern Religions

Studies of ancient Near Eastern and Mediterranean mythology all discuss stories of various gods, goddesses, and other mythical figures. For more focused studies, see Barbara S. Lesko, ed., *Women's Earliest Records: From Ancient Egypt and Western Asia* (Atlanta, GA: Scholars Press, 1989) and *The Remarkable Women of Ancient Egypt*, 3rd edn (Providence, RI: B. C. Scribe Publications, 1996); Mary Lefkowitz, *Women in Greek Myth* (Baltimore, MD: Johns Hopkins University Press, 1986); R. Hawley and B. Levick, eds., *Women in Antiquity: New Assessments* (London: Routledge, 1995); Lynn Roller, *In Search of God the Mother: The Cult of Anatolian Cybele* (Berkeley: University of California Press, 1999). For a fine source collection about women and religion in the ancient world, see Ross Kraemer, ed., *Maenads, Martyrs, Matrons, Monastics: A Sourcebook on Women's Religions in the Greco-Roman World* (Philadelphia, PA: Fortress Press, 1988).

There are, of course, many more analyses of Judaism than of other ancient Near Eastern religions. For two thought-provoking discussions of sexuality in Judaism, see Phyllis Trible, *God and the Rhetoric of Sexuality* (Philadelphia, PA: Fortress Press, 1978) and Howard Eilberg-Schwartz, *God's Phallus* (Boston: Beacon Press, 1994). See also David Biale, *Eros and the Jews from Biblical Israel to Contemporary America* (New York: Basic Books, 1992); Daniel Boyarin, *Carnal Israel: Reading Sex in Talmudic*

Culture (Berkeley: University of California Press, 1993); Michael L. Satlow, *Tasting the Dish: Rabbinic Rhetorics of Sexuality* (Atlanta, GA: Scholar's Press, 1995). For Jewish law see: Louis Epstein, *Marriage Laws in the Bible and the Talmud* (Cambridge, MA: Harvard University Press, 1942) and *Sex Laws and Customs in Judaism* (New York: Ktav Publishing House, 1948); Jacob Neusner, *A History of Mishnaic Law of Women* (Leiden: Brill, 1980); Rachel Biale, *Women in Jewish Law: An Exploration of Women's Issues in Halakhic Sources* (New York: Schocken, 1984). For collections that range over a long time period, see Judith Baskin, ed., *Jewish Women in Historical Perspective* (Detroit, MI: Wayne State University Press, 1991) and Ellen M. Umansky and Diane Ashton, eds., *Four Centuries of Jewish Women's Spirituality* (Boston: Beacon Press, 1992). For more recent developments, see: Susannah Heschel, *On Being a Jewish Feminist: A Reader* (New York: Schocken, 1983); Judith Plaskow, *Standing Again at Sinai: Judaism from a Feminist Perspective* (San Francisco: Harper and Row, 1990), and the magazine *Lilith*, which began publication in the 1970s.

Confucianism and Taoism

Discussion of gender in Chinese religions may be found in more general accounts of Chinese culture, such as Margery Wolf and Roxane Witker, *Women in Chinese Society* (Stanford, CA: Stanford University Press, 1975); Arthur P. Wolf, ed., *Religion and Ritual in Chinese Society* (Stanford, CA: Stanford University Press, 1974); George A. De Vos and Takao Sofue, *Religion and the Family in East Asia* (Berkeley: University of California Press, 1984). For more specialized studies, see: Alber Richard O'Hara, *The Position of Women in Early China According to Lieh Nu Chuan "The Biographies of Chinese Women"* (Taiwan: Mei Ya Publications, 1971); Edward H. Schaefer, *The Divine Woman: Dragon Ladies and Rain Maidens* (San Francisco: North Point Press, 1980); Tomas Cleary, ed., *Immortal Sisters: Secrets of Taoist Women* (Boston, MA: Shambhala, 1989).

Hinduism and Buddhism

There are several good studies of Hindu goddesses, including: John S. Hawley and Donna M. Wulff, eds., *The Divine Consort: Women and the Goddesses of India* (Delhi: Motilal Banarsidass, 1984); David Kinsley,

Hindu Goddesses: Visions of the Divine Feminine in the Hindu Religious Tradition (Berkeley: University of California Press, 1986); Kathleen M. Erndl, *Victory to the Mother: The Hindu Goddess of Northwest India in Myth, Ritual, and Symbol* (Oxford: Oxford University Press, 1993); Alf Hiltebeikel and Kathleen M. Erndl, eds., *Is the Goddess a Feminist? The Politics of South Asian Goddesses* (New York: New York University Press, 2000). For studies of actual people, see: Lynn Bennett, *Dangerous Wives and Sacred Sisters: Social and Symbolic Roles of High-Caste Women in Nepal* (New York: Columbia University Press, 1983); William S. Sax, *Mountain Goddess: Gender and Politics in a Himalayan Pilgrimage* (Oxford: Oxford University Press, 1991); Lindsey Harlan and Paul Courtright, eds., *From the Margins of Hindu Marriage: Essays on Gender, Religion, and Culture* (Oxford: Oxford University Press, 1994); John Stratton Hawley, ed., *Sati: The Blessing and the Curse: The Burning of Wives in India* (Oxford: Oxford University Press, 1994); Stephanie Jamison, *Sacrificed Wife/Sacrificer's Wife: Women, Ritual and Hospitality in Ancient India* (Oxford: Oxford University Press, 1996). For the complex relationship between gender and nationalism in India, see the entire issue of *Bulletin of Concerned Asian Scholars* 25: 4 (1993), "Women and religious nationalism in India."

For gender in historical and contemporary Buddhism, see: Diana Paul, *Women in Buddhism: Images of the Feminine in the Mahayana Tradition* (Berkeley: Asian Humanities Press, 1979); Lenore Friedman, *Meetings with Remarkable Women: Buddhist Teachers in America* (Boston, MA: Shambhala, 1987); Janice D. Willis, ed., *Feminine Ground: Essays on Women and Tibet* (Ithaca, NY: Snow Lion Publications, 1989); José Ignacio Cabezón, ed., *Buddhism, Sexuality and Gender* (Albany: State University of New York Press, 1992); Rita Gross, *Buddhism After Patriarchy: A Feminist History, Reconstruction, and Analysis of Buddhism* (Albany: State University of New York Press, 1993); Miranda Shaw, *Passionate Enlightenment: Women in Tantric Buddhism* (Princeton, NJ: Princeton University Press, 1994); Liz Wilson, *Charming Cadavers: Horrific Figurations of the Feminine in Indian Buddhist Hagiographic Literature* (Chicago: University of Chicago Press, 1996); Bernard Faure, *The Red Thread: Buddhist Approaches to Sexuality* (Princeton, NJ: Princeton University Press, 1998); Chatsumaru Kabilsingh, *Thai Women in Buddhism* (London: Parallax Press, 1991); Karma Lekshe Tsomo, ed., *Buddhist Women Across Cultures: Realizations* (New York: State University of New York Press, 1999); Ellison Banks Findly, ed., *Women's Buddhism, Buddhism's Women: Tradition, Revision, Renewal* (Boston, MA: Wisdom Press, 2000).

Christianity

Books on women and gender in Christianity number in the hundreds, so the following are just a few suggestions on where to start. Good essay collections or overviews include: Richard L. Greaves, ed., *Triumph Over Silence: Women in Protestant History* (Westport, CT: Greenwood Press, 1985); Sherrin Marshall, ed., *Women in Reformation and Counter-Reformation Europe: Public and Private Worlds* (Bloomington: Indiana University Press, 1989); Lynda L. Coon, et al., eds., *That Gentle Strength: Historical Perspectives on Women in Christianity* (Charlottesville: University of Virginia Press, 1990); Daniel Bornstein and Roberto Rusconi, eds., *Women and Religion in Medieval and Renaissance Italy* (Chicago: University of Chicago Press, 1996); JoAnn Kay McNamara, *Sisters in Arms: Catholic Nuns Through Two Millennia* (Cambridge, MA: Harvard University Press, 1996); R. N. Swanson, *Gender and Christian Religion* (London: Boydell and Brewer, 1998); Beverly Maine Kienzle and Pamela J. Walker, eds., *Women Preachers and Prophets through Two Millennia of Christianity* (Berkeley: University of California Press, 1999). For the early Church, see: Elaine Pagels, *Adam, Eve, and the Serpent* (New York: Random House, 1988); Peter Brown, *The Body and Society: Men, Women and Sexual Renunciation in Early Christianity* (New York: Columbia University Press, 1988); Deborah Sawyer, *Women and Religion in the First Christian Centuries* (London: Routledge, 1996). For the Middle Ages, see: James A. Brundage, *Law, Sex, and Christian Society in Medieval Europe* (Chicago: University of Chicago Press, 1987); Caroline Walker Bynum, *Holy Feast and Holy Fast: The Religious Significance of Food for Medieval Women* (Berkeley: University of California Press, 1987); Barbara Newman, *From Virile Woman to Woman Christ* (Philadelphia: University of Pennsylvania Press, 1995); Jane Schulenberg, *Forgetful of their Sex: Female Sanctity and Society, ca. 500–1100* (Chicago: University of Chicago Press, 1998). For the early modern period, see: Eve Levin, *Sex and Society in the World of the Orthodox Slavs, 900–1700* (Ithaca, NY: Cornell University Press, 1989); Lyndal Roper, *Oedipus and the Devil: Witchcraft, Sexuality, and Religion in Early Modern Europe* (London: Routledge, 1994); Joel Harrington, *Reordering Marriage and Society in Reformation Germany* (Cambridge: Cambridge University Press, 1995); Marilyn Westerkamp, *Women and Religion in Early America, 1600–1850* (London: Routledge, 1999); Merry E. Wiesner-Hanks, *Christianity and Sexuality in the Early Modern World: Regulating Desire, Reforming Practice* (London:

Routledge, 2000). For the modern period, see: Virginia Fabella and Mercy Amba Odulole, *With Passion and Compassion: Third World Women Doing Theology* (Maryknoll, NY: Orbis Books, 1988); Nancy A. Hardesty, *Your Sons and Your Daughters Shall Prophesy: Revivalism and Feminism in the Age of Finney* (New York: Carlson, 1991); Evelyn Brooks Higginbotham, *Righteous Discontent: The Women's Movement in the Black Baptist Church, 1880–1920* (Cambridge, MA: Harvard University Press, 1993); Susan Juster and Lisa MacFarlane, eds., *A Mighty Baptism: Race, Gender, and the Creation of American Protestantism* (Ithaca, NY: Cornell University Press, 1996); Rosemary Radford Ruether, *Christianity and the Making of the Modern Family* (Boston: Beacon Press, 2000),

Islam

An excellent very brief overview is Judith Tucker's *Gender and Islamic History* (Washington, DC: American Historical Association, 1995). Two widely read analyses of the roots of Muslim ideas of gender are: Leila Ahmed, *Women and Gender in Islam: Historical Roots of a Modern Debate* (New Haven, CT: Yale University Press, 1992) and Fatima Mernissi, *The Veil and the Male Elite: A Feminist Interpretation of Women's Rights in Islam*, trans. Mary Jo Lakeland (Reading, MA: Addison-Wesley, 1991). More detailed discussions of Islamic law and traditions are: M. E. Combs-Schilling, *Sacred Performances: Islam, Sexuality, and Sacrifice* (New York: Columbia University Press, 1989); Amire El Azhary Sonbol, ed., *Women, the Family and Divorce Laws in Islamic History* (Syracuse, NY: Syracuse University Press, 1996); Judith Tucker, *In the House of the Law: Gender and Islamic Law in Ottoman Syria and Palestine* (Berkeley: University of California Press, 1998); Miriam Cooke, *Women Claim Islam: Creating Islamic Feminism Through Literature* (London: Routledge, 2000). For recent collections of articles, see: Jane L. Smith, ed., *Women in Contemporary Muslim Societies* (London: Associated University Presses, 1980); Nikki R. Keddie and Beth Baron, eds., *Women in Middle Eastern History: Shifting Boundaries in Sex and Gender* (New Haven, CT: Yale University Press, 1991); Gavin R. G. Hambly, ed., *Women in the Medieval Islamic World: Power, Patronage, and Piety* (New York: St Martin's Press, 1998). Two of the few collections that directly compare religions are: Kari Elizabeth Borreson and Kari Vogt, eds., *Women's Studies of the Christian and Islamic Traditions: Ancient, Medieval, and Renaissance*

Foremothers (Dordrecht: Kluwer, 1993); Kristen E. Kvam, et al., eds., *Eve and Adam: Jewish, Christian, and Muslim Readings on Genesis and Gender* (Bloomington: Indiana University Press, 1999).

6 Political Life

The first histories written anywhere in the world were political, describing the actions of rulers and other leaders, and the relations – often violent – among various political entities. Rulers supported writers who recorded their deeds, and the court chronicles they produced are sometimes the only historical record available for a particular culture. Defining history primarily in terms of political events did not end with the ancient world, of course, but continues today. If you look at almost any history textbook you will find the story punctuated and periodized by politics: Chinese and Egyptian history is divided according to dynasties; Roman history divided into Republic and Empire; French, American, and Russian histories revolve around a revolution; African and South American history are divided into pre-colonial, colonial, and postcolonial eras. These long-range political developments are often further subdivided by civil or external wars and the rise and fall of various factions or political parties.

The story of politics and war has generally been told as one involving men only. In some ways this is understandable, for until the nineteenth (and in many areas until the twentieth) century, other than a few rulers and even fewer unusual cases, women did not have a formal political role. They did not hold office, sit in representative institutions, serve as judges, or in any other way participate in formal political institutions. Their absence from political life was matched by an absence from most works of political theory. Authors discussing political rights and obligations rarely mentioned women at all, setting up the male experience as universal and subsuming women's rights under those of the male heads of their household or family. If they did mention women it was to exclude them. Aristotle's treatise *Politics* famously begins with the line "man is a political animal" and his brief consideration of women (along with slaves and children) as a group to be ruled rather than to rule makes it clear he was not including women in this use of "man."

This assumption that politics only involves men has recently changed somewhat because of three historiographical trends. The first was a search for women who have exercised power in male-dominated institutions: women warriors, great queens, mighty empresses, and other "women worthies." This search has uncovered a surprising number of such extraordinary individuals, and also found examples of political systems in which women's power was built into the system.

The second was a broadening of the notion of "politics" to include groups and organizations other than formal institutions of government through which people expressed their opinions and shaped the world around them. Voluntary societies, clubs and associations, interest groups, religious organizations, self-help groups, and charitable foundations are now recognized as important actors in the political story, effecting political change on their own or through their influence on institutions of government. These organizations were also often themselves established and run in ways that are familiar to scholars of politics, with elections, presidents, committees, and so on. Both women and men were active in such groups, with women's participation or leadership a significant factor in their success long before women gained formal political rights.

The third and most radical change has been the recognition that anything in a society having to do with power relationships, not simply formal politics or organized groups, is political. Not only are the relationships between king and subject, monarch and parliament now viewed as political, but also those between master and servant, landlord and tenant, father and son, husband and wife. When this power is formally recognized and legitimated it becomes authority, but even if it is not, it is still power. This newer scholarship has pointed out that considerations of power are always relational, that is, they involve power *over* someone or something, along with power *to* carry out a certain action; thus to be complete, any study of power must pay attention to both the dominant and subordinate individual or group.

Within this broader notion of politics as power, women have figured on both the dominant and subordinate side. Though women had formal authority much less often than men, they clearly had power: Through the arrangement of marriages they established ties between influential families; through letters or the spreading of rumors they shaped networks of opinion; through patronage they helped or hindered men's political careers; through giving advice and founding institutions they shaped policy; through participation in riots and disturbances they demonstrated the weakness of male authority structures. Women's power has also been an important metaphor, usually viewed negatively as a sign of chaos and weakness, but sometimes positively as a symbol of individuals going beyond their normal abilities for the good of the state. Women's actual political subordination is, of course, easy to trace, and the newer political history has begun to explore its metaphorical dimensions. Joan Scott, for example, suggests that historians should investigate the ways in which gender figures in all political relationships, commenting that "gender is a primary way of signifying relationships of power." Even relationships that do not involve women often describe the dominant individual or group in masculine terms and the subordinate ones as feminized. Nations themselves are given gender characteristics, described as motherlands or fatherlands, and invasions or imperial conquests described as rapes.

This broader concept of the "political" means that all the chapters in this book have a clear political dimension, because all of them involve relations of power. As we have seen, families and organized religions were (and are) hierarchical structures of power, and for much of the world's history were intimately connected with, or were themselves, the formal institutions of government. As we saw in chapter 4, legitimate authority was often linked actually or metaphorically with fatherhood, and was thus clearly gendered. Similarly, work, education, and law all involved hierarchical power relationships, and in all of these realms gender was used as a way of representing positive and negative qualities. Consideration of the political dimensions of all of these areas would take another whole book, however, so this chapter will retreat somewhat from the broadest conceptualization of politics, and focus on local, territorial, and national structures of authority, and on groups organized to influence and shape those structures.

Kin Groups, Tribes, and Villages

The earliest power structures in human society were kin groups, in which decisions were made at the local level. Within these kin groups individuals had a variety of identities: they were simultaneously fathers, sons, husbands, and brothers, or mothers, daughters, wives and sisters. Each of these identities was relational (parent to child, sibling to sibling, spouse to spouse) and some of them, especially parent to child, gave one power over others. The interweaving of these relationships and their meaning varied from culture to culture, but one's status in one relationship affected one's status in the others, and often changed throughout one's life. A woman's situation as daughter or sister in a specific kin group, for example, shaped her relationship with her husband; her becoming a mother often further altered her status *vis-à-vis* her husband or other kin group members. A man's relationship with his father and his status in the kin group often changed when he married, and in some areas changed again if he became the father of a son. In many areas kin groups remained very significant power structures for millennia, and in some areas they still have control over major aspects of life, such as one's choice of a spouse or share of inheritance.

As we discussed in chapter 2, patterns of inheritance, residence, and membership in families and kin groups varied widely around the world, determining who one reckoned as kin and which specific individuals one had power over or owed obedience to. Kin groups themselves were conceptualized in many areas as parts of tribes or bands or peoples, and this larger unit also had power over its members – it might determine which kin group had claim to which area of land, or whether there would be war with another band. In some areas membership in a group came to revolve around language and other cultural traditions, what we conceptualize as "ethnicity," and to be enforced by endogamy, that is, by requiring that people marry within the group. Allegiance to an ethnic group continues to be extremely strong in many parts of the world today, of course, and is the source of some of the world's bitterest conflicts, such as those in the former Yugoslavia. (In many formerly colonial areas, divisions and hostilities between ethnic groups were enhanced by European colonial powers, and are not something that has existed for centuries.) Such ethnic allegiances also fed into the construction of national identities in the modern world, with national loyalties described in kin-group terms, as having "French blood" or "German blood."

In areas with agriculture, members of one kin group often settled with members of other groups in villages, which also developed structures of power to make decisions over issues of concern to the village, such as which crops would be planted or how disputes among villagers would be settled. These structures varied from autocratic, in which the leader of the most prominent family in the village made all decisions; to democratic, in which decisions were made by vote; to consensual, in which decisions were reached after a long discussion.

Kin, tribal, and village structures of power were almost always gender and age related, and in most parts of the world, adult men had the most power. The leader of a village was often termed the "big man" or some variant of this, and village or tribal councils or voting bodies were made up of adult male heads of household or heads of families. There are some cultures where this was not the case. Among some Native American groups kin groups were organized matrilineally and residence was matrilocal, so that one's mother's kin were more important than one's father's kin and related women often lived together. Some groups had a tribal council of adult women along with that of adult men, which had power over certain aspects of life, such as marital partners or the fate of prisoners captured from another tribe during warfare. Among the Cherokee, for example, the senior women in the clans were designated Beloved Women or War Women, and had a significant voice in decisions to end warfare. Some African peoples, such as the Igbo of Nigeria, also had separate women's councils that organized aspects of life in which women predominated, such as agricultural production and local trading networks.

The more egalitarian or complementary decision-making structures found in some cultures at the local level have led at times to romanticization, either of village life in general – as a place where the type of power wielded by women mattered – or of those cultures in which women had a formal role in decision-making. This is akin (and sometimes linked) to the search for primitive matriarchy noted in chapter 1, and often involves a rejection of contemporary western capitalist society and a search for a utopia elsewhere. Those who know village life well in the past and present warn against such romanticization, however, noting that even villages and groups that seem very isolated are usually enmeshed in larger political, economic, and ideological systems, which tend to privilege male power domains and limit women's ability to exert real power in local and family matters. Even in those cultures most often praised for political egalitarianism, such as the Iroquois of northeastern North America, women's decisions often had to be ratified by a group of men or were subject to male review.

Discussions about the history of local gender power relations are often enmeshed in debates about the influence of European colonialism and the sources of contemporary gender inequality, and can be very heated, with all sides creating stereotypes and inventing utopian (or dystopian) pasts. Many aspects of these debates will probably never be resolved because they revolve around issues of informal power that by their very nature did not leave a written record. Oral traditions can be of some assistance, but these change over time and are themselves, of course, only the part of the story that people chose to remember. Uncertainties about these issues may be one reason that political historians have generally focused on larger-scale political structures, viewing village life as the province for social historians, anthropologists, and folklorists.

Hereditary Aristocracies

In much of the world, kin, tribal, and village structures of power remained the primary political forces until the nineteenth or twentieth centuries, which has meant these areas have remained outside the purview of most traditional political history. This history has instead explored the larger-scale states that developed first in the ancient Middle East and North Africa, and then in India, China, the Mediterranean, Central and South America, and ultimately other parts of the world as well. All of these states developed hierarchies based on hereditary aristocracies. These aristocracies were kin groups themselves, of course, but they claimed authority over other kin groups based on ties with a divine or heroic figure, military prowess, economic dominance, or other distinguishing qualities. (In many areas hereditary aristocracies predated the development of written records, so that exactly how their authority was first established is not clear; by the time we learn about them, they are already in power.) This authority gave them special rights, privileges, and powers which were handed down from generation to generation, most prominently access to the labor of others. States based on hereditary aristocracies developed at widely different times in different parts of the world, from before the third millennium BCE to the eighteenth century CE. Some are still around today, of course, though the power of their hereditary rulers has often been limited by democratic or constitutional institutions of government.

The growth of hereditary aristocracies and larger-scale state governments affected relations between power and gender in ambiguous and sometimes contradictory ways. In many cases it led to restrictions on women and greater gender differentiation. Because the right to rule was handed down through inheritance it was extremely important to male elites that the children their wives bore were theirs. Elite women in many state societies were thus increasingly secluded, and strict laws were passed regarding adultery (defined as sex between a man and a married woman not his own wife), which in some cases affected non-elite women as well. Women's own kin connections often became less important than those of their husbands, which made their status more derivative and dependent than it had been in kin groups. These processes varied in their intensity, particularly in the rigidity of their control over female sexuality and their impact on ordinary women. Because they were dependent on the labor of others for their own power, however, hereditary aristocracies throughout the world intervened in the abilities of all kin groups, not simply their own, to make decisions regarding both production and reproduction. Thus both work and child-bearing became matters of state and not simply family concern, and village authorities or government officials – almost always male – intervened in issues in which women had previously often had a voice as members of a kin group.

The development of hereditary aristocracies did not uniformly limit women's power and status, however, but increased those of a small group of women and occasionally gave them legitimately sanctioned authority. Among the aristocracy itself, men were generally regarded as having more rights and power by virtue of their gender, but women were not completely excluded, and they could and did rule from time to time, from ancient Egypt to contemporary Britain. In fact membership in an elite family has continued to give women the opportunity for power in states that are officially democratic; Indira Gandhi in India and Benazir Bhutto in Pakistan, for example, followed in the footsteps of their fathers Jawaharlal Nehru and Zulfikar Bhutto and were elected as prime minister. (Indira's son Rajiv continued the family tradition after his mother was assassinated; after his own assassination, his wife, Sonya, who is actually Italian, and his daughter Priyanka, became significant political forces in India. Priyanka is described by her supporters as an avatar, or reincarnation and embodiment, of her grandmother Indira.)

The world's earliest recorded histories all mention a few powerful women among their long lists of male rulers, generals, and leaders. In Egypt, kingship was linked with divinity, and the ruler – who was eventually called the pharaoh – was regarded as divine. This divine force was found in all members of the pharaoh's family, and rulers or rulers-to-be occasionally married their sisters or other close relatives in order to increase the amount of divinity in the royal household. Whether or not they were sisters of the pharaoh, some Egyptian queens, such as Nefertiti in the first half of the fourteenth century BCE, wielded real power, particularly over religious institutions. There were several female pharaohs in Egypt's long history, such as Nitokerty, Sobekneferu, and Hatshepsut, although they were regarded as exceptions to the rule; Hatshepsut, for example, is always shown wearing the ceremonial beard which was a symbol of office for Egyptian rulers. In Mesopotamia, Sargon of Akkad's daughter Enheduanna was appointed by her father to an important position in the temple hierarchy, and there were a few other women from prominent families who were temple administrators, though their numbers were always very small compared to the number of men involved in positions of government. Several women, including Empresses Hamiko and Jingu, are mentioned among the early rulers of Japan, gaining power both through their family connections and their role as shamans or *miko* capable of hearing and transmitting the advice of the gods; accounts of their lives mix myth and history, but they became important parts of Japanese national traditions. In central America, Lady Ahpo-Katun, Lady Ahpo-Hel, and the Lady of Dos Pilas all ruled Maya city-states on their own, and the wives of rulers participated along with their husbands in the blood-letting rituals that were a key symbol of royal power.

Given the life expectancies in most premodern cultures, kings and emperors frequently began their reigns as children, with their mothers appointed as regents; particularly if these women came from powerful families or had family members controlling the army, religious institutions, or other important groups, they might hold actual power for many decades. The most famous of these from classical China was the Empress Lu, the wife of the first emperor of the Han dynasty and the mother of the second emperor. Her reign was apparently stable and popular, though later Confucian historians who wanted to legitimate their own ideas reported that she killed all her rivals and built up her own family's power through strategic appointments and marriages. The "Evil Empress Lu" became a prime example of what would happen when a woman ruled, and the positive aspects of her reign were forgotten. Even in periods in which there was not a mother serving as regent (termed an "empress dowager" in China), the women surrounding kings or emperors often served as a counter-balance to the power of the all-male official bureaucracy. Those male bureaucrats included historians and official record-keepers, so that such women are generally portrayed in court chronicles and other official histories as scheming and evil, with the stereotype of the weak ruler as one who let himself be advised by women. By the later Ming period in China high officials encouraged emperors to choose their spouses from among lower-ranking families so that they would not be as powerful, though this solution was not common elsewhere.

In western Africa the role of queen mother was institutionalized among some of the city-states of the Hausa people. She was titled the *magajiya* and could, with the permission of a senior council of male officeholders, depose the male ruler (*sarki*); she also acted as an intercessor with him in legal cases. The most famous *magajiya* was Queen Aminatu of Zazzau (later renamed Zaire after Aminatu's youngest daughter), who ruled from about 1536 to 1573 without a male co-ruler and expanded Zazzau's political boundaries and trading networks. Though her title meant queen mother, the *magajiya* was not necessarily the mother of the ruling *sarki*, but was actually chosen by the senior woman of the royal lineage, the *iya*, who acted in consultation with other female members of the royal family to pick the most capable woman; Aminatu, for example, was actually the daughter of the male ruler and was chosen as *magajiya* when she was sixteen. The *iya* was herself in charge of religious life in Daura before the introduction of Islam; a traditional religion termed *bori* centered on spirit-possession through which the royal family was thought to safeguard the health of the state.

Along with their positions as queen mothers, women occasionally ruled territories on their own in the classical and post-classical periods, contributing to the development of intellectual and cultural institutions, religious systems, and political structures. In Japan the early empresses were joined by a number of women who ruled during the Asuka and Nara periods (552–784 CE), all of them relatives of the previous emperor chosen as compromise candidates when warring factions were unable to agree on a successor; they often stepped down when a male candidate was finally chosen, but in two cases were recalled to rule when the male ruler proved incapable. In Europe the states that slowly developed after the disintegration of the Roman Empire began to favor primogeniture, the automatic handing down of a territory to the eldest son; this avoided the worst of battles over succession, but also meant that the king could be totally incompetent. In some states daughters could inherit if there were no sons, but in many they could not, a prohibition that was most extreme in France, where political theorists in the late Middle Ages invented a tradition termed the Salic Law. They claimed that earlier rulers had outlawed not only inheritance by a woman, but any inheritance through the female line, thus removing any sons of a princess from the succession. Other than in France, however, women ruled states and territories from time to time in Europe, and political theorists felt it necessary to consider the issue of female rulership, particularly at points where dynastic accidents left many women in charge.

One of these times was the sixteenth century, which saw Queen Isabella in Castile, Mary and Elizabeth Tudor in England, and Mary Stuart in Scotland as queens regnant, and Catherine de Medici and Anne of Austria in France as powerful queen mothers. The debate about female rulership was actually one about what we would term the social construction of gender, as writers discussed whether a woman's being born into a royal family and educated to rule could (and should) allow her to overcome the limitations of her sex. Which was, they wondered, and which should be, the stronger determinant of character and social role, gender or rank?

The most extreme opponents of female rule were Protestants who opposed the Catholic rulers Mary Tudor and Mary Stuart and argued that female rule was unnatural, unlawful, and contrary to Christian scripture. The Scottish reformer John Knox called rule by women "monstrous," echoing Aristotle's notion that the female sex in general is monstrous, and asserted that the subjects of female rulers needed no other justification for rebelling than their monarch's sex. Jean Bodin, a French jurist and political theorist, also based his opposition on scripture and natural law, but added a family-based argument: the state was like a household, and just as in a household the husband/father has authority and power over all others, so in the state a male monarch should always rule. The English theorist Robert Filmer carried this even further, asserting that rulers derived all legal authority from the divinely sanctioned fatherly power of Adam, just as did all fathers. Male monarchs in these period used husbandly and paternal imagery to justify their assertion of power over their subjects, as in the English and Scottish King James I's statements to parliament: "I am the Husband, and the whole Isle is my lawfull Wife. . . . By the law of nature the king becomes a natural father to all his lieges at his coronation. . . . A King is trewly *Parens patriae*, the politique father of his people." Criticism of monarchs was also couched in paternal language; pamphlets directed against the Crown during the revolt known as the Fronde in seventeenth-century France, for example, justified their opposition by asserting that the king was not properly fulfilling his fatherly duties.

Those who supported rule by women generally avoided such paternal imagery and also disputed scriptural and natural law arguments against female rulership. They argued that scriptural prohibitions of women teaching or speaking were only relevant for the particular groups to which they were addressed, and that a woman's sex did not automatically exclude her from rule just as a boy king's age or a handicapped king's infirmity did not exclude him. The English writer John Aylmer asserted that even a married queen could rule legitimately, for she could be subject to her husband in her private life, yet monarch to him and all other men in her public – a concept of a split identity that Aylmer and other political theorists described as the ruler's "two bodies" and what we might describe as a distinction between the queenship and the queen. A queen might be thus clearly female in her body and sexuality, but still exhibit the masculine qualities regarded as necessary in a ruler because of traits she had inherited or learned. In these arguments the defenders of female rule were thus clearly separating sex from gender, and even approaching an idea of androgyny as a desirable state for the public persona of female monarchs.

It is perhaps not very surprising that the most ardent defenders of female rule were writing during the reign of Queen Elizabeth I (1533– 1603), a monarch who astutely used both feminine and masculine gender stereotypes to her own advantage (and from whom they hoped to gain patronage). She is one of the few female rulers who has left us at least a few comments about her own situation. Like her Hausa con- temporary Aminatu, Elizabeth was an extremely effective ruler, who built up the national treasury, supported the navy and commerce, and encouraged the establishment of colonies and the disruption of Spanish trade with the New World. Most historians view her reign as one in which England first became a major world power, creating the basis for the later establishment of the British Empire. Though she had many suitors, Elizabeth never married, recognizing that if she did she would put herself in a very awkward position in a society that, despite Aylmer's arguments to the contrary, regarded husbandly and fatherly authority in the household as a model for good government in the larger political realm. Elizabeth used her unusual status as a virgin queen (immortalized in "Virginia," the name given originally by the English to all of North America not held by the Spanish or French) and as a person who combined masculine and feminine qualities skillfully in both her actions and words, noting: "I know I have the body but of a weak and feeble woman, but I have the heart and stomach of a king – and of a king of England too."

Though Elizabeth clearly recognized that her situation would have been very different had she been born a boy, she did nothing to change gender structures in England or to lessen the legal disabilities facing women. She clearly viewed her status as king as overriding her status as a woman, noting that "we Princes . . . [are] set on stages in the sight and view of all of the world." In this she followed the pattern of most queens throughout the world, who viewed their status as monarchs as overriding their status as women, and were not advocates of greater gender egalitarianism.

Warfare

Hereditary rulers, male and female, used war as a means of expanding and defending their territories, as have the various forms of government that have succeeded them; war has thus been a central part of political history since it was first written. From these earliest recorded histories, war has been profoundly gendered, with victors portrayed as masculine and virile, and losers as unmanly or feminized; conquests were sometimes ended with the symbolic or actual rape of the defeated soldiers, or in cultures where such homosexual contact was unacceptable, with the rape of women who were on the losing side. An English commentator attributed England's defeat in the American Revolution to the "loss of our ancient manners [and our] effeminacy," and an Irish commentator writing in the early twentieth century noted, "Bloodshed is a cleansing and sanctifying rite and the nation which regards it as a final horror has lost its manhood." Battle was often perceived as the ultimate test of both individual and collective manhood, and justified as defending those who could not defend themselves, especially children and women.

Stories about women engaged in combat generally serve to highlight the serious nature of certain battles – the situation was so desperate, that even women had to fight! – and to symbolize bravery beyond normal expectations. Many cultures have stories of androgynous warriors who disguised themselves as men to join – or lead – armies and save their state or community. Some of these, such as Hua Mulan of third century CE China, immortalized in the Disney cartoon feature, have become mythologized to a point where it is difficult to separate fact from fiction; she does appear in a number of early Chinese sources, however, serving in the imperial army with distinction for over a decade and thus appears to have been a real person. By contrast, Molly Pitcher, who supposedly took over an artillery position after her husband was killed in the battle of Monmouth during the American Revolution (and who has postage stamps, posters, and a stop on the New Jersey Turnpike named in her honor), was actually a creation of the centennial celebration of the American Revolution in 1876, though real women did help load and fire weapons in that war, and a few dressed as men to fight on a more regular basis.

Symbols such as Mulan and Molly Pitcher aside, the vast majority of those who have fought in organized warfare throughout history have been men (and boys), and professional military training has, until very recently, been closed to women. Contemporary historians have discovered that many more women have been involved in organized combat than wartime propaganda or traditional military history would lead one to expect, however, particularly in rear-guard and guerrilla actions. In medieval Europe women defended their castles and villages when their husbands were away, and in medieval Japan wives of samurai were trained to fight with long curved swords and expected to defend their estates in their husband's absence. During the twentieth century women fought in both Vietnam and Algeria to end French colonialism and in a number of other national revolutions and civil wars. In Zimbabwe, for example, women underwent military training and fought side by side with men in the war for independence which ended in 1980; they held positions of authority in the military command structure and may have made up as many as one-quarter of the fighters of the Zimbabwe African National Liberation Army.

Women have also been important in providing supplies, for until the development of modern armies with their own supply services and support personnel, armies generally lived off the land, with many more people engaged in finding and preparing food and maintaining clothing and equipment than in actual combat. Because of this, soldiers often brought women with them, who have been called "camp followers" and viewed primarily as providers of sexual services, but who were more often the wives, daughters, or even mothers of soldiers, who cared for all of their physical needs. Such women occasionally had official positions as laundresses, and military leaders from the Crusades through the American Civil War made provisions for their support. During the late nineteenth century many armies began to delegate provisioning, cooking, and cleaning to uniformed male personnel and to prohibit women from accompanying armies. They discouraged soldiers who were not officers from marrying, for as one British general put it (in a letter to his wife), a married soldier "is no longer whole-hearted in his pursuit of glory."

Though they frowned on marriage, the professional armies of the nineteenth and twentieth centuries continued to make non-marital sexual services available to soldiers through a variety of means. French and German armies regulated the sex trade in areas held by their troops, and during World War I mobile brothels drawn by horses accompanied the troops, often divided into those for officers and those for enlisted men. The Japanese in World War II forcibly conscripted 200,000 to 400,000 women, mainly from Korea, to serve as "comfort women" for their troops, and the United States Army in Vietnam established official military brothels within the perimeter of its base camps, with the women checked regularly by army doctors for venereal disease. In some cases these sexual contacts were linked with nationalist and ethnic loyalties; when Pakistan occupied Bangladesh in 1971, for example, troops raped Bengali women to "improve the genes of the Bengali people," and during the 1990s Serbian soldiers raped Muslim women in Bosnia under a policy of "ethnic cleansing," shouting "death to all Turkish sperm."

Though not always this extreme, links between heterosexual prowess, warfare, and manhood in official literature and popular culture were very strong in the twentieth century, beginning with the period leading up to World War I. British authors, politicians, and journalists saw the outbreak of war in 1914 as a great moment, when "the flashing of the unsheathed sword" could lift men from their "wish for indulgence and wretched sensitiveness." Much of the official propaganda early in the war focused on the plight of "brave little Belgium" invaded by the Germans, with Belgium portrayed in a highly feminized manner and depictions of German atrocities against Belgian women appearing in newspapers and on recruiting posters.

The arms race of the Cold War was another period when manhood and warfare were closely connected. A number of commentators have noted that this linkage – which the Australian physician and anti-nuclear activist Helen Caldicott wryly dubbed "missile envy" to parallel Freudian "penis envy" – was particularly strident because it no longer had any validity; nuclear missiles can be fired as easily by women as by men, and the doctrine of mutually assured destruction adopted by both sides turned the expected relations between combatants and non-combatants on its head. The women and children on both sides – who would be wiped out in a nuclear strike – made such action unthinkable, and so protected the men who were soldiers, rather than the other way around. In the last several decades warfare has been masculinized by stressing its technological nature, a circular process that also makes computer technology appear more male as it is linked to combat. (As noted in chapter 3, the computer industry was successful in regendering working at keyboard, linking it with mathematics and machinery instead of using a typewriter; the predominance of combat-based computer games has also been a factor in this.)

In the twentieth century military valor was connected to heterosexuality; the United States military disqualified homosexuals from serving for the first time in World War II, and is currently embroiled in long debates about how best to handle "gays in the military." These debates would no doubt have surprised military leaders from earlier times, for the first epics from many parts of the world portray male comradeship, often tested in battle, as the highest form of human connection, and see any attachment to women as weakening. This idea continued in western culture at least until the eighteenth century, for Shakespeare's history plays viewed extensive concern with heterosexual conquests – what today might be labeled being "macho" – as evidence of effeminacy, and Alexander Hamilton explained his departure for the army of the American Revolution to his new bride as an avoidance of "an unmanly surrender" to his love for her.

Not only were those with strong same-sex relations often regarded and portrayed as better soldiers, but so were those with no sexual relations at all, or at least no sexual relations that led to offspring. In several of the world's largest empires, including China and the Ottoman Empire, military leaders were often eunuchs, castrated at an early age to increase their opportunities for advance in the imperial bureaucracy. Eunuchs did not simply serve as guards for royal women, but could be found in many official and military positions, favored precisely because they could not have descendants and so were regarded as more loyal to the ruling hereditary aristocracy than men who thought about their own families. Their sexual status – along with their own abilities – was thus the reason for their power, and they can be seen as in some ways parallel to cross-dressing women warriors or queens who did not marry; in all of these cases, the individual's somewhat ambivalent gender position contributed to his or her political power.

War often creates dramatic alterations in gender structures, for it breaks down traditional norms of conduct, turning women into booty but also creating emergencies in which women carry out tasks normally done by men. This has been well-documented in twentieth-century wars; women's "contribution on the home front" during World War I was one of the reasons British politicians claimed women were finally given the vote right after the war, and their even greater contributions in terms of factory work in many countries during World War II allowed for astounding increases in production of weapons and military supplies crucial to the war effort. In the latter case, war was not followed by an expansion of women's political rights or opportunities; rather, as we saw in chapter 3, and particularly in the United States, wartime measures such as child-care centers, which had allowed married women to work, were revoked. This situation followed the more common pattern throughout history, in which war was viewed as an extraordinary situation calling for great sacrifices and bravery from all, with the peace that followed a time for a return to previous gender roles.

Citizenship and Suffrage

Villages, tribes, and hereditary aristocracies were the primary political structures encountered by most people throughout most of the world's history, but in a few cases in earlier times, and in many more in the last few centuries, these have been joined by forms of government in which individuals are regarded as citizens rather than members or subjects. The form of citizenship most familiar to us is national citizenship, which accompanied the development of nation-states in the early modern period. This type of citizenship was based on earlier smaller-scale forms, in which some of the residents of cities and villages began to form institutions of government based on residence, wealth, and personal status, rather than on tribal membership.

The earliest example of this in Europe is the city of Athens during the fifth and fourth centuries BCE, when various leaders transformed Athens from a government ruled by a few individuals into a limited democracy, one in which adult free males who held a certain amount of property and who had lived for several generations in the city made political decisions by voting directly. The easiest way to become a citizen was to be the son of one, with the handing on of citizenship from father to son symbolized by a ceremony held on the tenth day after a boy was born. A citizen father laid his son on the floor of the house and gave him a name; this ceremony, rather than his actual physical birth, marked a boy's legal birth, and was not carried out for girls. Women were not citizens in Athens and played no political role, other than in the comedies of the playwright Aristophanes – in which he portrays women with power as examples of democracy run amok – or the utopian writings of Plato, in which he proposes that the best form of government might be one in which talented men and women who lived independently from their families made all decisions. In both Athenian reality and Plato's *Republic*, having a political voice was linked with financial and legal independence; slaves and people who worked for a living were certainly not free enough, nor were women who were married or could marry, for marriage placed them in a dependent relationship.

The notion of citizenship – membership in an abstract body of individuals – continued in the Mediterranean after hereditary monarchies again came to power, though in both the Hellenistic monarchies and the Roman Empire citizenship primarily gave one legal privileges rather than a political voice. Women as well as men were officially described as citizens in legal cases, and in the Roman Empire even the children of former slaves could eventually become citizens. This more legal and economic form of citizenship emerged again in European towns and cities that developed in the Middle Ages. Being the citizen of a town gave one preferential legal treatment and certain privileges: one paid lower taxes than non-citizens, could live in the city and buy property there without seeking anyone's permission, and could claim certain services if one fell ill or became incapacitated, such as staying in a city hospital or receiving public support. (In short, urban citizenship brought many of the same benefits we associate with national citizenship today, particularly the ability to live and work undisturbed in a particular location.) Citizenship also brought obligations, such as the duty to pay taxes and to defend the city if it were attacked. As in the Roman Empire, both women and men were citizens, obligated, if they were heads of household, to swear oaths of loyalty and provide soldiers and arms for the city's defense. Some towns and villages had an annual oath-swearing, in which women did not participate, but the other obligations of citizenship were the same.

This rather off-hand acceptance of women as citizens began to change in the sixteenth century. Towns often became worried about the number of citizens who might claim public support, and increased fees for new citizens. (Worries about people moving in and becoming a burden on welfare rolls are not simply a modern phenomenon.) Greek philosophy and Roman law became more widely known and accepted, and both emphasized the mental weakness of women as a reason to exclude them from politics and limit their legal privileges. The middle-class men such as merchants or artisans who actually ran city governments increasingly regarded women having independent power not – as hereditary monarchs did – as a necessary expedient because there wasn't a son around, but as disruptive and disorderly; in their minds, women's authority was to be derivative only, coming from their status as wife or widow of the male head of household. They began to put more emphasis on the annual oath-swearing as a symbol of citizenship, and to regard women's citizenship as secondary and "passive," whereas men's was "active."

Concepts of national citizenship that developed in the seventeenth and eighteenth centuries built on this more gendered tradition. Women petitioned parliament in England during the period of the Civil War after the monarchy was overthrown, claiming "a proportional share in the Freedoms of this Commonwealth," but even the most radical groups in the English Civil War never suggested that ending the power of the monarch over his subjects should be matched by ending the power of husbands over their wives. The former was unjust and against God's will, while the latter was "natural," as the words of the radical parliamentarian Henry Parker make clear: "The wife is inferior in nature, and was created for the assistance of man, and servants are hired for their Lord's mere attendance; but it is otherwise in the State between man and man, for that civill difference . . . is for . . . the good of all, not that servility and drudgery may be imposed upon all for the pompe of one."

Eighteenth-century thinkers and political leaders began to add moral issues to women's inferior reason and wives' dependence in marriage as a grounds for denying women political rights. Thomas Jefferson noted: "Were our state a pure democracy, there would still be excluded from our deliberations women, who, to prevent deprivation of morals and ambiguity of issues, should not mix promiscuously in gatherings of men." Whether women ought to "partake in civil government dominions and sovereignty" was a topic of formal debate for the male students at Yale University in the 1770s, but there was little serious discussion of this in the founding of the new republic after the American Revolution. In a few cases in the early United States voting was based solely on property ownership and unmarried female property owners were allowed to vote, but these anomalies did not last long because they were not an intentional extension of voting rights to women, but simply accidental. By the nineteenth century such anomalies disappeared when voting rights in elections were specifically limited to males, leaving women along with children, criminals, and the mentally ill among the disenfranchised. The political role accorded to women was one of "republican womanhood," responsible for urging their husbands and sons to civic virtue, morality, and public service from the safety and tranquillity of their homes. This role was not limited to the United States, but was also that prescribed for women a century later in places such as Egypt or Iran, where women were urged by nationalist reformers to be nurturers of future citizens.

Most of the thinkers of the French Revolution agreed with Jefferson. There were a few exceptions – the Marquise de Condorcet, for example, commented: "Why should individuals subject to pregnancies and to brief periods of indisposition not be able to exercise rights that no one ever thought of denying to people who suffer from gout every winter or who easily catch cold?" But for most of the revolutionaries the possibility of getting pregnant created a type of distinction unlike any other. Whereas wealth, family background, social class, and status of birth were distinctions they increasingly took to be meaningless in terms of the limits of citizenship – the 1791 Constitution limited voting rights to those men who had some property, but by 1792 all men over 21 could vote – sex, remained, in their eyes, an unbridgeable chasm. Pierre-Gaspard Chaumette, a Parisian official, commented in 1792: "Since when is it permitted to give up one's sex? Since when is it decent to see women abandoning the pious cares of their households, the cribs of their children, to come to public places, to harangues in the galleries, at the bar of the Senate? Is it to men that nature has confided domestic cares? Has she given us breasts to feed our children?" (Parisian revolutionaries were obsessed with women's breasts – not only did they constantly use images of nursing mothers in their speeches and paintings, but in 1793 at the festival of Unity and Indivisibility honoring the new Republic, the deputies pledged their loyalty to the nation by drinking water spouting from the breasts of a large statue of an Egyptian goddess.)

Considerations – and rejections – of women's citizenship in 1792 did not simply arise out of abstract discussions of rights, but were in response to dramatic actions on the part of women, particularly in Paris, in the first years of the Revolution. Women drafted official grievance lists for elected deputies to take to the king, marched from Paris to Versailles, demanding that the king return to Paris, attended meetings and signed petitions concerning the future of the constitutional monarchy, participated in armed processions, and formed their own political society. Throughout all of these activities they identified themselves as "citizen" – *citoyennes* in the feminine in French – and as patriots. Women such as Olympe de Gouges wrote and spoke vigorously about the need for women to be part of political categories currently being discussed: "the nation," "the individual," "the people." This politicization of women shocked both conservatives and revolutionaries, and none of the various constitutions drafted during the Revolution allowed women to vote, though they did allow women some civil rights, such as divorce and property ownership. These were taken away again in Napoleon's Civil

Code of 1804 – which became the basis of many law codes in Europe with the Napoleonic conquests – which left adult unmarried women relatively free to engage in business and legal affairs, but, following the principle of coverture discussed in chapter 4, made married women totally subservient to their husbands and decreed that a wife's nationality should follow her husband's.

In many countries of Latin America as well as the United States and France, political and intellectual ferment led to democratic political revolutions. Educated people debated new ideas about justice, equality, and freedom, and discussed what qualities would be required for citizenship in states in which citizens had an actual voice in making political decisions. Women as well as men were involved in these discussions in cities ranging from San Juan in Puerto Rico to Caracas in Venezuela, hosting meetings in their homes where political grievances were aired and plans for reforms mapped out. Less elite women also worked for independence, serving as spies, carrying weapons and supplies, and caring for the wounded in field hospitals; a few dressed as men in order to engage in combat. Despite these efforts the constitutions of the new Latin American states did not allow women to vote, hold political office, be a witness in court, or be a guardian over minors (including their own children). Civil law codes heightened gender distinctions, generally forbidding married women to sign contracts, buy or sell, maintain bank accounts, or keep their own wages.

The exclusion of women from formal political rights in areas where political and nationalist revolutions established democratic governments sparked the movement for women's rights during the nineteenth century. This was one of many movements of reform and revolution at this time, as the social problems created by industrialism, combined with the rhetoric of political equality which grew out of the eighteenth-century revolutions and with reactions against colonialism, led many people in the nineteenth century to call for major social and political changes.

Because the movement for women's suffrage and political rights – what has since been termed the "first stage" of the women's movement – fit with traditional definitions of political history, it received attention from historians before many other issues involving gender and politics; indeed, it was often the only issue concerning women covered in college textbooks until several decades ago. The story that was told at that time focused primarily on the suffrage campaign in the United States and Great Britain, highlighting prominent individuals such as Susan B. Anthony and Sylvia Pankhurst, and organizations such as the National

Women's Suffrage Association and the Women's Social and Political
Union. Scholars noted that the tactics of women's rights groups varied
from country to country; those in England ultimately turned to militant
moves such as hunger strikes and other types of civil disobedience, while
in most other countries they used more moderate moves such as petition
drives (a political tool first developed by women's groups), lobbying, and
letters of protest.

More recent scholarship has made clear that the first wave of the
women's movement was international, not simply something emanating
from the Anglo-American world. The "woman question," which along
with suffrage debated the merits of women's greater access to education,
property rights, more equitable marriage and divorce laws, temperance,
and protection for women workers, was an international issue, though
with different emphases in different parts of the world. Reformers in India
urged an end to *sati*, female infanticide, and the prohibition of widow
remarriage; those in Europe worked for women's rights to own property
and control their own wages; those in the United States worked for
temperance and dress reform; those in Latin America sought improvements in working conditions and a restructuring of the civil codes which
limited women's economic rights.

As we saw in chapter 4, in the United States and Britain the key issue
was women's access to individual rights, while elsewhere, including
continental Europe, the emphasis was on women's duties and obligations. In most parts of the world reformers did not dispute ideas about
the centrality of marriage and motherhood in most women's lives, but
used the notion of women's responsibility for home and family as the
very reason that women should have an equal voice with men. Women,
they argued, needed the vote to ensure the well-being of their families
and children, and would clean up corrupt politics in the same way that
they cleaned up their households. They would end the sexual and
physical abuse of women, halt the spread of venereal disease, and reform
the sexual double standard. In several places reformers used ideas about
racial and class superiority to bolster their arguments, noting how much
more worthy and responsible honorable white middle-class women
were than working-class, immigrant, or non-white men. Such arguments are one of the reasons that white women were granted the vote
relatively early in Australia and New Zealand, and that one of the first
states to allow woman suffrage was conservative Utah, where Mormon
women argued their votes would outnumber those of non-Mormon
men.

By the middle of the nineteenth century groups specifically devoted to women's political rights began to be established in many countries of the world, and to communicate with each other in what became an international feminist movement; international meetings included ones in Washington, DC, in 1888 and in Buenos Aires in 1910. Suffragists were initially ridiculed and attacked physically, and in many countries anti-suffrage groups were formed whose tactics paralleled those of the suffrage groups; such groups included women as well as men, for women have been the only group in history to mobilize both for and against their own enfranchisement. The efforts of suffragists, combined with international events such as World War I, were ultimately successful, however, and suffrage rights were gradually extended to women around the world. Women were allowed to vote in national elections first in New Zealand in 1893 and in Finland in 1906; suffrage rights were granted in the United States and many European countries right after World War I, in Latin America, the Philippines, India, China, Japan, and the rest of Europe (except Switzerland) in the 1930s and 1940s. Women were allowed to vote on an equal basis with men in most of the constitutions of African and Asian states set up after World War II. In 2000 Kuwait was the only country that specifically limited voting to men, and there were protests against this by women in Kuwait in the 1990s because of women's active role in the Gulf War. (There are other countries which have no elected legislature so that neither women nor men vote.)

Though both supporters and opponents of women's suffrage expected women's voting patterns to differ sharply from those of men, in most elections they did not, and in some countries, such as Egypt, very few women actually voted. After gaining suffrage many women's groups turned their attention to other types of issues, such as educational, health, and legal reforms, or world peace.

By the 1960s women in many parts of the world were dissatisfied with the pace at which they were achieving political and legal equality, and a second-wave women's movement began, often termed the "women's liberation movement." Women's groups pressured for an end to sex discrimination in hiring practices, pay rates, inheritance rights, and the granting of credit; they opened battered-women's shelters, day-care centers, and rape crisis centers, and pushed for university courses on women and laws against sexual harassment. In western countries they pushed for abortion rights, and in India they mobilized against dowries and dowry-related deaths. By the early 1970s advocates of rights for homosexuals had also mobilized in many countries, sponsoring demonstrations, political action campaigns, and various types of self-help organizations. The United Nations declared 1975–85 to be the International Decade for Women, and meetings discussing the status of women around the world were held under UN auspices in Mexico City (1975), Copenhagen (1980), Nairobi (1985), and Beijing (1995). These meetings were sometimes divisive, pointing out the great differences in women's concerns around the world, with sexual orientation and female genital mutilation often the most explosive issues. The official Platform for Action of the Beijing Conference sought to avoid some of these divisions by calling for a general "empowerment of women," noting that this would mean different things in different areas of the world.

The reinvigorated feminist movement sparked conservative reactions in many countries, with arguments often couched in terms of "tradition." Women's rights, it was argued, stood against "traditional family values" and had caused an increase in the divorce rate, the number of children born out of wedlock, family violence, and juvenile delinquency; gay rights were even more dangerous. Such arguments were effective in stopping some legal changes – in the United States, for example, the Equal Rights Amendment was not ratified by enough states to become law, though Canada passed a similar measure in 1960 and Australia in 1984 – but the movement toward greater egalitarianism in political participation, education, and employment continued. In the United States the number of women in state legislatures quadrupled during the period 1970–90, and the number of female lawyers and judges went up almost as much. Around the world in the 1990s women held about 10 percent of the seats on national legislatures, though Sweden was the only country to have close to 50 percent of its legislators female.

Colonialism, Anti-colonialism, and Postcolonialism

Questions about the relationship between gender and political life in the nineteenth and twentieth centuries – or even earlier – did not play themselves out independently in any country, but were tied to international politics and issues of imperialism and colonialism. The study of colonialism and its aftermath has received a great deal of attention from historians recently, who initially focused on formal political structures and international relations but are increasingly investigating broader issues such as the development of national identities and the cultural construction of difference. This scholarship is often interdisciplinary in nature, combining artistic and literary evidence with more traditional historical documents, and because of its strong theoretical emphasis is labeled postcolonial theory. Historians of the United States and Europe are also now applying insights drawn from postcolonial theory as they investigate racial and ethnic minorities, viewing their relationships with dominant groups as a type of colonialism within one country.

Imperial power and ideas of the nation were explicitly and implicitly linked with gender and the cultural constructions of masculinity and femininity for both colonizers and colonized, beginning with the first European "colony" of the English in Ireland. For centuries English commentators described the Irish as both animal-like and feminized, the women showing "wild shamrock manners" because they did not wear corsets and the men both "brassy, cunning, and brutalized" and "easily subdued into docility." Even the mid-nineteenth century potato blight was their fault in the eyes of the English writer Thomas Carlyle, for their "laziness" had led to their "sluttishly starving from age to age."

Such opinions were even more strongly held by European (and later American) officials, merchants, and missionaries who established colonies beyond Europe. They often viewed women's less restrictive dress in tropical areas as a sign of sexual looseness, men's lack of facial hair or trousers as a sign of effeminacy, and any marital pattern other than permanent monogamy as a sign of inferiority. The English official Thomas Macaulay, for example, compared Bengali men in the 1750s to "women . . . enervated by a soft climate and accustomed to peaceful employments." Colonial powers often attempted to impose their own views of proper gender relations on their far-flung colonies, establishing schools to teach western values and using taxes, permits, and registration documents to impose western family structures. As we saw in chapter 2, racial hierarchies developed throughout the colonial world, and both individuals and governments used racial identity as a means of determining access to education, jobs, housing, voting rights, and other privileges.

Racial identity was used by colonial governments to enhance white privilege, and it remained important in the nationalist movements which opposed European colonization in the late nineteenth and early twentieth centuries. Part of creating and affirming a national identity was handling "the woman question," determining what the legal and social status of women would be. Colonial rulers, especially the British, often regarded customs that were harmful to women, such as child-marriage and *sati* in India or clitoridectomy in Kenya, as clear signs of the backwardness and barbarity of indigenous cultures and their need for outside rule. Nationalist reformers thus had to balance traditional customs and religious practices with their desires to appear modern enough to govern themselves.

Resistance to colonialism swept Africa and Asia after World War II, and both women and men were active in all types of opposition, though men usually emerged as the official voices of the nationalist movements and young men in particular formed the majority of all military units. (Even in the liberation war in Zimbabwe, for example, in which women formed a significant share of the fighting force, the majority were still men under the age of twenty-four.) Women participated in military actions (both independently and as members of guerrilla units), demonstrated for the relief of political prisoners, made speeches, and engaged in civil disobedience, boycotts, protests, and riots. In India both women and men were imprisoned for participation in boycotts and other types of non-violent protests against British rule in the 1930s. In the Algerian War against French rule (1954–62) women smuggled information and bombs under their long clothing, and some were tortured or executed for their activities. In South Africa both black and white women protested the imposition of apartheid and the forced relocation and dividing of African families.

Despite women's support of nationalist movements, and despite the support for women's issues expressed by some nationalist leaders such as Julius Nyerere of Tanzania, women's access to formal political power continued to be limited in most postcolonial states of Africa and Asia. Though women were often granted equal political rights in the constitutions of most newly independent states, women's concerns like more equitable marriage laws were generally not a high priority, and the few women who had high political positions were generally related to men with political power, such as Indira Gandhi or Benazir Bhutto, mentioned above. Carmen Pereira, an independence leader who fought the Portuguese in Guinea-Bissau in the 1970s, recognized this tendency, and noted that women were "fighting two colonialisms" – one of gender discrimination and one of nationalist struggle.

In some areas the relationship between women's rights and nationalist opposition to western political and cultural domination was the reverse of that envisioned by Pereira. Though young male nationalists were often successful at ending painful initiation rituals through which older men had held power over them, traditions which involved women were viewed positively. Opposition to the west was often described as a return to "tradition" or "authenticity," which generally meant a greater emphasis on women's role within the household and restrictions on their education, dress, movements, and opportunities. Efforts to change marriage laws or to end practices such as female genital mutilation were denounced as western imperialism, and women's modesty and sexual honor were linked with social stability and family loyalty. This linkage appealed to many women, particularly those who had gained little advantage from educational and economic changes, and women as well as men became exponents of "tradition." In Turkey, for example, one of the female legislators in the 1990s was refused her seat because she wished to wear a headscarf, a mark of conservative Islam, which in the opinion of most of her colleagues signified too great an intrusion of religion into the secular legislature.

Most communist countries in the twentieth century saw a disjuncture between theory and practice in terms of gender similar to that of many postcolonial states. As in nationalist movements, women played a variety of roles in the communist revolutions in Russia, China, Cuba, Vietnam, and elsewhere, and Marxist ideology proclaimed that men and women were equal. Mao Zedong, for example, asserted that women were bound by four ropes that should all be broken: political, clan, religious, and masculine authority. Educational opportunities for women were vastly improved in communist countries, and women entered certain professions such as medicine in numbers far exceeding those in western Europe or the United States. Women had (or have) equal rights in terms of property holding, marriage, divorce, and authority over their children, and they can be party members and officials. On the other hand, once blatant forms of oppression such as foot-binding in China were ended, issues perceived as "women's issues" such as access to birth control or programs to end family violence were not regarded as important. Almost all high political positions were held by men.

The end of communism in the Soviet Union and eastern Europe and the loosening of economic controls in China provided opportunities for some individuals, but these appear to be shaped by existing gender structures. Men were more able to gain capital with which to make investments and develop new business enterprises, and women were not hired because they were expected to want time off for pregnancy or the care of elderly relatives. For many women, especially in eastern Europe, the end of communism meant food shortages, an end to paid maternity

leave and government-supported day-care centers, increased street violence, and a huge growth in prostitution. Ultra-conservative nationalist
leaders in formerly communist countries often attributed social problems
to women: working women are the cause of unemployment; complain-
ing wives the cause of family violence, male alcoholism, and divorce;
selfish mothers the cause of disaffected young people and gangs. As in
postcolonial states, women's responses to eastern European nationalism
were varied; in the former Yugoslavia, for example, some women were
enthusiastic supporters of Serbian or Croatian nationalist leaders, while
others formed groups such as the Women's Lobby, Women in Black
Against War, and the SOS Hotline for Women and Children Victims of
Violence which campaigned against nationalist violence.

At the end of the twentieth century the economic and technological
changes discussed in chapter 3 led to an increasingly global economy,
with many observers commenting that international business and financial institutions were more important than any government in shaping
the lives of people around the world. This economic globalism was
accompanied by a proliferation of international agencies and organizations, both governmental and non-governmental, which set policy and
made decisions; indeed, at the UN World Conference on Women in
Beijing in 1995, there were about 5,000 official delegates and 30,000
representatives of non-governmental organizations, which included
large international agencies and tiny local grassroots groups. If we use
the broader definition of politics and include all relationships of power, it
is clear that the situation at the close of the twentieth century was
extremely complex, with men and women often enmeshed in a huge
number of power relationships, from kin and ethnic networks to interest
groups formed on the World Wide Web. These relationships sometimes
supported one another in promoting greater gender egalitarianism or
inequality, but they also often conflicted, making any generalizations
about the direction of trends around the world very difficult.

    The power of government – the narrower definition of politics – in
determining gender roles and structures is not completely irrelevant,
however, but generalizations are also difficult. About 75 percent of the
refugees fleeing political persecution and war around the world are
female, and the citizenship policies of nearly every country are still
gender-specific, making it more difficult for women than for men to
become legal residents. As we saw in chapter 4, more than twenty
countries, including the United States, have still not ratified the United

Nations Convention on the Elimination of All Forms of Discrimination Against Women, passed by the UN in 1979. The Taliban regime in Afghanistan has virtually eliminated all possibilities for education, public life, or employment for women. On the other hand, an amendment to the Indian constitution in 1992 required a third of the positions as village council-members and chiefs to be women, many from the country's lowest castes, and is beginning to have much more of an effect on both village life and gender relations than anyone predicted it would. France may soon follow the Indian example, because a new law of May 2000 requiring *parité* obliges the country's political parties to fill 50 percent of their candidacies in almost all races with women or lose their campaign funding. The nineteenth-century advocates of women's rights would certainly view such measures as welcome, though perhaps they would also wonder why such changes took so long. They might also caution against complacency given the major disparities between men's and women's opportunities that still exist in many parts of the world.

Further Reading

Because political issues have long been at the heart of history, most histories of women, particularly those that focus on one country in the modern period, include extensive discussion of politics and power; general political histories are much less likely to include considerations of gender than general social histories, however. A good general introduction to the more theoretical issues covered in this chapter is Anne Phillips, ed., *Feminism and Politics* (New York: Oxford, 1998).

Examinations of the political roles of kin groups and tribes include: Christine Gailey, *Kinship to Kingship: Gender Hierarchy and State Formation in the Tongan Islands* (Austin: University of Texas Press, 1987); Karen Sacks, *Sisters and Wives: The Past and Future of Sexual Equality* (Westport, CT: Greenwood Press, 1979); Irene Silverblatt, *Moon, Sun, and Witches: Gender Ideologies and Class in Inca and Colonial Peru* (Princeton, NJ: Princeton University Press, 1987); Laura F. Klein and Lillian A. Ackerman, eds., *Women and Power in Native North America* (Norman: University of Oklahoma Press, 1995); Ifi Amadiume, *Re-inventing Africa: Matriarchy, Religion and Culture* (London: Zed Books, 1997).

Studies of the interplay between gender and hereditary monarchy include: Leslie P. Peirce, *The Imperial Harem: Women and Sovereignty in the Ottoman Empire* (New York: Oxford University Press, 1993); John

Carmi Parsons, ed., *Medieval Queenship* (Manchester: Manchester University Press, 1998); Edna G. Bay, *Wives of the Leopard: Gender, Politics, and Culture in the Kingdom of Dahomey* (Charlottesville: University of Virginia Press, 1998). For an excellent study of Elizabeth I, see Carole Levin, *The Heart and Stomach of a King: Elizabeth I and the Politics of Sex and Gender* (Philadelphia: University of Pennsylvania Press, 1994).

A good place to begin for an overview of issues regarding warfare is Linda Grant De Pauw, *Battle Cries and Lullabies: Women in War from Prehistory to the Present* (Norman: University of Oklahoma Press, 1998). More specialized works include: Myrna Trustram, *Women of the Regiment: Marriage and the Victorian Army* (Cambridge: Cambridge University Press, 1984); Stephanie Urdang, *And Still They Dance: Women, War, and the Struggle for Change in Mozambique* (New York: Monthly Review Press, 1989); Michael C. Adams, *The Great Adventure: Male Desire and the Coming of World War I* (Bloomington: Indiana University Press, 1990); Irene Staunton, *Mothers of the Revolution: The War Experiences of Thirty Zimbabwean Women* (Bloomington: Indiana University Press, 1990); Catherine Clinton and Nina Silber, eds., *Divided Houses: Gender and the Civil War* (New York: Oxford University Press, 1992); Jacklyn Cock, *Women and War in South Africa* (Cleveland, OH: Pilgrim Press, 1993); Douglas Peers, *Between Mars and Mammon: Colonial Armies and the Garrison State in India, 1819–1835* (New York: St Martin's Press, 1995); Joy Damousi and Marilyn Lake, eds., *Gender and War: Australians at War in the Twentieth Century* (Cambridge: Cambridge University Press, 1995); Margaret S. Creighton and Lisa Norling, eds., *Iron Men, Wooden Women: Gender and Seafaring in the Atlantic World, 1700–1920* (Baltimore, MD: Johns Hopkins University Press, 1996); Billie Melman, ed., *Borderlines: Genders and Identities in War and Peace, 1870–1930* (London: Routledge, 1998); Kristin L. Hoganson, *Fighting for American Manhood: How Gender Politics Provoked the Spanish–American and Philippine–American Wars* (New Haven, CT: Yale University Press, 1998); Meredith Turshen and Clotilde Twagiramariya, eds., *What Women Do in Wartime: Gender and Conflict in Africa* (London: Zed Books, 1998); Susan R. Grayzel, *Women's Identities at War: Gender, Motherhood, and Politics in Britain and France during the First World War* (Chapel Hill: University of North Carolina Press, 1999).

Most of the research involving gender and citizenship has focused either on the United States or Europe. Good places to start are the general essay collection edited by Gisela Bock and Susan James, *Beyond Equality and Difference: Citizenship, Feminist Politics and Female Subjectivity*

(London: Routledge, 1992), Susan Moller Okin's general survey, *Women in Western Political Thought* (Princeton, NJ: Princeton University Press, 1979), or the more theoretical consideration of Carole Pateman's *The Sexual Contract* (Stanford, CA: Stanford University Press, 1988). The situation in Athens is explored provocatively in Eva Keuls's *The Reign of the Phallus: Sexual Politics in Ancient Athens* (New York: Harper and Row, 1985). For the United States, see: Mark E. Kann, *On the Man Question: Gender and Civic Virtue in America* (Philadelphia, PA: Temple University Press, 1991) and *The Gendering of American Politics: Founding Mothers, Founding Fathers, and Political Patriarchy* (Westport, CT: Praeger, 1999); Mary Beth Norton, *Founding Mothers and Fathers: Gendered Power and the Forming of American Society* (New York: Alfred A. Knopf, 1996); Kathleen M. Brown, *Good Wives, Nasty Wenches, and Anxious Patriarchs: Gender, Race, and Power in Colonial Virginia* (Chapel Hill: University of North Carolina Press, 1996); Linda K. Kerber, *No Constitutional Right to be Ladies: Women and the Obligations of Citizenship* (New York: Hill and Wang, 1998). For Europe, the French Revolution has received the most attention: Joan Landes, *Women and the Public Sphere in the Age of the French Revolution* (Ithaca, NY: Cornell University Press, 1988); Christine Fauré, *Democracy without Women: Feminism and the Rise of Liberal Individualism in France* (Bloomington: Indiana University Press, 1991); Harriet B. Applewhite and Darline Gay Levy, *Women and Politics in the Age of the Democratic Revolution* (Ann Arbor: University of Michigan Press, 1993); Genevieve Fraisse, *Reason's Muse: Sexual Difference and the Birth of Democracy* (Chicago: University of Chicago Press, 1994); Joan Scott, *Only Paradoxes to Offer: French Feminists and the Rights of Man* (Cambridge, MA: Harvard University Press, 1996).

Older works on the campaign for woman suffrage and the second-wave feminist movement also focused primarily on the United States or Europe, but this has begun to change. General surveys of women's movements worldwide include: Chandra Talpade Mohanty, Ann Russo, and Lourdes Torres, eds., *Third World Women and the Politics of Feminism* (Bloomington: Indiana University Press, 1991); Caroline Daly and Melanie Nolan, eds., *Suffrage and Beyond: International Feminist Perspectives* (Auckland: Auckland University Press, 1994); Amrita Basu, ed., *The Challenge of Local Feminisms: Women's Movements in Global Perspective* (Boulder, CO: Westview Press, 1995); Joan W. Scott, Cora Kaplan, and Debra Keates, eds., *Transitions, Environments, Translations: Feminisms in International Politics* (London: Routledge, 1997); Maroula Joannou and June Purvis, eds., *The Women's Suffrage Movement:*

New Feminist Perspectives (Manchester: Manchester University Press, 1998).

For the first and second-wave women's movements in the United States, see: Eleanor Flexner, *Century of Struggle: The Woman's Rights Movement in the United States* (New York: Atheneum, 1970); Sara Evans, *Personal Politics: The Roots of Women's Liberation in the Civil Rights Movement and the New Left* (New York: Vintage, 1979); Mary Ryan, *Women in Public: From Banners to Ballots, 1825–1880* (Baltimore, MD: Johns Hopkins University Press, 1990); Dorothy Salem, *To Better Our World: Black Women in Organized Reform, 1890–1920* (Brooklyn, NY: Carlson Publishing, 1990); Jane Sherron De Hart and Donald Matthews, *Sex, Gender and the Politics of the ERA: A State and a Nation* (New York: Oxford University Press, 1990); Robyn Muncy, *Creating a Female Dominion in American Reform, 1890–1935* (New York: Oxford University Press, 1991); Glenna Matthews, *The Rise of the Public Woman: Woman's Power and Woman's Place in the United States, 1630–1970* (New York: Oxford University Press, 1992); Roslayn Terborg-Penn, *African-American Women in the Struggle for the Vote* (Bloomington: Indiana University Press, 1998); Ruth Rosen, *The World Split Open: How the Modern Women's Movement Changed America* (New York: Viking, 1999). For a fascinating look at the opponents of suffrage, see Susan E. Marshall, *Splintered Sisterhood: Gender and Class in the Campaign against Woman Suffrage* (Madison: University of Wisconsin Press, 1997). For an excellent survey of the women's movements in Australia, see Marilyn Lake, *Getting Equal: The History of Australian Feminism* (St Leonards, NSW: Allen and Unwin, 1999). For further references to feminism see the list of further reading in chapter 4.

General collections on gender and colonialism include: Clare Midgley, ed., *Gender and Imperialism* (Manchester: Manchester University Press, 1998) and Ruth Roach Pierson and Nupur Chadhuri, eds., *Nation, Empire, Colony: Historicizing Gender and Race* (Bloomington: Indiana University Press, 1998). Works that look specifically at the role of women in imperialism include: Nupur Chaudhuri and Margaret Strobel, eds., *Western Women and Imperialism: Complicity and Resistance* (Bloomington: Indiana University Press, 1992) and Antoinette Burton, *Burdens of History: British Feminists, Indian Women, and Imperial Culture, 1865–1915* (Chapel Hill: University of North Carolina Press, 1994).

Most studies of the links between gender and empire focus on the British experience, including: Ronald Hyam, *Empire and Sexuality: The British Experience* (Manchester: Manchester University Press, 1990);

Graham Dawson, *Soldier Heroes: British Adventure, Empire, and the Imaging of Masculinity* (London: Routledge, 1994); Anne McClintock, *Imperial Leather: Race, Gender and Sexuality in the Colonial Contest* (London: Routledge, 1995); Felicity Nussbaum, *Torrid Zones: Maternity, Sexuality and Empire in Eighteenth-Century English Narratives* (Baltimore, MD: Johns Hopkins University Press, 1995); Mrinalini Sinha, *Colonial Masculinity: The "Manly Englishman" and the "Effeminate Bengali" in the Late Nineteenth Century* (Manchester: Manchester University Press, 1995); Revathi Krishnaswamy, *Effeminism: The Economy of Colonial Desire* (Ann Arbor: Univeristy of Michigan Press, 1998). Works that discuss other colonial settings include: Julia Clancy-Smith and Frances Gouda, eds., *Domesticating the Empire: Race, Gender and Family Life in French and Dutch Colonialism* (Charlottesville: University of Virginia Press, 1997); Nancy Rose Hunt, Tessie P. Liu, and Jean Quataert, eds., *Gendered Colonialisms in African History* (Oxford: Blackwell Publishers, 1997).

General studies of the interplay between feminism and nationalism in the postcolonial world include: Miranda Davis, ed., *Third World, Second Sex: Women's Struggles and National Liberation* (London: Zed Books, 1983); Kumari Jayawardena, *Feminism and Nationalism in the Third World* (London: Zed Books, 1986); Mary Ann Tetréault, ed., *Women and Revolution in Africa, Asia, and the New World* (Columbia: University of South Carolina Press, 1994); "Links across differences: gender, ethnicity and nationalism," special issue of *Women's Studies International Forum* 19, nos. 1/2 (1996); Ida Blom, Karen Hagemann, and Catherine Hall, eds., *Gendered Nations: Nationalism and Gender Order in the Long Nineteenth Century* (Oxford: Berg, 2000).

There is a large body of literature on gender and politics in the contemporary world, some of which has a historical dimension, such as: Cynthia Enloe, *Bananas, Beaches and Bases: Making Feminist Sense of International Politics* (London: Pandora, 1989); Barbara J. Nelson and Majma Chowdhury, eds., *Women and Politics Worldwide* (New Haven, CT: Yale University Press, 1994); Jan Jindy Pittman, *Worlding Women: A Feminist International Politics* (London: Routledge, 1996); Jill Stearns, *Gender and International Relations: An Intoduction* (New Brunswick, NJ: Rutgers University Press, 1997); Mary K. Meyer and Elisabeth Prügl, eds., *Gender Politics in Global Governance* (Lanham, MD: Rowman and Littlefield, 1999).

For studies of gender and politics in Latin America, see: Elsa Chaney, *Supremadre: Women in Politics in Latin America* (Austin: University of Texas Press, 1979); June E. Hahner, *Emancipating the Female Sex: The*

Struggle for Women's Rights in Brazil, 1850–1940 (Durham, NC: Duke University Press, 1990); Francesca Miller, *Latin American Women and the Search for Social Justice* (Hanover, NH: University Press of New England, 1991); K. Lynn Stoner, *From the House to the Streets: The Cuban Women's Movement for Legal Reform, 1898–1940* (Durham, NC: Duke University Press, 1991); Janet H. Momsen, *Women and Change in the Caribbean* (Bloomington: Indiana University Press, 1993); Steve Stern, *The Secret History of Gender: Women, Men, and Power in Late Colonial Mexico* (Chapel Hill: University of North Carolina Press, 1995); Elizabeth Dore, ed., *Gender Politics in Latin America: Debates in Theory and Practice* (New York: Monthly Review Press, 1997); Margaret Power, *Gendered Allegiances: The Construction of a Cross-class Right-wing Women's Movement in Chile, 1964–1973* (State College: Pennsylvania State University Press, 2000).

For specific studies of gender and politics in the recent history of Africa, see: Stephanie Urdang, *Fighting Two Colonialisms: Women in Guinea-Bissau* (New York: Monthly Review Press, 1979); June Goodwin, *Cry Amandla! South African Women and the Question of Power* (New York: Africana Publishing, 1984); Jane L. Parpart and Kathleen A. Staudt., eds., *Women and the State in Africa* (Boulder, CO: Lynne Rienner Publishers, 1989); Cora Ann Presley, *Kikuyu Women, the Mau Mau Rebellion, and Social Change in Kenya* (Boulder, CO: Westview Press, 1992); Sondra Hale, *Gender Politics in Sudan: Islamism, Socialism and the State* (Boulder, CO: Westview Press, 1996); Temma Kaplan, *Crazy for Democracy: Women's Grassroots Movements in the United States and South Africa* (New York: Routledge, 1996); Gwendolyn Mikell, ed., *African Feminism: The Politics of Survival in Sub-Saharan Africa* (Philadelphia: University of Pennsylvania Press, 1997); Susan Geiger, *TANU Women: Gender and Culture in the Making of Tanganyikan Nationalism, 1955–1965* (Portsmouth, NH: Heinemann, 1998); Obioma Nnaemeka, ed., *Sisterhood, Feminisms, and Power: From Africa to the Diaspora* (Trenton, NJ: Africa World Press, 1998)

For the Near East, see: Guity Nashat, ed., *Women and Revolution in Iran* (Boulder, CO: Westview Press, 1983); Earl L. Sullivan, *Women in Egyptian Public Life* (Syracuse, NY: Syracuse University Press, 1986); Mahnaz Afkhami and Erika Friedl, eds., *In the Eye of the Storm: Women in Post-Revolutionary Iran* (Syracuse, NY: Syracuse University Press, 1994); Deniz Kandiyoti, ed., *Women, Islam, and the State* (London: Macmillan, 1991); Lila Abu-Lughod, ed., *Remaking Women: Feminism and Modernity in the Middle East* (Princeton, NJ: Princeton University Press, 1998).

For Asia, see: Elisabeth Croll, *Feminism and Socialism in China* (New York: Schocken, 1980); Susan Pharr, *Political Women in Japan* (Berkeley: University of California Press, 1981); Rey Chow, *Women and Chinese Modernity* (Minneapolis: University of Minnesota Press, 1992); Tani Barlow, *Gender Politics in Modern China* (Durham, NC: Duke University Press, 1993); Christina Gilmartin, et al., eds., *Engendering China: Women, Culture and the State* (Cambridge, MA: Harvard University Press, 1994); Elaine Kim and Changmoo Choi, eds., *Dangerous Women: Gender and Korean Nationalism* (New York: Routledge, 1998); Raka Ray, *Fields of Protest: Women's Movements in India* (Minneapolis: University of Minnesota Press, 1999); Nivedita Menon, *Gender and Politics in India* (Delhi: Vedams, 1999).

For Australia, see: Marian Simms, ed., *Australian Women and the Political System* (Melbourne: Longman Cheshire, 1984); Miriam Dixson, *The Real Matilda: Women and Identity in Australia* (Sydney: University of New South Wales Press, 1999).

For western Europe, see: Joni Lovenduski and Pippa Norris, *Gender and Party Politics* (London: Sage, 1993); Patricia Hilden, *Women, Work and Politics: Belgium, 1830–1914* (Oxford: Clarendon Press, 1993); Diane Sainsbury, ed., *Gendering Welfare States* (London: Sage, 1994); Gisela Bock and Pat Thane, eds., *Maternity and Gender Politics: Women and the Rise of the European Welfare States, 1880s–1950s* (London: Routledge, 1994); Claire Duchen, *Women's Rights and Women's Lives in France, 1944–1968* (London: Routledge, 1994); R. Amy Elman, *Sexual Politics and the European Union: The New Feminist Challenge* (Berghahn, 1996); Susan Kingsley Kent, *Gender and Power in Britain, 1640–1990* (London: Routledge, 1999).

For the Soviet Union and eastern Europe, see: Mary Buckley, *Women and Ideology in the Soviet Union* (Ann Arbor: University of Michigan Press, 1989); Nanette Funk and Magda Mueller, eds., *Gender Politics and Post-Communism: Reflections from Eastern Europe and the Former Soviet Union* (New York: Routledge, 1993); Barbara Einhorn, *Cinderella Goes to Market: Citizenship, Gender, and Women's Movements in East Central Europe* (London: Verso, 1993); Barbara E. Clements, *Bolshevik Women* (New York: Cambridge University Press, 1997); Elizabeth Wood, *The Baba and the Comrade: Gender and Politics in Revolutionary Russia* (Bloomington: Indiana University Press, 1997).

7 *Education and Culture*

Since Paleolithic times human beings have expressed themselves through what we would now term the arts or culture: painting and decorating walls and objects, making music with their voices and a variety of instruments, imagining and telling stories, dancing alone or in groups. Many of these cultural creations had a larger purpose: they were created to honor and praise gods, spirits, or human leaders, to help people remember events and traditions, to promote good hunting. Some of these creations were easy to do, and everyone in a culture was expected to participate in some way: to dance in order to bring rain or give thanks for a good harvest, to listen when stories were told, to take part in processions on special feast days. Some of these creations required particular talents or training, and were undertaken only by specialists.

We cannot know for certain who made the art that has survived from the Paleolithic and Neolithic periods, or created the stories, songs, and dances from those eras that have long disappeared. In all cultures with written records and most of them without them, however, men and women had differing opportunities to create artistic and cultural products. In cultures without writing or formal schooling, these differences often related to the purpose of the creative product: certain dances were performed by men to bring luck in hunting, for example, while others were performed by women to assure safe childbirths; certain types of objects were made and decorated by men to be used in ceremonies and everyday work, while others were made by women; certain stories were told by women and were sometimes for women's ears only, while others were told and heard by men. In the same way that groups created widely varying family forms and kinship patterns and widely varying religious traditions, they also created a dizzying array of gender distinctions relating to cultural products and events.

Though the training required to make certain cultural products in any culture could be very extensive, the development of writing generally necessitated an even longer period of formal training. The earliest writing systems in the world were pictographic, and often used thousands of characters rather than the twenty to thirty letters of most modern alphabetic writing systems. Thus to learn these systems well, one had to spend years of study and practice, much of it rote memorization of symbols and phrases. Even after alphabetic systems became more common in some parts of the world, learning to read and write took a number of years (especially in areas such as Egypt where three or four different writing systems were used for different purposes, and a fully trained scribe had to know all of them). This meant that learning to read and write was generally limited to two sorts of people: members of the elite who did not have to engage in productive labor to support themselves, and those who could hope to support themselves by writing or for whom writing was required as part of their work. The first group was comprised of both women and men, for some elite women have been literate in almost all of the world's cultures. Initially the second group consisted of professional scribes, copiers, and record-keepers, and later it included people engaged in many other occupations. This second group was predominantly male, for until the last century or so people who wrote professionally or who used writing in their work have almost all been men. Though women were generally not prohibited from attending schools that taught reading and writing, because they could not take positions as officials, administrators, or scribes, parents were unwilling to pay for training daughters who had no prospects of later employment and whose education would thus be wasted; as the Late Period Egyptian scribe Ankhsheshonq put it, "Instructing a woman is like holding a sack of sand whose sides have split open."

As reading became the basis for the transmission of information on more and more subjects, women were also often excluded from formal schooling in all subjects, again either specifically through regulations barring them from attending or because they had no way of acquiring the background skills needed to attend. This limitation of formal schooling to men was based partly on the ideas about gender differences in terms of reason and abilities discussed in chapter 4, and partly on the greater opportunities available for men in most cultures to use any education they received. Opportunities for women to receive an education were often linked to very specific purposes; nuns in both Christianity and Buddhism, for example, often learned to read and write in order to copy religious literature or perform other religious functions, and some women in areas where women were secluded were allowed to study medicine in order to care for female patients. These gender differences in terms of access to education also came to include artistic training; artistic academies and musical training programs were frequently open to men only and groups that promoted literary production were often limited to male members.

Because of these differences in access to training, men's cultural products – their paintings, sculpture, poetry, philosophy, and musical compositions – have always vastly outnumbered those of women; of the 31,200 entries in the biographical dictionary of Chinese artists compiled in the 1980s by Yü Chien-hua, for example, only 1,046 are women. For some cultures, such as ancient Rome, no complete written works by a female author have survived at all, and very few appear to have been written by female authors in the first place. (We know there were a few from fragments that have survived or mention of these works in the works of male authors.) In addition, until very recently, works by men were almost always viewed as better than those by women, according to the standards of the culture in which they were produced; as the nineteenth-century Chinese editor Wu Hao commented, "the works of women should be judged by lower standards; we cannot be too picky." These assessments have made people angry, and some scholars have searched for "Old Mistresses," great women artists of the past to counter-balance the well-known Old Masters. The art historian Linda Nochlin and others have argued that such a search is futile, however; given gender differences in access to training, works by female artists (unsurprisingly) could not achieve the level of quality of those by male artists. The relationship between training and greatness has generally not been recognized openly, however; the smaller quantity and lesser quality of women's creative products have instead been used as further evidence of their inferior potential, and, with somewhat circular reasoning, as a reason to continue denying women access to training.

Value judgments such as "great" or even "good" in terms of art, literature, and music are, of course, highly subjective and change over time; your tastes in art and music are probably different from those of your parents, and even different from those of your peers. In the past (and perhaps even in the present) those value judgments have also been shaped by the gender of the artist, writer, or musician. Artistic and literary forms and styles generally produced by men have been judged superior to and more significant than those produced by women. In eleventh-century Heian Japan, for example, the most esteemed literature was poetry written in Chinese with Chinese characters; women did not learn this literary form or even how to write Chinese characters, so their works, written in prose and in *kana*, a script with Japanese syllabic characters, were viewed as clearly inferior. To take another example, in the United States in the nineteenth century the most highly regarded artistic form was the history painting, depicting a historical or classical scene by a male artist trained in Europe; women who wished to express themselves usually picked up a needle instead of a brush, making a quilt or sampler, both of which were not even considered "art." It is ironic that in both of these cases contemporary tastes have reversed the earlier value judgments: Japanese prose works, such as Murasaki Shikibu's *Tale of Genji* or Sei Shonagon's *The Pillow Book*, are regularly read in translation and taught in courses, while the Chinese poetry of their male contemporaries interests no one; quilts and samplers are displayed prominently in major museums and can fetch very high prices, while history paintings are often regarded as rather boring. Some of this re-evaluation may also be based on gender, of course, as many people now are particularly interested in works by women writers and artists.

Along with hierarchies based on gender, in many cultures there are additional artistic and literary hierarchies based on the style of a piece, the background of the artist, the market for which it is produced, and a number of other factors. These hierarchies are often described as a dichotomy between "learned" and "popular," or "high" and "low" forms of literature, art, and music. This division changes over time, particularly as forms that are considered popular or even vulgar in one century become "classical" in the next. In the twentieth century certain artists have also intentionally attempted to or accidentally succeeded in blurring the boundaries between popular and learned forms, and people have become more interested in the popular folk art of earlier centuries.

Along with artistic and literary hierarchies within one culture there are also hierarchies among cultures. Cultures with a strong sense of their own traditions and superiority often regard the literature and art of other areas as inferior. For example, European colonists from the sixteenth through the nineteenth centuries dismissed the art and music of the Americas and Africa as "primitive," the work of poorly trained craftsmen. They regarded the art and music of China, India, and other parts of the world in which there were institutions of higher education and artistic training as "exotic." These assessments were communicated to people living in colonial areas, and many artists and writers began to imitate European styles or to blend local and imported traditions, creating new artistic forms. Such blended styles often became commercially successful in both Europe and the colonies; religious paintings in European styles from Mexico and Japan were sold widely, as was white and blue porcelain – called "china" because that is where it was made – with scenes that mixed European and Chinese elements.

In the twentieth century people became more interested in indigenous styles in both the present and past. Western-trained artists were clearly influenced by art from around the world, and Europeanized or mixed forms from colonial areas went out of style in a search for what was judged to be "authentic." People's notions of what is authentic in, for example, Native American jewelry or west African carvings, may often be incorrect, but it shaped (and continues to shape) what was being produced (often in mass quantities) as this is what would sell.

These artistic hierarchies within and among cultures interweave with gender hierarchies. Because women were often excluded from formal training, their art and literature is by definition part of popular or folk culture; the names of those who created popular works are often unrecorded, leading one scholar to title a recent book "anonymous was a woman." In the colonial period women often had less access to European cultural forms and so did not produce works that blended styles. Thus the more recent search for "authentic" indigenous styles has often meant that work by women artists is particularly prized. The embroideries of Hmong women often support their immigrant families in North American cities, as do those of displaced Palestinian women now living in Lebanon or Jordan.

It is important to remember throughout this chapter that until very recently in most of the world's cultures artists did not sign their works, or musicians attach their names to compositions, or storytellers claim authorship of a particular myth or narrative, so we have no way of knowing the gender of the original creator. It is thus difficult to assess exactly how training in singing, dancing, or composing songs or poems was shaped by gender. As with many other aspects of life we have discussed in this book, historians often extrapolate backwards from more recent times or make inferences based on indirect evidence. Because the earliest formal education and training programs around the world were generally limited to men, some historians conclude that a strong gender hierarchy in terms of access to culture was already present before the advent of writing. Others point to contemporary groups, such as the Inuit and Navaho peoples of North America, in which women's and men's artistic products are equally valued, and regard formal education as the *cause* of gender divisions. Historians in the first camp regard this as romanticizing the past, akin to the search for a primitive matriarchy, and note that there are also more recent groups without formal schooling in which art, music, storytelling, and other aspects of culture are sharply divided according to gender.

Classical and Post-classical Cultures

Though there is dispute about gender distinctions in learning and artistic production in cultures with little or no formal schooling, there is no dispute about this in the world's classical and post-classical cultures. In all of these cultures the vast majority of men and women had no opportunity to learn to read or write, but among the elites who did, men's access to learning was much greater than women's. The philosophies and religions that developed in these cultures, particularly Confucianism and the Greek philosophy of Plato and Aristotle, clearly regarded women as both inferior in reason and dangerous to men's spiritual and intellectual development. Thus the schools, academies, and other institutions for training that developed were for men only. No woman attended Plato's academy or spoke in any of the dialogues written by Plato. We know the names of a few female poets among the ancient Greeks, such as Sappho and Erinna, but the painters, sculptors, playwrights, and philosophers whose names we know are all men. In China the imperial university established in the Han period to train scholars and bureaucrats in the Confucian classics had perhaps as many as thirty thousand students, all of them male. In the Tang period opportunities for positions as court officials or governors were determined by one's success in the imperial scholarly examinations; women could neither take the examination nor hold official positions. In India men trained as professional philosophers composed the Upanishads, collections of texts dating from 700–500 BCE which emphasized the importance of contemplation and personal self-control; though women appear to have taken part in early discussions of these texts, they were later barred from studying them or other sacred works. In Muslim areas schools attached to mosques trained boys to read the Qur'an and offered training to advanced scholars in science, medicine, Islamic law and theology; by the sixteenth century there were over 150 Quranic schools in the west African city of Timbuktu, open to male students only.

In all classical and post-classical cultures, however, there were always a few women who learned to read or write, or who even became highly learned. They generally followed one of three patterns: they were members of elite families whose fathers were open to women's education; they were nuns or members of religious groups that prized reading; or they were courtesans for whom training in music, dancing, or literature made them more attractive to powerful and wealthy men.

One of the most famous of the first type was Ban Zhao (*c*.50–*c*.115 CE), who took over as court historian for the Han dynasty in China after her brother who had held that position died. She wrote poetry, essays, memorials, and *Instructions for Women* (*Nü-chieh*), which became her best-known work. This short book of instructions for women was frequently recopied and elaborated on for hundreds of years, probably because it fully agreed with Confucian teachings about women; as late as the eighteenth century it was one of the "Four Books for Women," seen as a counterpart to the Confucian "Four Books" studied by men in preparation for the imperial examinations. Ban Zhao writes:

> Let a woman modestly yield to others; let her respect others; let her put others first, herself last. Should she do something good, let her not mention it; should she do something bad, let her not deny it. Let her bear disgrace, let her even endure when others speak or do evil to her. Always let her seem to tremble and to fear.... If a husband does not control his wife, then the rules of conduct manifesting his authority are abandoned and broken. If a wife does not serve her husband, then the proper relationship (between men and women) and the natural order of things are neglected and destroyed.

Not all learned women agreed with Ban Zhao, however, for her own sister-in-law apparently wrote a treatise disputing her ideas, which has been lost. Ban Zhao's own life also served as a counter-example to her words, for she was widowed young and did not simply retire into seclusion but took a very public position as historian, tutor, and adviser to the imperial household.

Islam, Buddhism, and Christianity all provide many examples of women who learned to read and write for religious reasons. As we saw in chapter 5 the major religious works in all of the world's text-based religions were written by male authors, but women also wrote a variety of works for other women and the larger world. Reading the Qur'an is a central religious practice in Islam, and from the thirteenth century to the fifteenth century a few women in the Muslim world became known for their learning, particularly in the interpretation of *hadith* (statements relating the Prophet's actions and sayings). Buddhist nuns from the first centuries of Buddhism composed poems describing the ways in which they used study and practice to achieve enlightenment, which were initially transmitted orally but were eventually written down and preserved as *Therigatha* (Psalms of the Nuns). Hildegard of Bingen (1098–1179) was the founder and abbess of two Christian monastic houses for women, a visionary, and a prolific author. She entered a monastery when she was eight and was the first woman encouraged by the pope to write works of theology, which she did along with plays, poetry, and scientific works. She was also a talented artist and composer of chants, liturgy, and other types of music. Many of her musical compositions have been recorded recently by various artists and are available on compact disk and on several websites; her writings have seen several recent editions and translations and are frequently studied not only for their historical interest but as a guide to developing personal spirituality, as are the writings of early Buddhist nuns.

Current interest in Hildegard of Bingen or Buddhist nuns celebrates their creativity, and makes it possible to overlook the constraints under which they lived and wrote. To keep their achievements in perspective, however, it might be helpful to compare Hildegard with her rough contemporary Thomas Aquinas (1225–74). Like Hildegard, Aquinas came from an elite family, and received his early education in monastic houses. (Religious institutions were one of the most important places of learning for boys and men as well as women and girls, often providing the only avenue for a boy who was not a member of the elite to gain an education.) When he was twenty he went to the relatively new University of Paris, where – as with all European universities until the late nineteenth century – attendance was limited to men. Aquinas was a brilliant lecturer and thinker and he began a steady climb up the academic ladder, eventually becoming a professor of theology and adviser at the papal court. He was the most important philosopher in the Middle Ages, particularly known for his attempts to demonstrate that reason and faith are not contradictory, but complement one another. He was canonized as a saint shortly after his death in 1323, and his philosophical system, termed Thomism, was declared the official philosophy of the Catholic Church in 1869. In the twentieth century philosophers such as Étienne Gilson applied his system of philosophy to more contemporary political and social issues in a movement usually called neo-Thomism. The respect and acclaim accorded Aquinas's ideas over the centuries would simply have been impossible for Hildegard, who was relatively unknown until the 1980s. This difference would not have been surprising to Aquinas, who noted in the *Summa Theologica*, his major work, "woman is naturally subject to man, because in man the discretion of reason predominates."

Despite the opinions of Aquinas and similar thinkers in many cultures, noblewomen with enlightened fathers and women who were nuns were sometimes able to demonstrate their learning and creativity without censure. This was not the case, however, with the third type of woman able to gain an education, the cultured courtesan. In some classical and post-classical cultures certain artistic forms and activities put one beyond the bounds of honor. Musicians, dancers, actors, and storytellers were often considered somewhat disreputable, particularly if they performed for common people or in public settings like marketplaces rather than before rulers at courts. This taint was particularly strong for women involved in these activities, who may (and were always thought to) have offered sexual services along with entertainment. Ironically, however, their already tarnished reputations often allowed such women access to more education and training than those whose reputations were guarded by families intent on a good marriage match. In Korea, for example, Neo-Confucian ideas about women's secondary status and seclusion were emphasized in the early Yi dynasty (1392–1910), but female entertainers termed *kisang* continued to learn and perform traditional songs, dances, and rituals at a time when men were adopting imported Chinese rituals; though the Korean state regarded *kisang* as the lowest social class, they still entertained at the royal court and could attend public events. In ancient Athens, while citizen women were secluded in their homes, courtesans termed *hetaerae* from outside Athens wrote and performed poetry and music as part of their services to the men who supported them. There is a story that the most famous of these, Aspasia, may have written the funeral speech spoken by her lover, the Athenian general Pericles, after a major battle in which many Athenians died during the Peloponnesian War. (If she did, her words to Athenian women are similar to those of Ban Zhao to Chinese women: "Greatest will be her [glory] who is least talked of among the men whether for good or for bad.")

The role of professional entertainer/hostess/courtesan continued for centuries in cultures like ancient Athens where husbands and wives did not socialize together, with the best-known example that of the geisha in Japan. Opinions about the origins of the geisha tradition are varied, but it is clear that by the Tokugawa period (1603–1867) certain parts of major cities, termed the *ukiyo* or Floating World, were set aside for entertainment. Here girls who were to become geisha – often sold or given by their parents or families into geisha houses – received many years of training in singing, storytelling, dancing, and playing musical instruments. Elite men socialized in geisha teahouses and paid large sums of money for their services, which might include sexual services but were often limited to conversation and entertainment; geisha sometimes performed customary dances and music in public as well. Connections with geisha were expected for Japanese political, military, and economic leaders until World War II, and are still found today among top executives or the very wealthy, as the enormous expense of geisha entertainment makes this a mark of status. Successful geisha who chose their patrons well could eventually become self-supporting and open their own houses, which offered a few women in Japan the chance for economic independence.

The link between dishonor and speaking or performing in public may have given some women greater opportunities, but in general it worked to restrict women's access to learning, and particularly their abilities to demonstrate their learning and talents. Women who spoke in public or circulated their writings so that others could see them were suspected of dishonor, particularly by men who were themselves educated. A fifteenth-century Italian humanist commented, "an eloquent woman is never chaste," a sentiment with which an eighteenth-century shogun in Japan agreed, noting, "To cultivate women's skills would be harmful." Such opinions were also shared more widely and reflected in popular sayings, such as one from China: "She who is unskilled in arts and literature is a virtuous woman." In both Europe and Asia there were also voices which argued the opposite, asserting that literacy would allow women to become *more* virtuous by reading instruction books and moral guides, but these were always in the minority.

The Renaissance

All of the world's classical and post-classical cultures made gender distinctions in terms of access to education and artistic training, and these were further rigidified during the early modern period. The situation in Europe has been particularly well studied in this era, in part because there are so many sources and in part because the institutions and value judgments developed in Europe shaped all later western developments. This is the period of the Renaissance, which began in Italy in the fourteenth century and is conventionally viewed as the beginning of the "modern" era in terms of culture. Though Christianity continued to be central to the lives of most Europeans, during the Renaissance art, music, and literature with secular subjects and themes also began to be appreciated by upper- and middle-class urban residents. A new attitude toward artists, writers, composers, and other creators of culture also developed. During the Middle Ages such individuals had been viewed as artisans just like shoemakers or bakers, and their products as the creations of a workshop, not an individual; this is the reason we know the names of so few medieval artists in Europe (and so few artists from elsewhere in the world). During the Renaissance the notion of the artist or writer as creative genius began to develop; artists started to sign their works, and certain branches of art – in particular painting, sculpture, and architecture – were deemed more significant than other types of art, such as needlework, porcelain manufacture, goldsmithing, and furniture making. This division hardened in the sixteenth century, particularly through the influence of Giorgio Vasari, who is often described as the first art historian. Painting, sculpture, and architecture were termed the "major" arts and everything else the "minor" or "decorative" arts. A similar split occurred in literature, with certain types of writing, such as poetry, history, and epics, now defined as "literature" and other types of writing, such as letters and diaries, excluded from this category.

The line between art and music by professionals and that by amateurs grew increasingly sharp, as did that between forms of art considered high art or serious literature, and those forms considered crafts or non-literary types of writing. This line between professional and amateur, art and craft, was one that was difficult for women to cross, for they were generally not accepted into programs for training artists or musicians, and were discouraged from publishing any written work that was not religious.

New institutions for the creation of culture also developed during the Renaissance in Europe. Though many visual artists and musicians still trained through apprenticeships, rulers also set up court-supported schools and hired large numbers of painters, sculptors, musicians, and composers. After the development of the printing press, journals which included and promoted the work of poets and other writers began to be published at regular intervals. Regional and national academies and societies which rewarded and supported creativity in science, literature, and the visual arts were established, usually with a very limited number of members. These journals, academies, and societies increasingly determined which artistic and literary genres and styles and which scientific theories would be judged praiseworthy, and thus which artists, writers, and scientists would get commissions or support from patrons.

All of these developments had dramatic effects on women's ability to participate in the creation of culture, particularly in those areas and genres judged most important. As in many cultures, women were often by regulation or practice excluded from schools and academies; their writings were also rarely accepted by literary journals. The self-promotion required by an artist, writer, composer, or thinker attempting to gain the support of a patron was judged unacceptable behavior when done by a woman. Europe's intellectuals debated whether women were capable of true creative genius, or had the rational capacity for scientific or philosophical insights. The major arts, the most celebrated forms of music and literature, and the most noted philosophical ideas were all regarded as tied to characteristics deemed masculine: forcefulness, strength, power, logic, singularity of purpose. The work which women artists, writers, and scientists did produce was often judged to be the result not of genius, but of nimble fingers, diligence in observation, skill at following the example of a male teacher, or bee-like industriousness, in other words, "craft," not "art" or "science." If her work could not be dismissed in this way, the woman was said to have "overcome the limitations of her sex" and set herself apart from all other women, or she was judged a hermaphrodite, or the work was attributed to her male teacher or a male member of her family.

The gender bias inherent in the Renaissance division of the visual arts into "art" and "craft" and "major" and "minor" meant that new genres which women created would never achieve the status of major arts, and genres in which substantial numbers of women continued to work would decrease in status. Two examples of the former are miniature portraits painted on ivory, invented by Rosalba Carriera (1675–1757) and paper collage, invented by Mary Delany (1700–88). One example of the latter is flower painting, which was originally an important branch of still life, but was later dismissed as trivial. The continuation of Renaissance values and their links with gender can be seen in the comments of the art historian Maurice Grant writing in the 1970s, who asserted that flower painting "demands no genius of a mental and spiritual kind, but only the genius of taking pains and specific craftsmanship"; the best proof of this, in his eyes, is that of all known flower painters "at least half of them are women."

The best example of loss of status in an art form is embroidery, which in the Middle Ages was practiced by both women and men often organized into male-directed craft guilds and paid on a scale equivalent to painting, but which throughout the Renaissance became increasingly identified as feminine. Middle- and upper-class girls were taught to embroider because embroidered clothing and household objects became signs of class status, and because embroidery was seen as the best way to inculcate the traits most admired in a woman: passivity, chastity, attention to detail, domesticity. As more embroidery was produced in the home for domestic consumption it was increasingly considered an "accomplishment" rather than an art, and those who embroidered for pay received lower wages, except for the male designers of embroidery patterns and the few men employed as court embroiderers by Europe's monarchs.

Along with changes in cultural institutions and values, technological changes increased the gender disparity in literacy and creativity in Renaissance Europe, and perhaps in other areas where similar technology was invented. The printing press with movable metal type was first developed in Korea in the thirteenth century, and independently in Germany in the fifteenth century. (Both of these inventions were inspired by Chinese printing with wooden blocks, which was much older.) In both of these places, printing made reading much easier, as printed texts were generally more legible than handwritten ones, and encouraged the growth of literacy. In Korea, printing combined with the new phonetic *han'gul* writing system in the fifteenth century to lay the foundation for a very high rate of literacy. In Germany, the Protestant Reformation, which began in the 1520s, encouraged Bible-reading, and religious reformers supported the establishment of schools. Formal schooling opportunities for boys increased steadily in urban areas, though schools were much slower in coming to rural areas and the number of schools was never as many as reformers hoped.

The establishment of schools for girls in cities and the countryside lagged far behind that of boys' schools in Germany and the rest of Europe. By 1580 in central Germany, for example, 50 percent of the parishes had licensed German-language schools for boys, and 10 percent for girls, while a survey of schools taken at the same time in Venice found about 4,600 male pupils, or about one-fourth of the school-age boys in the city, and only thirty girls. Opportunities for girls increased in the seventeenth century with the spread of the female teaching orders such as the Ursulines, but a count of school-age children in southern France in the late eighteenth century still found about two-thirds of boys receiving some schooling, compared to only one girl in fifty. Reading and writing were taught separately, with girls who were taught to read often not taught to write because they attended school for a shorter time than their brothers. Writing was also more expensive to learn, as pupils had to have some material on which to write, which parents were often unwilling to provide for their daughters. Teaching women to read but not write was the result not only of an economic decision on the part of parents, but also of contemporary notions about the ideal woman. Learning to read would allow a woman to discover classical and Christian examples of proper female behavior and to absorb the ideas of great (male) authors. Learning to write, on the other hand, would enable her to express her own ideas, an ability which few thinkers regarded as important and some saw as threatening. Higher education was, of course, even more gender specific; like their medieval counterparts, the new universities established in the sixteenth century were for male students only, as were the humanist academies founded in some Italian cities. This also appears to have been true in Korea, where the rise of Neo-Confucianism in the Yi dynasty meant that women were generally excluded from formal schooling, even though learning to read was now easier.

The fact that reading and writing were taught separately makes measuring literacy very difficult, as there is no way to tell that someone could read if he or she could not write. Historians often measure literacy by noting how many people signed their names on documents such as marriage contracts or wills, but the poor writing on such signatures, particularly those of women, suggests that their name might have been the only thing these people ever wrote. There is also a distinction between basic literacy and habitual book-reading, with the latter better measurable by the sale of books or indications of their ownership in wills and inventories than by signatures. Taken together, these various measures suggest that by the eighteenth century in Europe almost all upper-class men and women could read, and only a small minority of male or female peasants could. The gender gap was the greatest in the middle of the social scale, with about twice as many men as women able to write at least their name.

The gender patterns in education and culture established in the Renaissance accompanied Europeans wherever they set up colonies, with racial and ethnic hierarchies added to those of gender. Schools that were established for the children of colonists were often divided by gender, with higher education reserved for boys; in some areas, missionaries also ran schools for indigenous children, but those teaching more than basic reading and writing were limited to boys, who the missionaries hoped would later serve as pastors to their own people. In Catholic colonies convents offered a small number of indigenous girls the opportunity to gain literacy, though most local girls and women lived in convents as servants or lay-sisters, not as fully professed nuns, and so were not educated to the same level as European-background women.

In areas of the world that were not colonized in the early modern period, gender patterns in education developed in ways similar to those in Europe. By the eighteenth century in China, middle-class women in urban areas were more likely to be literate than they had been earlier; books of instructions for women, such as Ban Zhao's *Instructions for Women* and its many imitators, poured off of presses, and were discussed by women in literary discussion groups modeled after those of men. Women also read plays and other works of fiction, with the ardent female reader herself becoming a figure in literature and painting. Such readers sometimes wrote poetry themselves, although, as in Europe, the best poems were often ascribed to male ghostwriters. Doubts about the authenticity of various writings might even lead to doubts about the actual existence of a woman author; so many stories circulated about the most celebrated of these reader-poets, the doomed concubine Xiaoqing (1595–1612), that it is difficult to separate legend from life.

Democracy, Modernity, and Literacy in the Eighteenth to Twentieth Centuries

Beginning in the late eighteenth century, new ideas about the relations between education and the good of the state developed in many parts of the world, which eventually led to mass schooling and, by the nineteenth or twentieth century, to near total literacy in many countries. The expansion of schooling has often been viewed as part of the growth of democracy and industrialism, for the benefits of educating voters and workers are clear at the beginning of the twenty-first century. A problem with this explanation is that eighteenth- and early nineteenth-century democracies did not extend voting rights to the vast majority of the populace, nor did early industrialism depend on formal schooling, but often on the labor of children whom mandatory schooling would eventually remove from the workplace. Mass schooling actually developed earliest in countries such as Prussia and Sweden that were authoritarian politically and backwards economically; in these countries, schooling was explicitly linked to obedience to state authorities, religious orthodoxy, and the development of a modern army, in which soldiers would not only have the technical expertise to handle modern weapons but would also have learned from an early age to follow instructions and orders without question. In Sweden, for example, a royal decree from 1723 ordered parents to "diligently see that their children applied themselves to book reading and the study of the lessons in Catechism," and to teach farmhands and maidservants along with their own children. Parishes began to keep records of the reading ability of all inhabitants, with householders fined if their children could not read and those unable to read prohibited from marrying. By 1800 almost the entire population of Sweden was able to read at least simple religious texts, though it would take another hundred years before they could all write.

Both the democratic and the authoritarian model of the importance of education would seem to apply to boys and men only, for voters and soldiers (with the exception of a few women who dressed in men's clothing) were all male. Not surprisingly, there were more schools established for boys than for girls in countries that began to open publicly funded schools in the nineteenth century, but girls were not completely excluded. Educational reformers, whether democratic or authoritarian, regarded the schooling of girls as important, for these girls would eventually become mothers and thus responsible for the early upbringing of future soldiers and voters. In country after country in the nineteenth century women's education came to be linked with the good of the state. The Mexican legislator Justo Sierra, for example, noted that Mexican schools were "forming men and women for the home; this is our supreme goal. In doing it, we firmly believe that we are performing a service beyond comparison with any in the benefit of the Republic. . . . The educated woman will be truly one for the home; she will be the companion and collaborator of man in the formation of the family." The United States physician and politician Benjamin Rush agreed, commenting, "The equal share that every citizen has in the liberty and the possible share he may have in the government of our country make it necessary that our ladies should be qualified to a certain degree, by a peculiar and suitable education, to concur in instructing their sons in the principles of liberty and government." In Japan, education was to prepare girls to become "good wives and wise mothers," an aim so strongly supported by the government that by 1910, 98 percent of school-age boys and girls were enrolled in elementary school.

Political authorities in the nineteenth century were aware that mass schooling could be very expensive and sought ways to achieve their goals in the cheapest way possible. Sweden solved the problem by requiring parents to teach their children and dependents, a completely unpaid work force, but this was not a workable solution for most countries. They turned instead to the next cheapest thing: women. Religious schools increasingly turned elementary education over to nuns, who were paid nothing, and secular schools hired young women for wages that were next to nothing. School teaching, which had been a male profession in the eighteenth century, quickly came to be dominated by women; it has been estimated that about one out of every five white women in Massachusetts in the 1840s and 1850s was a teacher at some point in her life, and by the end of the century school teaching in Latin America as well was dominated by women. This regendering of school teaching followed the standard path of any type of cultural or economic activity: once women entered the field in great numbers, both salaries and prestige went down. School teaching was seen primarily as an occupation for young women; though male school teachers could marry, female school teachers who married were fired, a practice that continued until the mid-twentieth century in many areas. Defenders of this practice argued that a woman's teaching continued, of course, after marriage, with her most precious pupils – her own children. They provided books of instruction for mothers based on contemporary educational theories in what some historians have termed the "professionalization of motherhood."

Nineteenth-century school teachers were generally required to be little more than literate themselves, but reformers in the nineteenth century also pushed for the opening of secondary and advanced education to women. Those who opposed women's higher education did not link this with a loss of honor the way earlier writers had, but with a loss of something even more precious: reproductive capacity. They argued that using her brain too much would cause a woman to faint or her uterus to shrivel because it was deprived of blood. Reformers countered these arguments by continuing to stress that education would make women better mothers, enabling them to improve the lives of their families and children. Such arguments, combined with the practical need for female teachers and nurses and steady pressure by individual women, gradually led to more opportunities, with most European and many North and South American universities opening their doors to women in the late nineteenth or early twentieth centuries, though often with restrictions on what they could study and a quota sharply limiting their numbers; in 1913 there were about 4,000 female students at French universities compared to about 38,000 men. By the 1870s and 1880s women were also attending some medical schools in North and South America and Europe, though male students often protested, throwing mud and stones, or, in one instance in Scotland, bringing a sheep into the classroom with the comment that they had learned "inferior animals" were no longer to be excluded.

Opportunities for education for indigenous boys and girls in colonial areas during the nineteenth and early twentieth centuries were provided primarily by missionaries and religious orders, and parents hesitated to send their children as they feared they would convert. Such fears were well-founded, for nineteenth-century missionaries saw education as a way both to "civilize" and "Christianize" the people among whom they worked; the education they provided for girls thus included a heavy dose of domestic science, designed, in the words of Jules de Coppet, the governor-general of French West Africa, to "permit the evolution of the family...and permanently install our action within the indigenous society." In the United States such schooling extended to Native Americans in an attempt to compel an "evolution of the family"; as various tribes were forced off their lands and settled on reservations, officials and missionaries often removed children from their homes and sent them to boarding schools, thus disrupting family life completely.

Advocates of education for women often used conservative rhetoric about motherhood to achieve their aims, but they also viewed women's education as a sign of modernity and progress. In India, for example, male and female reformers advocated the opening of girls' schools along with other changes to improve the status of women, and a few schools were opened in major cities, largely to provide appropriately educated wives for western-educated Indian men. Graduates of these schools and other women who had received an education began to publish journals for women in Hindi, Urdu, and English. There were similar developments in Egypt, Turkey, Iran, and Tunisia, where women were actively recruited as teachers so that girls could learn in an all-female environment. In Egypt a separate school was opened for female health officers as early as the 1830s, with women trained in immunization and obstetrics as well as general medical care.

It is important to recognize that the expansion of educational opportunities for women in many colonial and non-industrialized areas was
limited to a tiny portion of the urban elite, in the same way that schools
in general reached very few people. In the Brazilian census of 1872, for
example, out of a population of roughly 10 million, roughly 1 million
free men and half a million free women could read and write, while only
about 1,000 enslaved men and 500 slave women could. Numbers in
India were even lower: the total number of women who were literate in
any language according to the 1901 census was 0.7 percent, rising by the
1946 census to 6 percent, with male literacy about double that of female.
Thus in most parts of the world until after World War II, social class and
family background were as important as gender in determining access to
education.

Most postcolonial states in Africa and Asia provided more access to
education than the colonial governments did, and literacy rates slowly
began to rise during the 1960s. As elsewhere in the world, however, girls
generally attended school less often and for a shorter period than boys,
with the widest gap in the poorest countries. Schools often charged fees
for attendance, uniforms, and books, and parents were more willing to
pay school fees for their sons than their daughters, for the employment
opportunities for educated young men are greater than those for educated young women. Statistics collected by UNESCO since the 1960s
indicate, not surprisingly, that the gender disparity is smallest in elementary education, and greatest in post-secondary education. Latin America
and east Asia broke with this pattern by the 1980s, however, with female
attendance at universities almost equaling that of male; in these areas, the
gender disparity in higher education was actually smaller than it was in
Europe and the United States at the time.

In Muslim countries cultural and economic factors limiting women's
education have been counter-balanced by the need for female professionals and, in countries such as Kuwait and Saudi Arabia, by enormous
oil revenues. In the 1970s and 1980s rates of higher education for
middle- and upper-class women rose dramatically; by 1987 in Kuwait,
for example, 21 percent of women and only 12 percent of men of
university age were enrolled in school, a gender disparity almost the
exact reverse of that of Japan, where 18 percent of the university-age
women and 28 percent of the university-age men were enrolled.
Women in Muslim areas have been most active in occupations where
they cater to women and girls, such as teaching and health care, but also
entered fields such as engineering and chemistry, in which they could

often work in sex-segregated workplaces. The opportunities for educated women in the Muslim world declined somewhat in the 1980s and 1990s when an economic slowdown led to calls for their returning home to their "natural" vocations as wives and mothers, but only in Taliban-held Afghanistan were professional women completely forced to stop working.

Equality of educational opportunities was an explicit goal of the communist governments established around the world in the twentieth century, and in all of them the literacy rates of men and women rose significantly and slowly became more equal; in 1978, for example, girls in China made up 45 percent of the primary school enrollment and 24 percent of college and university enrollment. Nadya Krupskaya, a leading Soviet thinker and Lenin's wife, was among many who linked women's education with the advance of socialism, arguing that women should study "agronomy, animal husbandry, sanitation, technology and so on. It is necessary for them to study those fields of production where a shortage of skilled workers threatens to have serious repercussions for the republic of workers and peasants." Many women in the Soviet Union followed her advice, for by 1968 women made up 72 percent of the medical doctors, 35 percent of the lawyers, and 30 percent of the engineers. (Comparable statistics in that year for the United States were 7 percent of the doctors, 3.5 percent of the lawyers, and 1 percent of the engineers.) Such statistics were often cited as an indication of the superiority of communism, but they overlooked the fact that medicine and law and to some degree engineering did not have the high status and high pay that they did in the western world; as we saw in chapter 3, status and privileges came from Party leadership, in which there were very few women.

As Krupskaya's words suggest, educated women in communist countries were expected to put the needs of "the republic of workers and peasants" first, above considerations of gender inequality; their writings, art, music, and other cultural products were to serve the goals of the state. This was also true to some degree in formerly colonial areas in the twentieth century, and most educated women joined educated men to focus on the themes of national liberation and the postcolonial condition in their poetry, plays, essays, novels, and songs. In both situations, however, some writers and artists explicitly criticized gender relations in political and family life. In 1979 in the Soviet Union a group of women wrote, typed, and circulated an underground publication *Woman and Russia: An Almanac to Women about Women* which included articles on abortion, child care, alcoholism and rape, and maternity hospitals, along with poetry and fiction. The editors and contributors were investigated and interrogated by the KGB and four of them were eventually exiled; Tatyana Mamonova, the chief editor, commented that they expected this, but did not expect the lack of support from male dissidents, who turned out to be "nonconformists only in their art; in their attitude toward women, they [were] absolutely conformist and sexist." In *Double Yoke* (1982) the Nigerian novelist Buchi Emecheta portrays a woman caught between traditional expectations of wifely obedience and contemporary values of achievement and independence. In *Woman at Point Zero* (1977), by the Egyptian physician and writer Nawal El-Sa'adawi, the main character is a woman forced to undergo a clitoridectomy and marry an abusive older husband; she later works as a prostitute and is ultimately deserted by the man she loves.

Writing by women in western countries during the 1970s also began to consider issues of gender more explicitly, in large part because of the development of feminist consciousness with the women's liberation movement. This led some theorists to explore the question of women's relationship to language itself. Most western languages are gender-inflected to some degree, and in all of them until the 1970s the male pronoun and other male words were used to stand for both men and women. Along with overt gender structures in language the historical dominance of the male point of view in all types of literature left a feeling of "speechlessness" in some European and American women writers, and they speculated about whether they could create a separate "women's language." This speculation led to a search for such a language in the past, and to considerations of instances in which women seemed to have developed separate rituals or even a separate culture; women's learning patterns, moral development, body language, and word choice were all described as distinct from those of men. This was accompanied by the creation of explicitly feminist music, art, sculpture, poetry, and other forms of creative expression. In some instances these new pieces were linked to historical examples of women's creativity; the visual artist Judy Chicago, for example, set up "The Dinner Party" with elaborate place settings of painted plates and embroidered table-runners for 39 educated and creative women, beginning with the Great Goddess and ending with Georgia O'Keeffe.

This search for and creation of a separate women's literary and artistic language struck many – including some feminist writers and artists – as misguided, for it seemed to be returning to notions of gender differences in creativity that had always limited women's creative opportunities in the past. The notion of a "women's language" or "women's art" appeared to them to be based on some sort of biological essentialism, linking the brain and the womb in ways that were acceptable to Aristotle or Aquinas or Wu Hao, but not to those advocating greater equality of opportunity. By the 1990s western theorists had largely moved away from even a whiff of essentialism in favor of a social constructionist point of view; if gender differences are to be regarded as socially constructed, historically changing, and perhaps even performative and easily manipulable, they argued, it made little sense to talk about any type of "women's language."

Discussions about a separate women's culture in the contemporary world may be more appropriate in areas of the world in which men and women are generally segregated and in which gender is clearly understood as rooted in unchanging male and female natures. Though highly educated women and men from all over the world increasingly share an international literary and artistic culture, separate rituals for men and women continue in many parts of the world. Women in Tunisian villages, for example, compose and sing lullabies to their children, expressing their hopes and dreams for the child. Bedouin women in Egypt tell elaborate stories, embellishing plots they have learned from their mothers and grandmothers. It is difficult to say what the further expansion of education, and of commercialized popular culture in the form of music, videos, and web programming from urban areas or from other countries will do to this type of traditional culture, though it has certainly been confronted with outside influences in the past without disappearing.

As with so many other of the topics considered in this book, the relationship between gender and culture at the beginning of the twenty-first century is full of contradictory tendencies. As measured by publication figures, school enrollments, artistic and musical production, and various other statistics, women's and men's opportunities are becoming more equal. In many of the countries of Latin America and the Caribbean the percentage of women in higher education exceeded that of men beginning in the 1980s, which also happened in the United States for the first time in 1998. Though only 5 percent of the art hanging in New York museums was by women in 1990, nearly 20 percent of art in galleries (which feature contemporary artists) was by women. On the other hand, gender inequities still exist at all levels.

Only 11 percent of the full professors in US colleges and universities in 1993 were female, though more than 50 percent of the part-time work force at those colleges was female. Though women now have 20 percent of the art in galleries, more than half the artists and two-thirds of those earning bachelors' degrees in Fine Arts are women, so female artists continue to have greater difficulties in getting their work shown. Even at the most elite level, gender disparities are very clear. Many more of the highest paid movie stars in the world – those commanding over $20 million a picture in 2000 – are men rather than women. Among the highest paid sports stars – certainly a significant part of contemporary cultural life – the disparities are even greater.

Some of these disparities are the result of accumulated years – or centuries – of gender distinctions, and may eventually disappear. Prophets of the new information technologies also predict that older cultural forms – the university, the gallery, the musical recording – will disappear in the near future, replaced by computer-housed forms of training, display, and distribution. Advocates of these developments praise the possibilities, arguing that this will democratize culture, making it open to anyone with creative ideas and access to a computer. Critics note that access to a computer is at present impossible for most of the world's population, for the majority have still never used a telephone, much less a keyboard; if and when they do gain such access this will also link them with global commercialization and lead to an end to individual local cultures, not their flourishing. Disagreements about how the new information technologies will shape gender are similarly sharp. Will the striking initial disparity in boys' and girls,' men's and women's computer use continue, making access to new forms just as gender-related as access to older forms? (This disparity can only partially be accounted for by the high percentage of web traffic devoted to pornography.) Or will the internet and the web, in which one's identity can so easily be hidden, accomplish what centuries of women writing under male names could not, a valuation of creative productions based on the product alone and not the producer? If this happens will it be a good thing, or will something be lost?

Further Reading

Feminist criticism has led the way in understanding the relationship between gender and genre, and between gender and cultural concepts such as genius, professionalism, originality, and talent. See, for example: Linda Nochlin, "Why are there no great women artists?" in Elizabeth C. Baker and Thomas B. Hess, eds., *Art and Sexual Politics: Women's Liberation, Women Artists and Art History* (New York: Macmillan, 1973), pp. 1–43; Rozsika Parker and Griselda Pollock, *Old Mistresses: Women, Art and Ideology* (New York: Pantheon Books, 1981); Berenice A. Carroll, "The politics of 'originality': women and the class system of the intellect," *Journal of Women's History* 2 (1990): 136–63; Norma Broude and Mary D. Garrard, eds., *Expanding Discourse: Feminism and Art History* (New York: HarperCollins, 1992); Fredrika H. Jacobs, *Defining the Renaissance Virtuosa: Women Artists and the Language of Art History and Criticism* (Cambridge: Cambridge University Press, 1997); Bonnie Smith, *The Gender of History: Men, Women, and Historical Practice* (New York: Oxford University Press, 1998); Judy Chicago and Edward Lucie-Smith, *Women and Art: Contested Territory* (London: Weidenfeld and Nicolson, 1999).

There are many collections of the works of women artists, most of which include discussion of the social context within which the women worked. For general overviews, see: Wendy Slatkin, *Women Artists in History from Antiquity to the 20th Century*, 2nd edn, (Englewood Cliffs, NJ: Prentice-Hall, 1990); Nancy G. Heller and Nancy Grubb, eds., *Women Artists: An Illustrated History* (New York: Abbeville Press, 1997); Whitney Chadwick, *Women, Art, and Society* (London: Thames and Hudson, 1996). For artists working in Europe and North America, see: Eleanor Tufts, *Our Hidden Heritage: Five Centuries of Women Artists* (New York: Paddington Press, 1974); Ann Sutherland Harris and Linda Nochlin, *Women Artists: 1550– 1950* (New York: Alfred A. Knopf, 1976); Charlotte Rubinstein, *American Women Artists: From Early Indian Times to the Present* (New York: Avon, 1982). For Asia, see: Marsha Weidner, *Flowering in the Shadows: Women in the History of Chinese and Japanese Painting* (Honolulu: University of Hawaii Press, 1990). Rozsika Parker's *The Subversive Stitch: Embroidery and the Making of the Feminine* (London: Woman's Press, 1984) places women's embroidery over many centuries within its ideological and social context. For a work that uses gender as a tool of analysis without focusing specifically on women artists, see Gladys Engel Lang and Kurt Lang, *Etched in Memory: The Building and Survival of Artistic Reputation* (Chapel Hill: University of North Carolina Press, 1990). For a really fun revisionist view of art history, see *The Guerrilla Girls' Bedside Companion to the History of Western Art* (New York: Penguin Books, 1998), put together by the Guerrilla Girls, a group of women artists and art professionals who use posters and actions (in which they wear gorilla masks) to expose sexism and racism in the art world.

There are fewer studies of music than the visual arts, though more are appearing every year. For broad overviews of women musicians, see: Carol Neuls-Bates, *Women in Music: An Anthology of Source Readings from the Middle Ages to the Present* (New York: Harper and Row, 1982); Jane Bowers and Judith Tick, eds., *Women Making Music: The Western Art Tradition, 1150–1950* (Urbana: University of Illinois Press, 1986); Ellen Koskoff, ed., *Women and Music in Cross-cultural Perspective* (New York: Greenwood Press, 1987); Kimberly Marshall, ed., *Rediscovering the Muses: Women's Musical Traditions* (Boston, MA: Northeastern University Press, 1993). For more focused studies, see: Susan C. Cook and Judy S. Tsou, *Cecelia Reclaimed: Feminist Perspectives on Gender and Music* (Urbana: University of Illinois Press, 1994); Lucy O'Brien, *She Bop: The Definitive History of Women in Rock, Pop, and Soul* (New York: Penguin Books, 1996); Lucy Green, *Music, Gender, Education* (Cambridge: Cambridge University Press, 1997); Ralph P. Locke and Cyrilla Barr, eds., *Cultivating Music in America: Women Patrons and Activists since 1860* (Berkeley: University of California Press, 1997).

While the interplay between music and gender has only recently begun to be studied, that between literature and gender has been the focus of a huge number of studies. This is particularly so for studies of women writers, which must number in the thousands; those titled "women writers in . . ." or "women authors in . . ." alone number in the hundreds, and can be easily searched on-line. Studies of men writers are, of course, not identified as such, and only a few of the most recent have begun to consider the gender of their subject. For studies of women writers, the following bibliographies and guides can provide some introduction: Graciela N. V. Corvalán, *Latin American Women Writers in English Translation: A Bibliography* (Los Angeles: Latin American Studies Center, California State University, 1980); Diane E. Marting, *Women Writers of Spanish America: An Annnotated Bio-bibliographical Guide* (New York: Greenwood Press, 1987); Gwenn Davis and Beverly A. Joyce, *Personal Writings by Women to 1900: A Bibliography of American and British Writers* (Norman: University of Oklahoma Press, 1989); Debra Adelaide, *Bibliography of Australian Women's Literature, 1795–1990* (Port Melbourne, Victoria: Thorpe, 1991); Kristina R. Huber, *Women in Japanese Society: An Annotated Bibliography of Selected English Language Materials* (New York: Greenwood Press, 1992); Betty S. Travitsky and Josephine A. Roberts, *English Women Writers, 1500–1640: A*

Reference Guide (1750– 1996) (New York: G. K. Hall, 1997); Sharon Ouditt, *Women Writers of the First World War: An Annotated Bibliography* (London: Routledge, 2000).

Most studies of formal schooling until very recently made little or no mention of the fact that this was limited to boys and men. For general studies that do consider women's and girls' education, see: O. W. Furley, *A History of Education in East Africa* (New York: NOK Publishers, 1978); Teshome G. Wagow, *Education in Ethiopia: Prospect and Retrospect* (Ann Arbor: University of Michigan Press, 1979); S. Alexander Rippa, *Education in a Free Society: An American History* (New York: Longman, 1988); Paul F. Grendler, *Schooling in Renaissance Italy: Literacy and Learning, 1300– 1600* (Baltimore, MD: Johns Hopkins University Press, 1989); H. Warren Button, *History of Education and Culture in America* (Englewood Cliffs, NJ: Prentice-Hall, 1989); Michael Alexander, *The Growth of English Education, 1348–1648* (University Park: Pennsylvania State University Press, 1990); John F. Cleverley, *The Schooling of China: Tradition and Modernity in Chinese Education* (Sydney: Allen and Unwin, 1991); Benjamin A. Elman and Alexander Woodside, eds., *Education and Society in Late Imperial China, 1600– 1900* (Berkeley: University of California Press, 1994); Pavla Miller, *Transformations of Patriarchy in the West, 1500– 1900* (Bloomington: Indiana University Press, 1998); Stephen Tozer, et al., *School and Society: Historical and Contemporary Perspectives* (Boston, MA: McGraw-Hill, 1998); Peter N. Stearns, *Schools and Students in Industrial Society: Japan and the West, 1870–1940* (Boston, MA: Bedford Books, 1998); R. A. Houston, *Literacy in Early Modern England: Culture and Education 1500–1800*, 2nd edn (London: Longman, 2001).

There are a number of studies that focus specifically on women's education. For Europe, see: Christine Johansen, *Women's Struggle for Higher Education in Russia, 1855–1900* (Kingston and Montreal: McGill-Queens University Press, 1987); Dale Spender, ed., *The Education Papers: Women's Quest for Equality in Britain, 1850–1912* (New York: Routledge, 1987); Gerda Lerner, *The Creation of Feminist Consciousness: From the Middle Ages to 1870* (Oxford: Oxford University Press, 1993); Christine Ruane, *Gender, Class, and the Professionalization of Russian City Teachers, 1860–1914* (Pittsburgh, PA: University of Pittsburgh Press, 1994); Sharif Gemie, *Women and Schooling in France, 1815–1914: Gender, Authority, and Identity in the Female Schooling Sector* (Keele: Keele University Press, 1995); Anne T. Quartararo, *Women Teachers and Popular Education in Nineteenth-Century France: Social Values and Coroporate Identity at the Normal School Institution* (Newark: University of Delaware Press,

1995); Sara Delamont, *A Woman's Place in Education: Historical and Socio-logical Perspectives on Gender and Education* (Aldershot: Avebury, 1996); Kenneth Charlton, *Women, Religion and Education in Early Modern England* (London: Routledge, 1999); Barbara J. Whitehead, ed., *Women's Education in Early Modern Europe: A History 1500–1800* (New York: Garland, 1999); Jane Martin, *Women and the Politics of Schooling in Victorian and Edwardian England* (London: Leicester University Press, 1999). For the United States, see: Lynn Gordon, *Gender and Higher Education in the Progressive Era* (New Haven, CT: Yale University Press, 1990); John L. Rury, *Education and Women's Work: Female Schooling and the Division of Labor in Urban America* (Albany: State University of New York Press, 1991); Catherine Hobbs, ed., *Nineteenth-century Women Learn to Write* (Charlottesville: University Press of Virginia, 1995); Amy McCandless, *The Past in the Present: Women's Higher Education in the Twentieth-Century American South* (Birmingham: University of Alabama Press, 1999). For Africa, see: Marianne Bloch, et al., eds., *Women and Education in Sub-Saharan Africa: Power, Opportunities, and Constraints* (Boulder, CO: Lynne Riemer, 1990). For Asia, see: Barbara Rose, *Tsuda Umeko and Women's Education in Japan* (New Haven, CT: Yale University Press, 1992); Dorothy Ko, *Teachers of the Inner Chambers: Women's Culture in Seventeenth-Century China* (Stanford, CA: Stanford University Press, 1994); Carol Chapnick Mukhopadhyay and Susan Seymour, eds., *Women, Education, and Family Structure in India* (Boulder, CO: Westview Press, 1994); Gail Minault, *Secluded Scholars: Women's Education and Muslim Social Reform in Colonial India* (Oxford: Oxford University Press, 1998); Kaye Haw, *Educating Muslim Girls: Shifting Discourses* (Milton Keynes: Open University Press, 1997). For Latin America, see: Francine Rose Masiello, *Between Civilization and Barbarism: Women, Nation, and Literary Culture in Modern Argentina* (Lincoln: University of Nebraska Press, 1992); Nelly P. Stronquist, ed., *Women and Education in Latin America: Knowledge, Power, and Change* (Boulder, CO: Lynne Rienner, 1992).

There are several good studies that place current issues in gender and education in developing countries in historical perspective: Jill Ker Conway and Susan C. Bourque, eds., *The Politics of Women's Education: Perspectives from Asia, Africa, and Latin America* (Ann Arbor: University of Michigan Press, 1993); Elizabeth M. King and M. Anne Hill, eds., *Women's Education in Developing Countries: Barriers, Benefits, and Policies* (Baltimore, MD: Johns Hopkins University Press, 1993); Grace C. L. Mak, *Women, Education and Development in Asia* (New York: Garland,

1996); Christine Heward and Sheila Bunwaree, eds., *Gender, Education, and Development: Beyond Access to Empowerment* (London: Zed Books, 1998); Sheena Erskine and Maggie Wilson, *Gender Issues in International Education: Beyond Policy and Practice* (New York: Falmer Press, 1999).

8 Sexuality

Most of the chapters in this book opened with a brief discussion of the ways in which historians studied the topic under discussion – politics, work, religion, education – before they began to consider gender. Sexuality is different, for it became a topic of extensive historical inquiry only after the development of women's history; the best marker for new fields is a specialized journal, and the *Journal of the History of Sexuality* began publication in 1990. Even though some of the most prominent theorists of historical sexuality, such as the French philosopher Michel Foucault, focused primarily on the male experience just as traditional history had, both because of the timing of their emergence as historical fields and the nature of their subject, gender and sexuality are often closely related. Indeed, sexuality may have the opposite problem from other areas of historical inquiry, in that scholars may need to be reminded of distinctions between gender and sexuality rather than con-vinced of the importance of gender as a category of analysis when exploring sexuality.

Such distinctions are themselves historically and culturally variable; in some cultures, for example, sexuality may be understood primarily as a gendered orientation – as desiring and having sexual relations with individuals who are regarded as one's own or the opposite sex – while in others it may be thought of primarily in terms of the number or age of one's sexual partners, or the role one takes in sexual intercourse. (These roles are generally described as "active," meaning the person who inserts something – usually a penis – in another's bodily orifice, and "passive," the person in whom something is inserted. Such terms are highly gendered, of course, and derived from the male experience.) Conversely, gender in many cultures is viewed as an outgrowth of sexuality – men are defined as those who have sex with women, women as those who have sex with men and bear the children that result from this sex – though this is not always the case. As we discussed in the Introduction, some cultures assign individuals to a third gender category on the basis of their clothing and tasks, regardless of the identity of their sexual partners.

The sources, limits, and meanings of sexuality are just as contested as those of gender. The word "sexuality" – currently defined as "the constitution or life of the individual as related to sex" or "the possession or exercise of sexual functions, desires, etc." – is itself quite new, coming into English and most other western languages in about 1800. At that point new ideas about the body, changes in marriage patterns, new concepts of gender differences, and new methods of controlling people's lives converged in western countries to create what scholars usually call "modern sexuality," which will be discussed in more detail below. Some historians argue that this shift in thinking did not simply create *modern* sexuality, but sexuality itself, for people in earlier centuries did not think of themselves as having a "sexuality" or classify as sexual things that to us seem obviously to be so. These scholars point out that ancient Greek and medieval Latin did not even have words for "sex" or "sexual," and advocate avoiding the word "sexuality" when discussing earlier periods. The same is true for "gender," of course, as we have used it in this book, but using modern categories to explore the past is not an unacceptable practice as long as we use them carefully, because investigations of the past are always informed by present understandings and concerns. Thus this chapter will use the term "sexuality" as it is commonly understood today, and investigate some of the intersections between sexuality and gender.

One of the ways in which gender and sexuality have been linked is that both were trivialized and viewed as questionable or marginal areas of scholarly inquiry. Vern Bullough, one of the first investigators of European medieval sexuality, reports that throughout the 1960s – that decade of the "Sexual Revolution" – his research on such topics as homosexuality, prostitution, and transvestism was rejected by historical journals as unsuitable, while books which avoided any discussion of sex, such as Edith Hamilton's *The Greek Way*, were bestsellers. This attitude began to change in the 1970s with the advent of social history and women's studies. The history of women's bodies and sexual lives became a significant area of study within feminist scholarship, which often argued that sexual relationships – in the past or present – are power relationships, an idea captured in the slogan "the personal is political."

The study of sexuality within feminist scholarship has produced several areas of sharp controversy. One involves the degree to which the body, sexual desire, and the experience of motherhood can be sources of power for women. Should women celebrate their bodies, the mother–daughter bond, and their sexual feelings, or do these actions overlook differences among women and reinforce the nefarious notion that "biology is destiny"? A second debate concerns pornography and sexual practices such as sado-masochism. Are these necessarily harmful to women, or can there be "feminist" pornography or sado-masochism? Does pornography limit women's civil rights, or is censorship of pornography, like any censorship, ultimately more dangerous than the material it prohibits? A third area of controversy, one which more often draws on historical and religious examples from history and religion than the others, addresses the valuation of sexual activity: Can a life of chastity and celibacy be a freeing option, or is it always an example of repression? Does our contemporary emphasis on finding and expressing one's "sexual identity" lead scholars to misrepresent the lives of women in the past? And finally: How are sexuality and gender related; that is, how do cultural definitions of what it means to be a man or woman relate to such matters as sexual identity, erotic desire, and sexual activities?

The relationship between gender and sexuality is also a key issue in gay and lesbian studies, an academic discipline originating in the 1970s, and in queer theory, which began as a field in the 1990s. Many of the issues found in the study of sexuality or in feminism also occur in queer theory: To what degree is sexual identity socially constructed? To what extent can sexual or gender identity (or even sex) be intentionally blurred or hidden, making it simply a "performance" rather than part of one's essential nature? To what extent *should* sexuality or gender be blurred? Queer theorists often argue in favor of fluidity in both gender and sexuality, criticizing dichotomous understandings of a clear split between heterosexual and homosexual and even finding the more varied categories of gay, lesbian, bisexual, and transsexual (sometimes abbreviated with the acronym "GLBT") too limiting. Other scholars wonder whether denying that a group has an essential identity – that is, something that makes it clearly homosexual (or women, or African-American) – makes it difficult to argue in favor of equal treatment or an end to discrimination.

In the same way that the development of women's history led scholars to start exploring men's experiences in history *as men* (rather than simply as "the history of man" without noticing that their subjects were men), gay and lesbian studies has led a few scholars to explore the historical construction of heterosexuality. Recognizing the constructed nature of heterosexuality has been just as difficult for many historians as recognizing that most history was actually "men's history," however. The cultural analyst Eve Sedgwick wryly notes that "making heterosexuality historically visible is difficult because, under its institutional pseudonyms such as Inheritance, Marriage, Dynasty, Domesticity, and Population, heterosexuality has been permitted to masquerade so fully as History itself."

Along with issues originating in feminist and queer theory, the historical study of sexuality has been shaped by the ideas of Michel Foucault, who in 1976 began publication of a multivolume *History of Sexuality,* intended to cover the subject in the west from antiquity to the present. Though only three volumes were published before his death in 1984, the first book, along with Foucault's other works on prisons, insanity, and medicine, greatly influenced later historians.

Foucault argued that the history of sexuality in the west was not characterized by the increasing repression of a free biological drive, but instead by the "transformation of sex into discourse." This process began with the Christian practice of confessing one's sins to a priest, during which first acts and then thoughts and desires had to be described in language. This practice expanded after the Reformation as Catholics required more extensive and frequent confession and Protestants substituted the personal examination of conscience for oral confession to a priest. During the late eighteenth century, Foucault argued, sexuality began to be a matter of concern for authorities outside religious institutions: political authorities tried to encourage steady population growth; educational authorities worried about masturbation and children's sexuality; and medical authorities both identified and pathologized sexual "deviance" and made fertility the most significant aspect of women's lives. Foucault traced this expansion of discourses about sex into the present, when, he noted, "we talk more about sex than about anything else," and it was this discourse that created modern "sexuality" as we now understand the term. Before people learned to talk about sex so thoroughly, there was sex, according to Foucault, but not sexuality. Modern sexuality is closely related to power, not simply the power of authorities to define and regulate it, but also the power inherent in every sexual relationship. This power – in fact, all power, in Foucault's opinion – is intimately related to knowledge and to "the will to know," the original subtitle of the first volume of his *History of Sexuality.*

Historians of sexuality after Foucault have often elaborated on his insights by defining what is specific to modern western sexuality (many scholars now see the sharpest break with the past in the nineteenth rather than the eighteenth century, with the development of the notion of a "sexual identity"); exploring the mechanisms that define and regulate sexuality; and investigating the ways in which individuals and groups described and understood their sexual lives. Other scholars have pointed out gaps or weaknesses in Foucault's theories, and address issues that he largely ignored, among them women's sexuality, the relationship between race and European notions of sexuality, and the ways in which economic power structures shaped sexual ideas and practices.

The debates about the relationship between sex and gender traced in chapter 1 have also emerged in scholarship on sexuality, with biology, anthropology, psychology, and history all leading scholars to denaturalize sexuality, that is, to emphasize its social construction and historical variability. In some cases the body itself has been denaturalized, with historians asserting that because people in past times perceived and experienced their bodies differently, those bodies really *were* different. Much "body history" is thus part of the New Cultural History with its emphasis on discourse, though a few historians use the body to counter-act that emphasis, arguing that people's lives included physical experiences that were not or could not always be expressed in words. These embodied experiences are difficult to recapture or study, but neglecting them, they argue, leads to a history that is sanitized and cerebral rather than one that takes pain or pleasure seriously.

The history of sexuality, and particularly its relationship with gender, is closely linked with many of the issues we have already discussed in this book: most families are, of course, founded with a sexual relationship; all of the world's religions take a stance on sexual conduct; the laws, norms, and ideals concerning gender often have a sexual component; political authorities regulate sexual behavior. Because sexuality is such a new field of historical inquiry these linkages have been studied quite well for some of the world's cultures, and are only beginning to be investigated for others. As with so many other aspects of gender, the vast majority of historical scholarship has dealt with the western experience, though there are large numbers of anthropological studies of non-western cultures which include extensive discussions of sexuality. Such studies have often been used to criticize western sexuality as repressed and unhealthy (or as obsessive and thus also unhealthy), though anthropologists warn against such simplistic dichotomies. They stress that the sexual norms and practices of all cultures, and not simply the west, change over time because of contacts with other cultures and internal developments. Historians are now beginning to explore sexuality in more of the world's cultures, using traces of information from a large range of sources in the same way that historians of women have been doing.

Classical Eurasia

The sexual ideas and practices of much of classical Eurasia were shaped primarily by religious systems such as Hinduism, Buddhism, and Christianity, which we have already discussed in chapter 5. One of the few places where religious ideas played less of a role was ancient Athens, which has received extensive attention from historians because it has left so many sources in comparison to other ancient cultures and because it has traditionally been regarded as a foundation of western culture.

The sources surviving from ancient Athens provide a great deal of information about attitudes toward sexuality among the educated male elite. Plato and Aristotle, the two most important philosophers of ancient Athens, were both suspicious of the power of sexual passion, warning that it distracted men from reason and the search for knowledge. Both men praised a love that was intellectualized and non-sexual, the type of attachment we still term "platonic." (Neither Plato nor Aristotle were concerned about what sex does to women except as this affects men.) Plato developed a dualistic view of humans and the world, arguing that the unseen realm of ideas was far superior to the visible material world, and that the human mind or soul was trapped in a material body. This mind/body split was a gendered concept, with men associated more with the mind and women with the body. Women's bodies were also viewed as more influenced by their sexual and reproductive organs than men's; Plato described the womb as an "animal" that wandered freely around the body, causing physical and mental problems. (This is why the words "hysteria" and "hysterectomy" both have the same Greek root.)

The mind/body split did not originate with Plato, but his acceptance and elaboration of it helped to make this concept an important part of western philosophy from that time on, and led some groups (though not Plato) to reject sexual activity completely. In Aristotle the mind/body split is reflected in the process of procreation (what he termed "generation"), with the male providing the "active principle" and the female simply the "material." (The Greek physician and medical writer Galen disagreed with this formulation, however, and regarded both parents as providing "active principles.") As we saw in chapter 4, the categories "male" and "female" were not completely dichotomous to Aristotle or Plato, however, but part of one hierarchical continuum, with men at the more positive end.

In classical Athens part of an adolescent citizen's training in adulthood was supposed to entail a hierarchical sexual and tutorial relationship with an older man, who most likely was married and may have had other female sexual partners as well. The key sexual distinction was not the sex of one's partner, but one's role in the sexual act itself; Athenians thus differentiated between active and passive, between penetrator and penetrated, with the latter positions appropriate only for slaves, women, and boys. (There is some dispute about whether penetration was involved in male–male sex involving free men, or whether sex was generally intercrural, that is, between the thighs.) These pederastic relations between adolescents and men were often celebrated in literature and art, in part because the Athenians regarded perfection as possible only in the male. The perfect body was that of the young male, and perfect love that between an adolescent and an older man, not that between a man and an imperfect woman; this love was supposed to become intellectualized and "platonic" once the adolescent became an adult. How often actual sexual relations between men or between men and women approached the ideal in Athens is very difficult to say, as most of our sources are prescriptive, idealized, or fictional.

Whatever their impact on the real sexual lives of Athenians, Athenian ideas and practices were influential in the later Roman Republic and Empire. Many Romans agreed with Plato that sexual passion was disruptive and saw sexual relationships as an important area of government concern; Roman lawmakers frequently enacted statutes dealing with sexual offenses. The most serious transgressions were those which might upset the social order: adultery (which was defined as sex with a married woman not one's wife); sexual relationships involving young upper-class unmarried women (particularly if the man was from a lower social group); marriages which crossed social boundaries; and rape or abduction of girls or boys. Roman law drew increasingly sharp lines between categories of women based on their sexual relationships with men: there were wives, whose children could inherit; concubines, who had some legal rights but usually could not marry their sexual partners because they were slaves or freed slaves, had a dishonorable occupation such as being an actress, or were over fifty (and thus beyond child-bearing years); and prostitutes, defined as women who were sexually available to a large number of people, whether or not they charged for their services. The legal category of prostitute in Rome also included men, which is a good example of the ways in which gender and sexuality can intersect; male prostitutes were not viewed as women, but they were also not fully men, which in Rome meant being an adult married man whose children could be of service to the state.

Roman literature often celebrated sexual relationships of all types in a way Roman law did not. The only two sexual activities uniformly condemned in literature were men taking the passive role in homosexual acts – viewed as unmanly and unworthy of a Roman citizen, and suitable only for slaves and prostitutes – and women taking the active role, which was seen as usurping a masculine privilege. In Rome, as in Athens, there was not a sharp line between heterosexuality and homosexuality, for one's role in sexual relations, not the sex of one's partner, was what mattered. Most scholars conclude that people did not have a "sexual identity" as it is currently defined, and some even suggest that talking about "sexuality" at all when discussing classical cultures is misleading.

In classical China as well, the idea of a life-long sexual identity based on the sex of one's sexual partners was not well established, though at certain times there were male homosexual subcultures in which men participated throughout their lives. The best-studied of these is one which developed among imperial officials, intellectuals, and actors in the Sung dynasty (960–1279), and male homosexuality was not prohibited until the beginning of the Qing dynasty in 1644.

Sexual activity that could lead to children was another matter, however. During the Neo-Confucian movement of the Song dynasty educated officials put great emphasis on the disruptive power of heterosexual attraction, viewing it as so strong that individuals alone could not control it; walls, laws, and strong social sanctions were needed to keep men and women apart and to preserve order within the family. In many parts of China women of the middle and upper classes were increasingly secluded, and even peasant houses were walled; boys and girls were cheap to hire as servants for tasks that needed to be done outside the walls. As we saw in chapter 4, female seclusion was also accomplished through footbinding, a practice whose origins are obscure and debated, for contemporary official documents rarely discuss it. Footbinding does appear frequently in pornography, however, where the pointed shape that bound feet assumed was compared to lotus blossoms – an erotically charged image – and where the hobbled walk of women with bound feet was described as increasing their sexual prowess by lubricating their genitals. That sexual prowess was to be limited to the men on whom they were dependent, however, for unbound feet were seen as a sign of sexual freedom.

Though Confucian notions of hierarchy and order found strong resonance in Japan, Japanese culture never adopted footbinding, and many ideas about sexuality found in other Asian cultures were simply absent from Japan: virginity in brides was not a preoccupation and marriage was not regulated by either church or state. Japan was religiously pluralistic, with traditional Japanese religion (termed Shinto) mixing with Buddhism and other imported religious beliefs. Many of these belief systems held ambivalent ideas about sexuality: women carried out important religious rituals, yet were also regarded as sources of pollution through menstruation and childbirth; Buddhist monks were encouraged to abstain from all sex, yet homosexual relationships between monks and acolytes were common and sometimes celebrated in Buddhist monasteries. As in China, male homosexuality in both Japan and Korea was largely tolerated among certain groups, such as officials, the military aristocracy, actors, and intellectuals. In other Southeast Asian and Oceanic cultures various types of same-sex relationships, such as those between older men and boys, or those involving individuals regarded as shamans, were also widely accepted; in some cultures coming-of-age ceremonies for boys involved ingesting the semen of an older man, thus taking in his essence. In all classical Eurasian cultures references to same-sex relations among women are very sparse. This cannot be taken as evidence that they did not exist, however; as we have seen repeatedly, most of those who produced all types of written records were male, and not very interested in any aspect of women's lives if it did not intersect significantly with the lives of men.

The Americas

Learning about sexuality (or at least male sexuality) in classical Athens, Rome, China, or Japan is relatively easy, as there are extensive written records about norms and to some degree about practices; these records only present information from a particular point of view, of course – most often that of learned males – and they never provide answers to all one's questions, but they still contain a great deal. This is much more difficult for the rest of the world before the modern period. Many cultures developed systems of writing, but used them only for very limited purposes, such as recording the deeds of great kings or hymns of praise to deities. We can infer various things about sexuality from these records, but do not have direct statements about sexual mores or practices. Some cultures' systems of record-keeping have yet to be deciphered, so we are not sure what they might reveal. Other cultures did not develop writing on their own, but only after contact with outsiders; all information thus comes from archeological evidence, writings by outsiders, or oral traditions recorded much more recently. This was the case, for example, with the ancient Germanic cultures of northern Europe. We have a number of comments about Germanic sexual habits from the Roman historian Tacitus, but these were colored by Tacitus's desire to contrast the Germans, who he described as virtuous and plain-living, with his own Roman compatriots, who he saw as corrupt, debauched, and immoral. Similar problems occur in many other cases where the only sources come from outside a culture; perhaps more than in any other aspect of life, observations about sexuality are shaped by one's own background, purposes, motives, and norms, and rarely even attempt to be objective observation.

The problem of bias in reports on sexuality is not always solved when indigenous people themselves begin to write, as they frequently were taught to read and write by outsiders, learning the values of these outsiders as well as their techniques. This issue is clearest in the case of the Americas. A number of native peoples in central America and the Andes had systems of writing or record-keeping, but those that have been deciphered primarily record the deeds of kings or gods and provide few direct comments about the sexual activities of ordinary people. (In part this is because of the nature of what has survived; those from the Maya, for example, are primarily carved in stone, because all but four pre-conquest Maya books were destroyed by Spanish Christian authorities in the sixteenth and seventeenth centuries, who considered Maya writing to be demonic.) Most of the peoples in South and Central America and all of those in North America did not keep written records, however, so that indigenous authors learned to read and write from European clergy after European conquest. There is thus great debate among historians about how "authentic" their voices are, how much they were seeing and recording their original cultures through eyes that were already acculturated to Christian and European ways. At least in part, indigenous authors adopted views of Indian sexuality held by Europeans, which usually emphasized either innocence or lasciviousness.

Thus their works, along with those of European missionaries and colonists, tend to fit what they observed into a preconceived model.

Because the record is often so thin and involves layers of interpretation, historians disagree about a great many aspects of sexual life in the Americas before European colonialism. All agree that there was wide variety, though a few traditions which most cultures shared: all groups had some sort of marriage ceremony, with marital partners generally chosen by the family or community rather than the individuals themselves. The marriage was sometimes preceded by a period of trial marriage in which the potential husband lived and worked in his father-in-law's house; sexual relations might begin during this period. Among some groups divorce was frowned upon after children had been born, but among many it was quite easy for either spouse to initiate. Marriage was often monogamous, although more powerful men in some groups had more than one wife and rulers sometimes had a great many wives. Individuals abstained from sexual relations at different times for ritual purposes, but life-long chastity was regarded as bizarre and most people married at some point in their lives. Some cultures linked control of the body with order and control in society and the cosmos, with excessive sexual energy or activity in both women and men viewed as harmful; in a few cultures all sexual activity was seen as disruptive, so that sexual intercourse occurred outside houses or other buildings.

Some scholars suggest that the more highly organized and stratified societies, such as the Aztec and Inca, were more strict than those which did not have strong centralized political control. Among the Nahua peoples of central Mexico – which included the Aztecs – adultery (defined as sex with a married woman), abortion, living together without marrying, and incest were at least in theory harshly punished. The proper life was seen as a balance between order and disorder, so that the sexual ideal was moderation, not abstinence. Some Aztec religious rituals linked human sexuality and fertility with agricultural fertility in ways that the Spanish missionaries and authorities found shocking, including (most famously) human sacrifice and ritual cannibalism, and young male priests processing with erect penises or dressed in the flayed skin of a woman. (Most Nahua peoples and other residents of Mexico did not carry out ceremonies of large-scale human sacrifice, which were part of the Aztec state cult of the sun.)

The Inca also had a cult of the sun, in which certain young women were chosen as *acllas* (women dedicated to the sun), and either remained virgin-priestesses in special buildings or married the king of the Inca or

one of his favorites. In Inca society everyone except the *acllas* was
expected to marry, and marriages, except for those of the Inca king
and his favorites, were monogamous. Fertility and procreation were
viewed as extremely important, with a girl's first menstruation marked
by a special ceremony giving her her adult name and clothing. The
coming-of-age ceremony for a boy also included his being given his
adult name and a loincloth, and having his ears pierced for large ear
spools, so that he shed blood the way a girl did at menstruation.

Third Genders

Among many groups in the Americas there were – and in a few cases still
are – individuals who combined the clothing, work, and other attributes
of men and women. Most of these individuals are morphologically male,
and, as noted in chapter 1, the Europeans who first encountered them
thought they were homosexuals and called them "berdaches," from an
Arabic word for male prostitute. This term can still be found in older
scholarly literature, but the preferred term today is "two-spirit people."
Though Europeans focused on their sexuality, two-spirit people were
distinguished from other men more by their clothing, work, and religious roles than their sexual activities; their difference was thus one of
gender rather than sexuality. Among many groups two-spirit people are
actually thought of as a third gender rather than effeminate males, so that
sexual relations between a two-spirit person and a man may have not
been understood as "same-sex" in any case. (In a very few instances there
were also two-spirit people who were morphologically female but
carried out male tasks and wore male clothing; groups with such individuals thus had four gender categories.) Two-spirit people often had
special religious and ceremonial roles because they were regarded as
having both a male and female spirit rather than the one spirit which
most people had; they could thus mediate between the male and female
world and the divine and human world. Among most tribes such
individuals were honored and accepted, although among some they
were ridiculed, with the reasons for this diversity of treatment not yet
clear.

The Americas were not the only area of the world in which there
were individuals regarded as neither men nor women, or both men and
women, or in some other way transcending dichotomous gender classifications. In some cases these individuals appear to have been physically

hermaphroditic, either from birth or as the result of castration, though in others their distinctiveness or androgyny was purely cultural, and might be either permanent or temporary. (And we have seen in chapter 1 the ways in which the physical and the cultural are interwoven to the point where the distinction between them often collapses.) In some cultures such individuals engaged in sexual activities or had permanent or temporary sexual relationships, while in others they did not; their ambiguous or mixed gender definition means that such relationships often fell outside of a dichotomous scheme, so that categorizing them as homosexual or heterosexual is not appropriate.

The gender and sexuality of such individuals is thus complex and highly variable, but in almost all cultures where they are found they had special ceremonial or religious roles. In the Philippines religious leaders termed *baylans* or *catalonans* were generally married older women, regarded as to some degree androgynous because they were no longer able to have children. They were thought to be able to communicate with both male and female spirits, and this, in addition to their lack of fertility, gave them greater freedom of movement than younger women had. When men performed rituals as *baylans* or *catalonans* they wore women's clothing or a mixture of men's and women's clothes. In South Sulawesi (part of Indonesia) individuals termed *bissu* carried out special rituals thought to enhance and preserve the power and fertility of the rulers, which was conceptualized as "white blood," a supernatural fluid that flowed in royal bodies. The *bissu* were linked to the androgynous creator deity; they could be women, but were more often men dressed in women's clothing and performing women's tasks. In northern India divine androgyny is replicated in the human world by religious ascetics termed *hijra*, impotent or castrated men dedicated to the goddess Bahuchara Mata; they are regarded as having the power to grant fertility and so perform blessings at marriages and the births of male children. In Polynesian societies *mahus* perform certain female-identified rituals, do women's work, and have sex with men, as do the *xanith* in Oman; both of these groups are effeminate men, but they can also throw off these roles and become men when they choose, marrying in the same way a man would.

Both historical and contemporary examples of third genders and third (or fourth or fifth) categories of sexual orientation are receiving a great deal of study today, and are often used by people within the gay rights and transgender movements to demonstrate both the extent of non-dichotomous understandings and the socially constructed and historically variable nature of all notions of gender and sexual difference. In some areas there has been a blending of older third-gender categories and more recent forms of expressing homosexual identity, as gay rights groups assert their connections with older traditions within their own culture to stress that demanding rights for homosexuals is not simply a western import.

The Colonial World: Sex and Race

Current academic and popular interest in third gender/sex groups around the world stands in sharp contrast with the attitudes of westerners when they first encountered them during the colonial period. Colonial officials and missionaries generally classified them as homosexuals and regarded them with horror, as a sign of the depravity and inferiority of non-European cultures. Other sexual practices were also regarded as markers of inferiority, including polygyny, incest, same-sex relations not involving third gender individuals, concubinage, and temporary marriage, and were frequently invoked as a justification for European conquest and imperialism.

Over the last decade historians have paid great attention to the ways in which both the discourse and the reality of colonialism were both gendered and sexualized. As with many other issues we have discussed in this book, it is hard to understand how this could have been over-looked for so long, for the evidence is clear and frequent in standard sources. In a number of woodcuts and engravings from the sixteenth and seventeenth centuries, for example, America was depicted as a naked woman in a feather headdress. In his description of the discovery of the South American country of Guiana, Sir Walter Ralegh, the English explorer, described the land as "a country that hath yet her maidenhead [that is, still a virgin].... It hath never been entered by any armie of strength."

Not only was colonial territory itself (particularly the "New World") described or portrayed in sexualized metaphors, but the stories of colonization that captured people's imaginations – and in some cases still do – were those involving love and/or sex between individuals of different groups. One of these was the story of Thomas Inkle, an English trader, and Yarico, a young Indian woman, which was told in at least sixty different versions in ten European languages during the eighteenth century. According to the story, Inkle was rescued by Yarico after he was shipwrecked; the two became lovers, and he promised to take her back to England and marry her. When she hailed a passing ship, they sailed to Barbados, where he sold her into slavery. The account was first told in a single paragraph in *A True and Exact History of the Island of Barbados* (1657) by the English gentleman Richard Ligon, who reported that he heard it directly from Yarico, now a slave in the house in which he was staying; he describes her as "of excellent shape and colour... with small breasts, with the niples of a porphyry colour." The story was retold in 1711 by Richard Steele in an essay in *The Spectator*, a very widely read periodical, who fleshed it out considerably; he transformed Yarico into a princess (a detail he may have taken from the related story of Pocahontas) and made her pregnant with Inkle's child at the time he sold her, which caused him to demand more for her. Steele used the story primarily to argue that women were more constant in love than men, but in its later incarnations – as poetry, essays, several plays performed in Paris and Philadelphia, and even a comic opera (in which it was given a happy ending) – it was often used to criticize the slave trade, with Yarico sometimes changed into an African, or referred to as both Native American and African in the same text.

Steele and later authors do not go into the details that Ligon does about Yorico's breasts, but they generally make it clear that she was naked or nearly naked. European accounts of exploration and travel almost always discuss the scanty clothing of indigenous peoples, which was viewed as a sign of their uncontrolled sexuality. Hot climate – which we would probably view as the main influence on clothing choice – was itself regarded as leading to greater sexual drive and lower inhibitions. By the eighteenth century leading European thinkers such as Adam Smith and David Hume divided the world into three climatic/sexual zones: torrid, temperate, and frigid (words that still retain their double climatic/ sexual meaning). They and many other European writers and statesmen worried about the effects of tropical climates on the morals as well as the health of soldiers and officials, and devised various schemes to keep Europeans sent to imperial posts from fully "going native," adopting indigenous dress, mores, and who knew what else. They also linked this climatic/sexual schema with the advancement of civilization; in the torrid zones, heat made people indolent and lethargic as well as lascivious, whereas a temperate climate (like Britain) encouraged productivity and discipline along with sexual restraint and respect for women.

The aspect of "going native" that most concerned colonial authorities was, not surprisingly, engaging in sexual relations with indigenous people, and the colonial powers all regulated such encounters. In some cases, such as the earliest Spanish and Portuguese colonies, sexual relations and even marriage between Europeans and indigenous peoples were encouraged as a means of making alliances, cementing colonial power, and increasing the population; rape and enforced sexual services of indigenous women were also a common part of conquest. Because initially almost all Europeans in colonial areas were men, such relations did not upset notions of superiority. Once more women began to immigrate, official encouragement and even toleration of mixed marriages generally ceased, though informal relations ranging from prostitution through concubinage continued.

Attitudes toward sexual relations between certain types of individuals, and the policies and practices that resulted from those attitudes, were shaped by notions of difference that, as we saw in chapter 2, were often conceptualized physically as blood. In North America a binary system of racial classification developed in which "one drop of [black] blood" made one black. In Latin America the complex system of socio-racial categories termed *castas* led to an assignment of race based largely on outer appearance, though in theory based on the mix of African, European, and Native American blood in one's veins. Racial hierarchies also developed in the parts of Africa and Asia that became colonies during the nineteenth century, with "scientific" ideas about racial differences refueling earlier theories about blood.

Whatever the national, religious, class, or racial boundaries regarded as significant in a particular area, they were maintained by regulating sexual activity. This was done through laws prohibiting inter-group marriage or sexual contacts, and done more effectively through the creation and maintenance of traditions and other types of internalized mechanisms of control. If children are taught very early who is unthinkable in terms of a marriage partner, and unattractive in terms of a sexual partner, the maintenance of boundaries will not depend on laws or force alone. This is something that nearly all human societies have recognized, for the maintenance of all types of hierarchies depends on those in power marrying people which that society defines as "like themselves." If they do not, the distinction between elites and non-elites literally disappears, whether those elites are defined in racial, class, ethnic, or religious terms.

Colonial societies sometimes allowed elite men to marry or (more often) to have non-marital sexual relationships with non-elite women, placing various types of restrictions on the children of those unions. The reverse was much rarer, for the sexual activities of elite women were those most closely monitored in colonial, and, in fact, in nearly all societies. Thus socially defined categories of difference such as race and class are not only sexual ones, but also gendered. The story of Inkle and Yarico would have been told much differently if their races had been reversed; instead of a noble symbol of love and loyalty, she would have been degraded and dissolute, the type of woman the West Indian planter Edward Long warned about in 1772 with his comment "the lower class of women in England are remarkably fond of the blacks."

Long's brief comment manages to bring together sex, gender, race, and class, and he was far from alone in his thinking. A number of historians have pointed out the various ways in which these conceptual categories were linked in the period of colonialism and imperialism, not only in colonial areas but also in Europe and in places that became independent, such as the United States and Latin America. Indigenous peoples were often feminized, described or portrayed visually as weak and passive in contrast to the virile and masculine conquerors, or they were hypersexualized, regarded as animalistic and voracious (or sometimes both). Racial hierarchies became linked with those of sexual virtue, especially for women, with white women representing purity and non-white women lasciviousness. Dispelling such stereotypes was extremely difficult and took great effort; African-American women in the early twentieth-century United States, for example, took great care to hide the sexual and sensual aspects of their lives and emphasize respectability in what the historian Darlene Clark Hine has called a "culture of dissemblance."

In the colonial world sexual and racial categories were viewed as permanent moral classifications supported by unchanging religious teachings. They were not viewed as socially constructed, but as undergirded by an even more fundamental boundary, that between "natural" and "unnatural." Thus same-sex relations were defined as a "crime against nature" and often tried in church courts. This link between natural and godly began to lessen in intensity during the eighteenth century, but the importance of nature in setting boundaries only intensified, and "nature" came to lay at the basis of modern understandings of sexuality.

Modern Sexuality

Much of the earliest scholarship in the history of sexuality – which means that of the 1980s, as this is such a new field – posited a clear break between "modern" sexuality (by which it meant modern western sexuality) and that which came before. The beginning of modern sexuality was located sometime between the late eighteenth and the early twentieth centuries, with those who argued for an earlier transition highlighting the rise of scientific ideas about the body and those arguing for the later transition highlighting the beginning of the notion of a "sexual identity." As with all schemes of periodization in history, particularly those that argue for one single transition, this view is now seen as overly simplistic, not cognizant enough of class, racial, and gender differences within the west, to say nothing of those involving other cultures. Many scholars have thus given up looking for a single transition point or marker, and instead point to a number of changes that went on over the "long nineteenth century," stretching from the French Revolution to World War I. (The concept of the "long nineteenth century" developed first in political history, but it works in other areas of study as well.)

One of these was a change in the basic paradigm of sexuality from religion to science. As we have seen, all religions of the world regulate sexual conduct, regarding sexual behavior as part of a moral system. In some religions, acts alone are regulated, while in others – including Judaism and Christianity – one's motivations as well as one's acts determine the moral content of behavior, and sometimes motivations or thoughts alone are deemed immoral. (Former President Jimmy Carter's self-critical comments to *Playboy* magazine about having "lust in his heart" are an example of this.) Over the course of the eighteenth century, though harsh laws regarding sexual conduct remained on the books, they were enforced only sporadically and selectively. The concern with sexual thoughts and motivations rather than simply conduct actually grew more intense, however. Pornographic literature, for example, which had been a significant share of printed works in Europe since the development of the printing press in the mid-fifteenth century, was not legally banned because of its sexual content until the mid-nineteenth century with laws such as the Obscene Publications Act passed by the British parliament in 1857. (Some earlier pornography had been banned or confiscated, but this was because it included stories or gossip about the sexual activities of powerful people and thus had political content.) This concern gradually became a scientific rather than a religious issue, however, with sexual desires and actions that deviated from the expected norm now viewed not as sin but as "degeneracy," a term coined by the French asylum doctor Bénédict-Augustin Morel in 1857, or as "perversion," a term which became common in both medical and popular literature.

These desires, and the actions that resulted from them, were now studied, categorized, and classified as part of the natural world. Desires and actions judged to be too harmful or deviant might be corrected or prevented, but this was to be done through the assistance of scientifically trained professionals, not that of pastors or priests. The most important professionals in this new scientific understanding of sexuality were medical doctors, for sex was increasingly regarded as an aspect of health, with doctors determining what was "normal" and "abnormal." Western governments sought to promote a healthy society as a way of building up national strength, and anything that detracted from this became a matter of official and often public concern. Masturbation, prostitution, hysteria, and venereal disease all came to be viewed primarily as sexual issues and health problems, as did what were regarded as more extreme perversions, such as sadism, fetishism, masochism, exhibitionism, nymphomania, and "inversion," a common nineteenth-century term for same-sex desire. These various sexual disorders were labeled and identified in the German physician and neurologist Richard von Krafft-Ebing's landmark book *Psychopathia sexualis* (1886), the first important study in the new medical specialty of sexology.

Medical and political discussions of such issues, and their actual control and treatment, were profoundly gendered, and also shaped by class and racial hierarchies. Hysteria, for example, was an illness primarily in women marked by behaviors that deviated from or exaggerated what was acceptable in women, so that both emotional coldness and weeping fits were read as symptoms; hysteria in middle- and upper-class women was viewed as the result of too little sexual activity, and in lower-class women as the result of too much, particularly if the women were prostitutes. Exhibitionism, on the other hand, was a male malady, judged perverse by sexologists because by exposing his penis a man allowed himself to be viewed by others in a way that was proper only for women. The law itself confined the crime of exhibitionism to men, and Angus McLaren has found that more men were jailed for exhibitionism in early twentieth-century Chicago than for any other crime.

Masturbation was a matter of concern in both males and females, but particularly in boys and men, for whom the too early or too frequent spilling of sperm might cause them to become, in the words of the French doctors Fournier and Béguin, "weakened, pallid beings, equally feeble in body and mind... incapable of defending the nation or of serving it by honorable or useful work." The notion that men had only a limited amount of sperm – often labeled the "spermatic economy" – was based on the older idea of bodily humors that medicine had largely rejected by the nineteenth century, but it undergirded an obsession with masturbation that continued well into the twentieth century. This fixation was shaped by notions of race and class as well as gender; lower-class and non-white servants were often accused of teaching white, middle-class children to masturbate. A British soldier in Kenya, Robert Baden-Powell, founded the Boy Scouts in 1908 explicitly to teach British boys what he regarded as the right sort of manly virtues and keep them from masturbation, effeminacy, physical weakness, and homosexuality. These were traits he regarded as particularly common among the non-white subjects of the British Empire, and also among the residents of British industrial cities. If they were not counteracted with a vigorous program of physical training and outdoor life, Baden-Powell and numerous other writers, physicians, politicians, and church leaders predicted an inevitable "race degeneration" or even "race suicide."

Prostitution also came to be regarded primarily as a threat to men's health; prostitutes in Italy, France, and parts of Germany were required to register with the police and be examined regularly by doctors, who used unwashed syringes and speculums – labeled by French prostitutes the "government's penis" – and so helped to spread venereal diseases even more quickly. Beginning in 1864 Britain passed a series of Contagious Diseases Acts through which women in any port city of Britain and its empire who were simply suspected of being prostitutes could be arrested and sent to a "lock hospital" to be examined and treated for venereal disease. When the English social reformer Josephine Butler suggested that men who frequented prostitutes also ought to be examined, the royal commission in charge was shocked at the suggestion, noting: "there is no comparison to be made between prostitutes and the men who consort with them. With the one sex the offense is committed as a matter of gain; with the other it is an irregular indulgence of a natural impulse." The gender- and class-specific handling of venereal disease meant that efforts at control were completely ineffectual, and finally in 1884 efforts by women such as Butler led to the repeal of the Contagious Diseases Acts, though the registration of prostitutes continued in continental Europe. In both Europe and its colonies prostitution was generally viewed as a necessary evil, a regrettable concession to the strong sexual needs of lower-class men, certainly preferable to masturbation or same-sex relationships. Commentators in this era – the high point of the

Industrial Revolution – often used industrial or mechanical metaphors when talking about sex, describing sexual drives as surging through the body in the same way steam did through engines or water through pipes. This "hydraulic model" of sex led them to worry about what would happen (to men) who did not have an outlet; would such "repression" cause them to explode the same way that pipes or engines would if they were blocked?

As they worried about repression and its consequences, sexologists frequently turned their attention to same-sex desire in the decades around 1900, initially labeling this "inversion," though eventually the word "homosexuality," devised in 1869 by the Hungarian jurist K. M. Benkert, became the common term. Sexologists expected "inverts" to exhibit the tastes, behaviors, clothing preferences, habits, and abilities of the other sex, and often searched for physical signs, such as an enlarged clitoris or well-developed muscles in a woman, or the lack of a beard in a man. During the nineteenth century individuals had often expressed same-sex desire in very passionate terms, but these were generally regarded as "romantic friendships," expected as a part of growing up and, especially in women, not a sign of deviancy even if they continued throughout an individual's life. The Young Men's Christian Association (YMCA), for example, began in England in 1848 as a Christian men's movement in which young unmarried men were expected to strengthen their character and morality through passionate attachments to one another, a union of souls that would lead to greater love for God. Historians debate whether such friendships should be labeled "homosexual" because this was not yet a category in people's minds, but the medicalization of same-sex desire as a form of sexual deviancy changed attitudes toward them, and intimacy between girls or between boys was increasingly regarded with distrust. By the 1920s the YMCA's official statements condemned same-sex attraction and espoused a "muscular Christianity," centered on basketball (invented at a YMCA), swimming, and other sports, and on "normal" heterosexual relationships.

In the early twentieth century same-sex desire may have been expressed less openly in Europe and North America than it had been earlier, but it also became more often something which linked individuals in homosexual subcultures, a matter of identity rather than simply actions. Historians have discovered homosexual subcultures and communities – with special styles of dress, behavior, slang terms, and meeting places – developing among men in European cities as early as the seventeenth century, but these became more common in the twentieth century, and more often involved women as well as men. These communities varied tremendously depending on social class, race, and other factors, with differing patterns in the way gender and sexuality interacted. In turn-of-the-century New York City, male "fairies" dressed in flamboyant effeminate clothes and makeup gathered in the Bowery, while in the 1920s Harlem nightclubs and parties were popular with "bulldagger" women and "sissy" men, as well as those simply seeking good music and vibrant nightlife. In many US cities during the 1950s women who frequented lesbian bars developed norms of clothing and behavior that highlighted gender dichotomy, choosing to identify either as "butch" – with short hair and men's clothing – or as "fem" – wearing traditional women's clothing.

Heterosexuality also became a matter of identity in the early twentieth century, of a permanent "sexual orientation" that eventually became a legal as well as medical term and a central part of modern western notions of the self. The word "heterosexual" was originally used by sexologists to describe individuals of different sexes who regularly engaged in non-procreative sex simply for fun; it was thus a type of perversion, though a mild one. Increasingly the term came to be used for those who were sexually attracted to the "opposite" sex, with the proper development of this attraction a matter of physical and psychological health. "Normal" heterosexual development was also determined by gender, most famously in the ideas of the Austrian psychiatrist Sigmund Freud. Freud developed the notion that human behavior is shaped to a great extent by unresolved sexual conflicts which begin in infancy; these sexual conflicts are gendered, with girls suffering primarily from penis envy (the recognition that they are lacking something their brothers have) and boys from an Oedipus complex (the desire to kill their fathers so that they can possess their mothers). Freud's ideas were vigorously attacked, sometimes by his former associates, but they had a wide impact in fields far beyond psychology such as literature, art, and education.

These scientific and medical studies of sexual attitudes and behavior led to two somewhat contradictory ideas about sexuality. On the one hand, one's choice of sexual partners or other aspects of one's sexual behavior were increasingly regarded as a reflection of a permanent orientation rather than simply individual acts, so that one had what came to be termed a "sexual identity" as a homosexual or heterosexual determined by object choice, not sexual role. On the other hand, homosexuality and other types of "deviant" sexuality were defined as physical or psychological illnesses which could be cured through drugs, surgery, or psychoanalytical analysis. By the late nineteenth century sexual offenders were no longer executed, but they might be jailed, imprisoned in mental hospitals, or forced to undergo unwanted surgical or psychological treatments. Popular and learned books advised readers about how to achieve a "healthy" sex life, and efforts were made to prevent sexual deviance as well as cure it.

Contradictory ideas and differences of opinion about sexuality and its relation to gender continued throughout the twentieth century. Some medical researchers investigated a "gay" gene and variations in brain structure, while others criticized their findings as logically and methodologically flawed, shaped by notions of gender that continued to view homosexual men as in some ways feminized. (Most research on homosexuality in the twentieth century, like most medical research in general, focused on men.) At the same time that discrimination on the basis of sexual orientation was prohibited in many areas – largely as a result of the gay rights movement that began in the 1970s – many people (including some gay rights' activists) argued that sexual orientation, sexual identity, and perhaps even gender identity were completely socially constructed and could or should be changed, adapted, and blended at will. They asserted that "sexual orientation" and "gender identity" had indeed been part of "modern" ideas about sexuality, but in a postmodern world such concepts were just as outmoded as Plato's "wandering womb."

As you can see, we are in some ways back where we started in chapter 1, noting the huge range of contemporary opinion about the complex relationship between sex and gender. This chapter has added further complications, for the patterns, precepts, and practices of sexuality have clearly intersected in a huge variety of ways with gender, as well as with every other topic considered in earlier chapters. I noted at the beginning of this chapter that it is often difficult for scholars to keep gender and sexuality distinct, and I realized when writing it just how true my words were. Perhaps this lack of a clear line between gender and sexuality is part of the "postmodern condition," in which we all recognize that our identities and selves are not unitary wholes, but complex and changing. The frequency with which I found myself in earlier chapters asking you as readers to move around the book for more information rather than march straight through it supports this sense of complexity as well. When we use gender as a lens, we end up not limiting our view, but both sharpening and widening the picture; thus, though it may not be possible in optics, we simultaneously achieve the benefits of both a telephoto and a wide-angle lens.

Further Reading

Because of the close relationship between gender and sexuality in historical studies over the last several decades, many of the general and theoretical works cited in the list of readings following the Introduction also contain extensive discussion of sexuality; this list does not include anything mentioned there. An excellent starting point for western sexuality is Robert Nye, ed., *Sexuality* (New York: Oxford University Press, 1999), which includes discussions ranging from antiquity to the present, arranged chronologically; there is no similar study which is global in perspective. The many books of Vern Bullough, including *Sexual Variance in Society and History* (New York: John Wiley, 1976) and Vern Bullough and Bonnie Bullough, *Cross Dressing, Sex, and Gender* (Philadelphia: University of Pennsylvania Press, 1993) and *Sexual Attitudes: Myths and Realities* (New York: Prometheus, 1995) do sometimes range beyond the west. (There are several very dated books titled *Sex in History* which are not viewed as authoritative any more.) There is a good survey of the development of the history of western sexuality in the introduction to Domna Stanton, ed., *The Discourses of Sexuality: From Aristotle to AIDS* (Ann Arbor: University of Michigan Press, 1992). A summary of the new history of the body may be found in the chapter by Ray Porter in Peter Burke, ed., *New Perspectives on Historical Writing* (Cambridge: Polity Press, 1991); this book also contains a survey of women's history by Joan Scott. Several other useful general essay collections are: Peter Laslett, et al., eds., *Bastardy and its Comparative History* (Cambridge, MA: Harvard University Press, 1980); Philippe Aries and André Bejin, eds., *Western Sexuality: Practice and Precept in Past and Present Times* (Oxford: Blackwell Publishers, 1985); Jean-Louis Flandrin, *Sex in the Western World: The Development of Attitudes and Behavior*, trans. Sue Collins (Chur, Switzerland: Harwood, 1991); Pat Caplan, ed., *The Cultural Construction of Sexuality* (London: Tavistock, 1987); Kathy Peiss and Christina Simmons, eds., *Passion and Power: Sexuality in History* (Philadelphia: University of Pennsylvania Press, 1989); Roy Porter and Mikuás Teich, eds., *Sexual Knowledge, Sexual Science: The History of Attitudes to Sexuality* (Cambridge: Cambridge University Press, 1994); Nikki R. Keddie, ed., *Debating Gender, Debating Sexuality* (New York:

New York University Press, 1996). The newest research can always be found in the *Journal of the History of Sexuality* and in the books in the University of Chicago series, *Sexuality, History, and Society*.

Foucault's most influential work on sexuality is also his briefest: *The History of Sexuality I: An Introduction*, trans. Robert Hurley (New York: Random House, 1990). An excellent summary of Foucault's thought is Alan Sheridan's *Michel Foucault: The Will to Truth* (London: Routledge, 1990) and a good collection of his writings is David Couzens Hoy, ed., *Foucault: A Critical Reader* (Oxford: Blackwell Publishers, 1986). Discussions of the relationship between Foucault and feminism have been largely in the form of collections of articles, such as Caroline Ramazanoglu, ed., *Up Against Foucault: Explorations of Some Tensions Between Foucault and Feminism* (New York: Routledge, 1993) and Susan Hekman, ed., *Feminist Interpretations of Michel Foucault* (University Park: Pennsylvania State University Press, 1996). Lois McNay provides a longer analysis in *Foucault and Feminism: Power, Gender and the Self* (Boston, MA: Northeastern University Press, 1993).

Theoretical discussions of the constructed nature of gender and sexual identity include Teresa de Lauretis, *Technologies of Gender* (Bloomington: Indiana University Press, 1987), Jonathan Ned Katz, *The Invention of Heterosexuality* (New York: Dutton Books, 1995), and the works of Judith Butler cited in the Introduction. The debate within feminism about pornography and sado-masochism is discussed in Carol Vance, ed., *Pleasure and Danger: Exploring Female Sexuality* (New York: Routledge, 1984). Many recent theoretical works on the body do not have a historical component. Several which do are: Michael Feher with Ramona Nadoff and Nadia Tazi, *Fragments for a History of the Human Body*, three parts (New York: Zone Books, 1989–91); David Hillman and Carla Mazzio, *The Body in Parts: Fantasies of Corporeality in Early Modern Europe* (London: Routledge, 1997)

Sexuality in the ancient Mediterranean has been analyzed in: Eva Keuls, *The Reign of the Phallus: Sexual Politics in Ancient Athens* (New York: Harper and Row, 1985); Aline Rouselle, *Porneia: On Desire and the Body in Antiquity*, trans. Felicia Pheasant (Oxford: Blackwell Publishers, 1988); David M. Halperin, John J. Winkler, and Froma I. Zeitlin, eds., *Before Sexuality: The Construction of Erotic Experience in the Ancient Greek World* (Princeton, NJ: Princeton University Press, 1990); John J. Winkler, *The Constraints of Desire: The Anthropology of Sex and Gender in Ancient Greece* (New York: Routledge, 1990); Wayne R. Dynes and Stephen Donaldson, eds., *Homosexuality in the Ancient World* (New York: Garland, 1992).

This chapter has not included much discussion of medieval and early modern Europe, as this area was covered at some length in chapters 2 and 5, but there are excellent resources for further reading not listed in those chapters. The best places to begin for studying sexuality in Europe during the Middle Ages are Joyce E. Salisbury, *Medieval Sexuality: A Research Guide* (New York: Garland, 1990) and Vern L. Bullough and James A. Brundage, *Handbook of Medieval Sexuality* (New York: Garland, 1996). Important recent essay collections include: Karma Lochrie, Peggy McCracken, and James A. Schulz, eds., *Constructing Medieval Sexuality* (Minneapolis: University of Minnesota Press, 1996); Jacqueline Murray and Konrad Eisenbichler, eds., *Desire and Discipline: Sex and Sexuality in the Premodern West* (Toronto: University of Toronto Press, 1996); Louise Fradenburg and Carla Freccero, eds., *Premodern Sexualities* (New York: Routledge, 1996). More specialized medieval analyses include: Guido Ruggiero, *Boundaries of Eros: Sex Crime and Sexuality in Renaissance Venice* (Oxford: Oxford University Press, 1985); Caroline Walker Bynum, *Fragmentation and Redemption: Essays on Gender and the Human Body in Medieval Religion* (New York: Zone Books, 1991). For early modern Europe, see: Rosalind Mitchison and Leah Leneman, *Sexuality and Social Control: Scotland 1660–1780* (London: Blackwell Publishers, 1989); Robert Purks Maccubbin, ed., *'Tis Nature's Fault: Unauthorized Sexuality during the Enlightenment* (Cambridge: Cambridge University Press, 1987); Isabel V. Hull, *Sexuality, State, and Civil Society in Germany, 1700–1815* (Ithaca, NY: Cornell University Press, 1996); Tim Hitchcock, *English Sexualities, 1700–1800* (New York: St Martin's Press, 1997); Randolph Trumbach, *Sex and the Gender Revolution, Vol. 1: Heterosexuality and the Third Gender in Enlightenment London* (Chicago: University of Chicago Press, 1998).

Information on gender and sexuality in the pre-Columbian Americas is often part of newer general studies, such as: Inga Clendinnen, *Aztecs: An Interpretation* (Cambridge: Cambridge University Press, 1991); Constance Classen, *Inca Cosmology and the Human Body* (Salt Lake City: University of Utah Press, 1993); Matthew Restall, *The Maya World: Yucatec Culture and Society, 1550–1850* (Stanford, CA: Stanford University Press, 1997).

The classic study of two-spirit people in North America is Walter L. Williams's *The Spirit and the Flesh: Sexual Diversity in American Indian Culture* (Boston, MA: Beacon Press, 1986). A newer collection is Sue-Ellen Jacobs, Wesley Thomas, and Sabine Lang, eds., *Two-Spirit People: Native American Gender Identity, Sexuality, and Spirituality* (Urbana: University of Illinois Press, 1997). For transgendered people outside North America, see: Serena Nanda, *Neither Man nor Woman: The Hijras of India* (Belmont, MA: Wadsworth Publishing, 1990); Stephen O. Murray, ed., *Oceanic Homosexualities* (New York: Garland, 1992); Gilbert Herdt, ed., *Third Sex, Third Gender: Beyond Sexual Dimorphism in Culture and History* (New York: Zone Books, 1994).

There are many studies published over the last decade that investigate sexuality and gender in the colonial world. In addition to those listed in chapter 5, see: Ann Laura Stoler, *Race and the Education of Desire: Foucault's History of Sexuality and the Colonial Order of Things* (Durham, NC: Duke University Press, 1995); Robert Young, *Colonial Desire: Hybridity in Theory, Culture, and Race* (London: Routledge, 1995); Richard Trexler, *Sex and Conquest: Gendered Violence, Political Order, and the European Conquest of the Americas* (Ithaca, NY: Cornell University Press, 1995). Many of the texts that retell the Inkle and Yarico story have been collected in Frank Felsenstein, ed., *English Trader, Indian Maid: Representing Gender, Race, and Slavery in the New World* (Baltimore, MD: Johns Hopkins University Press, 1999).

A good overview of the development of "modern" sexuality is Carolyn Dean's *Sexuality and Modern Western Culture* (New York: Twayne, 1996). See also: Jeffrey Weeks, *Sex, Politics, and Society: The Regulation of Sexuality Since 1800* (London: Longmans, 1981); Catherine Gallagher and Thomas Laqueur, eds., *The Making of the Modern Body: Sexuality and Society in the Nineteenth Century* (Berkeley: University of California Press, 1987); John C. Fout, ed., *Forbidden History: The State, Society, and the Regulation of Sexuality in Modern Europe* (Chicago: University of Chicago Press, 1992). The writings of early sexologists have been gathered and analyzed in Lucy Bland and Laura Doan, eds., *Sexology Uncensored: The Documents of Sexual Science* and *Sexology in Culture: Labelling Bodies and Desires* (Chicago: Universty of Chicago Press, 1998).

Important studies of same-sex relations over a long time period include: Salvatore J. Licata and Robert P. Peterson, eds., *Historical Perspectives on Homosexuality* (New York: Haworth Press, 1981); Lillian Faderman, *Surpassing the Love of Men: Romantic Friendships and Love between Women from the Renaissance to the Present* (New York: William Morrow, 1981); David Greenburg, *The Construction of Homosexuality* (Chicago: University of Chicago Press, 1988), which has a bibliography of more than a hundred pages; Martin Duberman, Martha Vicinus, and George Chauncey, Jr., eds., *Hidden From History: Reclaiming the Gay and Lesbian Past* (London: Meridian, 1989); David Higgs, ed., *Queer Sites: Gay Urban Histories Since*

1600 (New York: Routledge, 1999). More specialized studies and collections include: Judith C. Brown, *Immodest Acts: The Life of a Lesbian Nun in Renaissance Italy* (Oxford: Oxford University Press, 1986); Kent Gerard and Gert Hekma, eds., *The Pursuit of Sodomy: Male Homosexuality in Renaissance and Enlightenment Europe* (New York: Harrington Park Press, 1989); Bret Hinsch, *Passions of the Cut Sleeve: The Male Homosexual Tradition in China* (Berkeley: University of California Press, 1990); Emma Donoghue, *Passions Between Women: British Lesbian Culture 1668–1801* (London: Scarlet Press, 1993); George Chauncey, *Gay New York: Gender, Urban Culture, and the Making of the Gay Male World, 1890–1940* (New York: Basic Books, 1994); Gary Leupp, *Male Colors: The Construction of Homosexuality in Tokugawa Japan* (Berkeley: University of California Press, 1995); Michael Rocke, *Friendly Affection, Nefarious Vices: Homosexuality, Male Culture and the Policing of Sex in Renaissance Florence* (Oxford: Oxford University Press, 1995); Brett Beemyn, ed., *Creating a Place for Ourselves: Lesbian, Gay, and Bisexual Community Histories* (New York: Routledge, 1997); John Donald Gustav-Wrathall, *Take the Young Stranger by the Hand: Same-sex Relations and the YMCA* (Chicago: University of Chicago Press, 1998); Gregory M. Pflugfelder, *Cartographies of Desire: Male–male Sexuality in Japanese Discourse, 1600–1950* (Berkeley: University of California Press, 1999). Several important historical studies that look at Christianity and homosexuality are: John Boswell, *Christianity, Social Tolerance and Homosexuality: Gay People in Western Europe from the Beginning of the Christian Era to the Fourteenth Century* (Chicago: University of Chicago Press, 1981) and *Same-Sex Unions in Pre-Modern Europe* (New York: Villard Books, 1994); Bernadette J. Brooton, *Love Between Women: Early Christian Responses to Female Homoeroticism* (Chicago: University of Chicago Press, 1996); Mark D. Jordan, *The Invention of Sodomy in Christian Theology* (Chicago: University of Chicago Press, 1997) and *The Silence of Sodom: Homosexuality in Modern Catholicism* (Chicago: University of Chicago Press, 2000).

The best place to start in exploring sexuality in the United States is John D'Emilio and Estelle B. Freedman's *Intimate Matters: A History of Sexuality in America*, 2nd edn (New York: Harper and Row, 1997). Another good, more focused introduction is Leila Rupp's aptly titled *A Desired Past: A Short History of Same-sex Love in America* (Chicago: University of Chicago Press, 1999). Other major collections and analyses include: Kevin White, *The First Sexual Revolution: The Emergence of Male Heterosexuality in Modern America* (New York: New York University Press, 1993); Martha Hodes, *White Women, Black Men: Illicit Sex in the*

Nineteenth Century South (New Haven, CT: Yale University Press, 1997); Angus McLaren, *The Trials of Masculinity: Policing Sexual Boundaries, 1870–1930* (Chicago: University of Chicago Press, 1997); Merril D. Smith, ed., *Sex and Sexuality in Early America* (New York: New York University Press, 1998); Martha Hodes, ed., *Sex, Love, Race: Crossing Boundaries in North American History* (New York: New York University Press, 1999); Jennifer Terry, *An American Obsession: Science, Medicine, and the Place of Homosexuality in Modern Society* (Chicago: University of Chicago Press, 1999). There is also infomration about sexuality in Nancy Shoemaker, ed., *Negotiators of Change: Historical Perspectives on Native American Women* (New York: Routledge, 1995) and David Barry Gaspar and Darlene Clark Hine's *More than Chattel: Black Women and Slavery in the Americas* (Bloomington: Indiana University Press, 1996).

Works in English (and actually in any language) focusing on areas outside western Europe and North America are far fewer in number. Some of these primarily look at European reactions to sexual behavior in other cultures, including Rudi Bleys's *The Geography of Perversion: Male-to-Male Sexual Behavior outside the West and the Ethnographic Imagination, 1750–1918* (New York: New York University Press, 1995) and several of the essays in Stuart Schwartz, ed., *Implicit Understandings: Observing, Reporting, and Reflecting on the Encounters Between Europeans and Other Peoples in the Early Modern Era* (Cambridge: Cambridge University Press, 1994).

The older works by Robert H. van Gulik, *Sexual Life in Ancient China* (Leiden: E. J. Brill, 1961) and Basim Musallam, *Sex and Society in Islamic Civilization* (Cambridge: Cambridge University Press, 1983) are still widely consulted. For newer studies of Asia, see: José Ignacio Cabezón, ed., *Buddhism, Sexuality and Gender* (Albany: State University of New York Press, 1992); Lenore Masterson and Margaret Jolly, eds., *Sites of Desire, Economies of Pleasure: Sexualities in Asia and the Pacific* (Chicago: University of Chicago Press, 1997). For eastern Europe, see Jane T. Costlow, Stephanie Sandler, and Judith Vowles, eds., *Sexuality and the Body in Russian Culture* (Stanford, CA: Stanford University Press, 1993) and Eric Naiman, *Sex in Public: The Incarnation of Early Soviet Ideology* (Princeton, NJ: Princeton University Press, 1999).

Afterword

At the end of the introduction I warned you that this book might make you feel angry, depressed, or defensive. I made this comment because those are reactions I often get from students when I teach courses that focus on women and gender, or when I discuss the differences between men's and women's experiences in more general history courses. The first two emotions are ones I have often felt myself, and sometimes continue to feel despite nearly thirty years of studying women and gender. Women's history can easily, as my students say, be a downer or leave you pissed off. Investigating certain topics also leaves me, as a middle-class woman of Euro-American background, feeling defensive; it is always more comfortable (and comforting) to explore issues of male privilege than what Peggy McIntosh has called "the invisible knapsack of white privilege."

At times I have also felt defensive about doing women's history at all. In the nineteenth century professional historians in European and American universities sought to make history into a science, one that engaged, as the natural sciences were understood to do, in the unearthing and marshaling of facts and the "objective" retelling of a story. That notion of what history was about continued to shape the teaching of history for a very long time, particularly in graduate schools. We were warned against investigating topics about which we could not be objective; better, for example, if we were a strong Catholic to study a Protestant group, or better yet to stay away from religious issues altogether. Ideal topics were those in which we were not emotionally, spiritually, intellectually, or philosophically invested, and perhaps not even very interested. The best might be one that was simply assigned by our dissertation adviser, which would allow us to achieve the necessary objectivity as well as the even-more-necessary excellent letter of recommendation.

This was a situation in which a number of my friends found themselves, but I was fortunate to have a dissertation adviser (such an individual is called a "Doctor-father" [*Doktorvater*] in the telling German phrase) who did not demand such filial obedience of his academic offspring. I also came into graduate school right at the point when doing research on women did not seem utterly bizarre, though there were not yet any courses in women's history taught by regular faculty. (There were also no tenured women in a department of more than fifty, although the quota on the percentage of incoming graduate students who could be female, found in many history departments into the 1960s, had been lifted.) I certainly internalized the notion of objectivity to a great degree, however, and, along with other historians of women, set out to prove that I could be as objective as the next man. We particularly guarded ourselves against the feelings of anger or depression our materials often provoked in us, ever defensive against charges of "bias" or "having an agenda." Even when many of us came to accept and assert that all history has an agenda, that every historian decides what is important enough to study for personal and political reasons (including the desire to get a job), we were still very careful in our language. We recognized the temptation to make unreflective ethical judgments about the past – as Barbara Newman has put it, the temptation to idealize, pity, or blame – and fought it. We highlighted the complexity of women's experience, and tried to avoid making generalizing statements about whether certain developments were good or bad for women. (A friend of mine calls this the Glinda test, after the question posed to Dorothy by Glinda, the good witch in *The Wizard of Oz*: Are you a good witch, or a bad witch?)

Women's history thus had a self-contradictory task, to highlight women yet assert that studying them was no different than studying anything else. Joan Scott has pointed out that this was also a paradox in feminism, for in order to eliminate sexual difference, feminists first had to proclaim that difference, to point out women's "otherness" within political and intellectual structures based on the individual male citizen. This was not simply an issue of theoretical perspective, because it confronted those of us who were teachers every time we made up a course syllabus: should we, for example, be more interested in separate courses in women's history, or in integrating women into general history courses? If we did the former, we were ghettoizing women, but we were better able to evaluate their experiences with the complexity they deserved. If we did the latter, we never had enough time to differentiate sufficiently among women, and also encountered student hostility: "I thought this course was going to be about history, not *women's* history." This contradiction was particularly strong every March, when Women's History Month rolled around – we wanted to see events and exhibits celebrating women, yet often winced at their lack of sophistication and wondered whether we should participate.

In many ways the turn to gender was a relief; "gender" sounded much more elegant and allowed for greater intellectual distancing than "women," in the same way that "man" had earlier sounded cultivated and scholarly. (*The Ascent of Men* just doesn't have the same ring as *The Ascent of Man*.) As "gender" became more common, it also allowed us to avoid using the word "sex"; as scholars we dropped it because we wanted to be free of the taint of essentialism and prove that we understood the socially constructed and historically variable nature of all categories. (Our lead was followed by people who designed registration forms, driver's license applications, and other documents, but that was to avoid hinting at the other meanings of sex, not to assert that gender was socially constructed; so far, I have not seen a form that has boxes to check for male, female, other, and none.)

Though all scholars studying women had to confront these issues, they became very acute for me when I began to write and edit surveys, readers, and other books designed for classroom use. I became quite skilled at presenting material in the relatively bland manner expected in such materials, suggesting areas about which there is historical debate, but not participating in the debate myself. You have no doubt noticed that kind of reluctance at certain places in this book, in phrases such as "scholars disagree about . . ." or "there is a variety of opinion about . . ." That tendency became even stronger as I wrote books on broader and broader topics, for my graduate school training had taught me that the only topics on which I could be fully authoritative were those in which I had done archival research in the original languages: certainly an impossibility when I wrote *Women and Gender in Early Modern Europe* (my command of Portuguese or Polish is pretty slim), and even more so with this book.

Despite the years of practice at presenting a balanced picture, however, I found when writing this book that there was no way to avoid letting in my own convictions, particularly as I decided to end each chapter with a brief discussion of current issues. Precisely because I read so widely in periods and geographic areas that were new to me, the anger and sadness my students often feel hit me a number of times as I was researching and writing, and idealization, pity, and blame certainly crept in. In this I am not alone, neither in expressing my beliefs nor worrying about that expression. Peter Stearns, who has written many more surveys and textbooks than I have (and probably more than any other living historian), felt it necessary to comment in the introduction to a recent book on gender, "Evaluations in the book assume that relative equality between the sexes is a 'good' thing, which is a modern and not uncontested value." It is hard to imagine another category of difference or aspect of life about which such a statement would appear, at least in books printed by reputable presses designed for classroom use. Would we feel it necessary to explain that we viewed poverty or racism as a "bad" thing, or regarded access to medical care and education as a "good" thing?

It is precisely the contested nature of gender that made me initially decline but ultimately accept the suggestion of Constantin Fasolt – the editor of the series of which this book is a part – to write this personal afterword. Though I cautioned you in the introduction about your response to the material in this book, I must in fairness also note that I hoped all along it would provoke some emotional reactions, at least incredulity and puzzlement if not anger or despair. Investigating gender in the past is a political act, an assertion that the story we have been told is not only incomplete (all history is, of course, incomplete), but to some degree intentionally incomplete. Studying gender involves saying "no, *this* also matters, *this* also is part of history," whether "this" is the experience of a wife or a husband, a prostitute or her client, a priest or a spirit medium, an architect or an embroideress. I often end my books and articles, as I did the introduction to this one, with a one-sentence admonition to my readers, allowing myself that small break with my usual measured authorial voice. My reflections are a bit longer this time, but I will end in a voice that those who know me (or who have read this book carefully) will also recognize, one of cautious optimism. I would hope that the information in this book will lead you to engage in your own political acts, and know that if it does, aspects of your life that mirror the chapters you have read – your work, religious worship, creative outlets, sexuality, and family relationships – may not be the same.

Further reading

Peggy McIntosh's essay has been widely reprinted, most recently in Richard Delgado and Jean Stefanic, eds., *Critical White Studies* (Philadelphia: Temple University Press), pp. 291–9 For discussions of the development of professional history, see Peter Novick, *That Noble Dream: The "Objectivity Question" and the American Historical Profession* (Cambridge: Cambridge University Press, 1988), and Bonnie G. Smith, *The Gender of History: Men, Women, and Historical Practice* (Cambridge, MA: Harvard University Press, 1998). Barbara Newman's thoughts on temptations in feminist historical practice can be found in *Exemplaria: A Journal of Theory in Medieval and Renaissance Studies* 2/2 (October 1990), 687–715, and Joan Scott's on contradictions in feminism in *Only Paradoxes to Offer: French Feminists and the Rights of Man* (Cambridge, MA: Harvard University Press, 1996). The quotation from Peter Stearns can be found in his *Gender in World History* (London: Routledge, 2000), p. 7.

Index